I0522300

Brandee Jankoski

# *Season's Eatings*

## A Year-Round Holiday Cookbook

Copyright © 2023 by Brandee Jankoski
All rights reserved. No part of this publication may be reproduced, stored or transmitted in any form or by any means, electronic, mechanical, photocopying, recording, scanning, or otherwise without written permission from the publisher. It is illegal to copy this book, post it to a website, or distribute it by any other means without permission.
First edition

# Contents

## 3   *Super Bowl Party Time*

# 4    Valentine's Day Delights

## 5  *Easter Feasts*

# 6  *Fourth of July Favorites*

# 7    *Hauntingly Delicious Halloween Delight*

## 8  *Thanksgiving and Christmas Classics*

# 9 Leftover Magic

# Introduction

# Welcome to a Year of Celebration in Your Kitchen

As you turn the pages of "Season's Eatings: A Year-Round Holiday Cookbook" embark on a culinary journey that celebrates the year's most cherished moments. This cookbook is more than just a collection of recipes; it's an invitation to explore the rich tapestry of flavors and traditions that accompany each holiday.

From the clinking glasses on New Year's Eve to the warm, spiced aromas of Christmas, holidays are the milestones of our lives, marked by shared tables and cherished recipes. In this book, we've gathered an array of dishes that honor these special days, ensuring that no matter the occasion, you'll have the perfect recipe at your fingertips.

Whether you're a seasoned chef or a kitchen novice, these recipes are designed to inspire joy and creativity in your cooking. We've included classic favorites that evoke nostalgic memories, as well as innovative twists to surprise and delight your palate. From hearty Thanksgiving feasts to light and refreshing summer soirees, each chapter is a testament to the diverse ways we come together to celebrate.

This book is not just about the food—it's about the stories, the laughter, and the connections forged over shared meals. It's about transforming your kitchen into a place of celebration, no matter the day. As you explore these pages, we invite you to create new traditions, relive cherished memories, and savor the joy of cooking for those you love.

So preheat your ovens, gather your ingredients, and get ready to explore the wonders of "Season's Eatings: A Year-Round Holiday Cookbook." Let's make every day a celebration!

# The Significance of Celebrating Holidays Through Food

Celebrating holidays with food is a practice as old as civilization itself, deeply rooted in the human experience. The act of preparing and sharing meals during these special times is more than just a ritual; it's a profound expression of culture, connection, and tradition. Let's explore why food plays such an integral role in our holiday celebrations:

1. Cultural Heritage and Identity: Holidays often reflect the history and traditions of a culture. The foods we eat during these times serve as a link to our ancestry, connecting us to the past and preserving our heritage. Each dish can tell a story, whether it's a centuries-old recipe or a modern adaptation. These culinary traditions help maintain a sense of identity and continuity across generations.

2. Connection and Community: Food has the unique power to bring people together. Holiday meals are communal affairs where families, friends, and even strangers gather around

a shared table. This act of coming together strengthens bonds, fosters a sense of belonging, and creates a community. It's a time when people set aside differences to celebrate commonalities.

3. Joy and Celebration: Holidays are synonymous with joy, and food is one of the greatest sources of pleasure. Preparing and enjoying festive dishes is a celebration of the senses. The flavors, aromas, and presentations of holiday meals contribute significantly to the overall ambiance and spirit of the occasion.

4. Memory and Nostalgia: Food has a powerful way of evoking memories and emotions. The taste of a particular holiday dish can transport us back to childhood, remind us of loved ones, and evoke cherished memories. These nostalgic experiences enrich the holiday and provide continuity between past and present.

5. Symbolism and Meaning: Many holiday foods carry symbolic meanings. For example, eating apples and honey for Rosh Hashanah symbolizes the wish for a sweet new year, while the Thanksgiving turkey represents gratitude and abundance. These symbolic foods add depth and significance to the celebrations.

6. Creativity and Innovation: Holidays are also times for culinary creativity and innovation. Chefs and home cooks alike take pride in experimenting with recipes, incorporating new ingredients, or fusing different culinary traditions. This innovation keeps holiday meals exciting and allows for the creation of new traditions.

7. Teaching and Learning: Holiday cooking is often a communal activity, where culinary skills and family recipes are passed down through generations. This transfer of knowledge is not just about teaching cooking techniques; it's about imparting values, stories, and family history. In essence, the celebration of holidays through food is a multifaceted experience that nourishes not only our bodies but also our souls. It's an expression of who we are, where we come from, and what we cherish. Food, in the context of holidays, becomes more than sustenance; it becomes a vessel for celebration, connection, and the enduring human spirit.

# Tips for Holiday Cooking and Preparation

When it comes to holiday cooking, the key is to balance tradition with simplicity, allowing you to enjoy both the process and the celebration. Whether you're preparing a feast for a crowd or an intimate dinner, these tips will help you navigate the holiday kitchen with ease and joy.

1. Plan Ahead: Organization is crucial for holiday cooking. Plan your menu well in advance, considering the number of guests and their dietary preferences. Make shopping lists and don't leave grocery shopping to the last minute. Pre-order specific items if necessary, like a Thanksgiving turkey or specialty ingredients.

2. Prep in Advance: Do as much prep work as possible ahead of time. Chop vegetables, measure out ingredients, and make sauces or marinades in advance. Some dishes can be made entirely ahead of time and frozen or refrigerated until needed.

3. Delegate Tasks: Don't hesitate to delegate tasks. Cooking a holiday meal is a big undertaking, and it's okay to ask for help. Assign family members or guests with tasks like setting the table, chopping vegetables, or making a simple dessert.

4. Stick to What You Know: Holidays might not be the best time to experiment with complex or unfamiliar recipes. Stick to recipes you're comfortable with, and consider making one or two new dishes if you're feeling adventurous.

5. Keep It Simple: It's easy to get carried away with an elaborate menu, but simplicity often wins. Choose dishes that can be easily prepared in large quantities and that appeal to a wide range of tastes.

6. Use Time-Saving Gadgets: Make use of kitchen gadgets like slow cookers, pressure cookers, and food processors to save time and effort. These tools can be especially helpful for preparing large quantities of food.

7. Cook in Stages: Not everything has to be cooked at once. Utilize your oven, stovetop, and other appliances efficiently by cooking dishes in stages. Keep in mind the cooking time and temperature of each dish.

8. Don't Forget the Presentation: The presentation of your dishes can make a big difference. Take a little extra time to garnish and present your food in a way that makes it feel special.

9. Keep Dietary Restrictions in Mind: Be mindful of guests' dietary restrictions or allergies. Offer a variety of dishes that cater to different dietary needs, ensuring that everyone has something to enjoy.

10. Enjoy the Process: Finally, remember that holiday cooking is about more than just food; it's about creating memories and celebrating with loved ones. Enjoy the process, and don't stress about perfection.

By following these tips, you can make holiday cooking a more manageable, enjoyable, and delicious experience. Remember, the goal is to create a festive atmosphere and make lasting memories with your loved ones.

# New Year's Celebrations

*As the clock strikes midnight and the calendar turns to a fresh page, there's an undeniable sense of hope and anticipation that fills the air. New Year's Eve is a time for reflection, for setting new goals, and most importantly, for celebrating with loved ones. In this chapter of our cookbook, "New Year's*

*Celebrations," we invite you to embrace the spirit of new beginnings and revel in the joyous moments that come with the arrival of a brand new year. Whether you're hosting a grand New Year's Eve party or enjoying a cozy night in with family, this chapter is your culinary guide to creating memorable and delicious dishes that will kick off the year with a burst of flavor and excitement. From elegant appetizers and sparkling beverages to Traditional New Year's Day Meals for Luck and Prosperity, we've curated a collection of recipes that are sure to inspire your New Year's culinary journey.*

*Join us in exploring the diverse flavors and culinary traditions from around the world, as we toast to new beginnings, express gratitude for the past, and savor the promise of the year ahead. Whether you're looking for classic comfort food or innovative twists on traditional favorites, "New Year's Celebrations" has something for everyone to enjoy. So, let's raise our glasses and embark on a culinary adventure that will make your New Year's celebration truly special and unforgettable.*

# Appetizers and finger foods perfect for New Year's Eve parties

# Crispy Bruschetta with Tomato and Basil

**Serving Size:**

Makes about 24 pieces

**Instructions:**

1. Preheat your oven to 350°F (175°C).
2. Arrange baguette slices on a baking sheet and brush lightly with olive oil.
3. Bake for 10-15 minutes until golden and crisp.
4. In a bowl, mix tomatoes, garlic, basil, and olive oil. Season with salt and pepper.
5. Top each bread slice with the tomato mixture.
6. Drizzle with balsamic glaze before serving, if desired.

**Ingredients:**

- 1 baguette, sliced into ½-inch rounds
- 2 cups cherry tomatoes, finely chopped
- 1 clove garlic, minced
- ¼ cup fresh basil, chopped
- 2 tbsp olive oil
- Salt and pepper, to taste
- Balsamic glaze (optional)

# Mini Spinach and Feta Puff Pastry Rolls

**Serving Size:**

Makes about 20 rolls

**Instructions:**

1. Preheat oven to 400°F (200°C).
2. Mix spinach and feta cheese in a bowl.
3. Roll out puff pastry and cut into small rectangles.
4. Place a spoonful of the spinach and feta mixture on each rectangle.
5. Roll the pastry over the filling and seal the edges.
6. Brush each roll with beaten egg.
7. Bake for 15-20 minutes until golden brown.

**Ingredients:**

- 1 sheet puff pastry, thawed
- 1 cup spinach, cooked and drained
- ½ cup feta cheese, crumbled
- 1 egg, beaten

# Sweet and Spicy Meatballs

Serving Size:

Makes about 30 meatballs

Instructions:

1. Preheat oven to 375°F (190°C).
2. Mix meat, egg, breadcrumbs, milk, salt, and pepper. Form into small meatballs.
3. Place meatballs on a baking sheet and bake for 20-25 minutes.
4. In a saucepan, combine barbecue sauce, honey, and sriracha. Simmer for 5 minutes.
5. Toss baked meatballs in the sauce and serve.

Ingredients:

- 1 lb ground beef or turkey
- 1 egg
- ½ cup breadcrumbs
- ¼ cup milk
- Salt and pepper, to taste
- 1 cup barbecue sauce
- ½ cup honey
- 2 tbsp sriracha sauce

# Caprese Skewers

Serving Size:

Makes about 20 skewers

Instructions:

1. Thread a cherry tomato, basil leaf, and mozzarella ball onto a skewer.
2. Repeat until all ingredients are used.
3. Drizzle with balsamic glaze and season with salt and pepper.

Ingredients:

- Cherry tomatoes
- Fresh mozzarella balls
- Fresh basil leaves
- Balsamic glaze
- Salt and pepper, to taste

# Smoked Salmon and Cream Cheese Cucumber Bites

**Serving Size:**

Makes about 24 bites

**Instructions:**

1. Spread cream cheese on each cucumber round.
2. Top with a piece of smoked salmon.
3. Garnish with dill.

**Ingredients:**

- 1 cucumber, sliced into rounds
- 4 oz smoked salmon, cut into small pieces
- 4 oz cream cheese, softened
- Fresh dill, for garnish

# Baked Parmesan Zucchini Fries

**Serving Size:**

Makes about 4 servings

**Instructions:**

1. Preheat oven to 425°F (220°C).
2. Mix breadcrumbs, Parmesan, salt, and pepper in a bowl.
3. Dip zucchini fries in egg, then coat with breadcrumb mixture.
4. Bake for 20-25 minutes until crispy.

**Ingredients:**

- 2 zucchinis, cut into fries
- 1 cup panko breadcrumbs
- ½ cup grated Parmesan cheese
- 1 egg, beaten
- Salt and pepper, to taste

# Mini Quiche Lorraine Bites

Serving Size:

Makes about 24 mini quiches

## Instructions:

1. Preheat oven to 350°F (175°C).
2. Cut puff pastry into small circles and press into mini muffin tins.
3. Whisk together eggs, cream, salt, and pepper.
4. Place bacon and cheese in each pastry cup, then fill with egg mixture.
5. Bake for 15-20

## Ingredients:

- 1 sheet puff pastry, thawed
- 4 eggs
- 1 cup heavy cream
- 1 cup cooked bacon, chopped
- 1 cup shredded Swiss cheese
- Salt and pepper, to taste

# Traditional New Year's Day Meals for Luck and Prosperity

# *Roast Beef with Garlic Mashed Potatoes and Glazed Carrots*

Prep Time:  2 hours
Cooking Time: 1.5 hours
Total Time: 3.5 hours

Servings:
6 people

Ingredients:

For the Roast Beef:

- Beef roast (about 3-4 pounds)
- 2 tablespoons olive oil
- Salt and pepper to taste
- 4 cloves garlic, minced
- 1 tablespoon rosemary, chopped
- 1 tablespoon thyme, chopped

For the Garlic Mashed Potatoes:

- 3 pounds potatoes, peeled and quartered
- 4 cloves garlic, minced
- 1/2 cup milk
- 1/4 cup butter
- Salt and pepper to taste

For the Glazed Carrots:

- 6 large carrots, peeled and sliced
- 2 tablespoons butter
- 2 tablespoons brown sugar
- 1 teaspoon cinnamon
- Salt to taste

Instructions:

Roast Beef:

1. Preheat the oven to 375°F (190°C).
2. Rub the beef with olive oil, garlic, rosemary, thyme, salt, and pepper.
3. Place in a roasting pan and roast for about 1.5 hours, or until the internal temperature reaches 135°F for medium-rare.
4. Let the beef rest for 15 minutes before slicing.

Garlic Mashed Potatoes:

1. Boil the potatoes in salted water until tender, about 20 minutes.
2. In a small saucepan, heat milk and garlic over low heat.
3. Drain potatoes and return them to the pot.
4. Mash the potatoes, adding the garlic-infused milk and butter gradually.
5. Season with salt and pepper.

Glazed Carrots:

1. In a skillet, melt butter over medium heat.
2. Add carrots, brown sugar, cinnamon, and salt.
3. Cook until carrots are tender and glazed, about 15 minutes.

Serving Suggestions

Serve the slices of roast beef alongside the garlic mashed potatoes and glazed carrots. Garnish with fresh herbs if desired.

# Herb-Crusted Rack of Lamb served with Rice Pilaf and Steamed Broccoli

Prep Time: 15 minutes
Cooking Time: 25 minutes
Total Time: 40 minutes

Servings:
4 people

## Herb-Crusted Rack of Lamb

Ingredients:

- Rack of lamb (8 ribs)
- 2 tbsp Dijon mustard
- 2 cloves garlic, minced
- 1/4 cup fresh bread crumbs
- 2 tbsp fresh rosemary, chopped
- 2 tbsp fresh thyme, chopped
- Salt and pepper, to taste
- Olive oil

Instructions:

1. Preheat Oven: Preheat your oven to 400°F (200°C).

2. Prepare Lamb: Season the rack of lamb with salt and pepper. In a skillet, heat a bit of olive oil and sear the lamb on all sides until golden brown.

3. Herb Crust: Mix together bread crumbs, rosemary, thyme, garlic, and a pinch of salt and pepper. Brush the lamb with Dijon mustard and then press the herb mixture onto the mustard.

4. Bake: Place the lamb in a roasting pan and bake for about 20-25 minutes for medium--rare. Let it rest for 10 minutes before slicing.

## Rice Pilaf

Ingredients:

- 1. 1 cup long-grain rice
- 2. 2 tbsp butter
- 3. 1 small onion, finely chopped
- 4. 2 cups chicken broth
- 5. Salt and pepper, to taste

Instructions:

1. Sauté Onion: In a saucepan, melt butter and sauté onion until translucent.

2. Cook Rice: Add rice and cook for 2-3 minutes. Pour in chicken broth, bring to a boil, then reduce heat to low. Cover and simmer for 18-20 minutes, or until liquid is absorbed.

3. Rest: Remove from heat and let it sit, covered, for 5 minutes. Fluff with a fork before serving.

## Steamed Broccoli

Ingredients:

- 1 head of broccoli, cut into florets
- Salt, to taste

Instructions:

1. Steam Broccoli: In a steamer, steam the broccoli florets for about 4-5 minutes or until they are tender but still crisp.

2. Season: Season with a bit of salt.

Serve the sliced herb-crusted rack of lamb with a side of rice pilaf and steamed broccoli for a delicious and elegant meal. Enjoy!

# Seafood Paella

Prep Time: 30 minutes
Cooking Time: 40 minutes
Total Time: 1 hour 10 minutes

Servings:
6 people

## Ingredients:

- 2 cups paella rice
- 4 cups fish stock
- 1 cup white wine
- 1 onion, chopped
- 2 cloves garlic, minced
- 1 red bell pepper, sliced
- 1/2 pound shrimp, peeled and deveined
- 1/2 pound mussels, cleaned
- 1/2 pound clams, cleaned
- 1/2 pound squid, sliced
- 1 teaspoon saffron
- Olive oil
- Salt and pepper to taste
- Lemon wedges for garnish

## Instructions:

1. In a large pan, sauté onion, garlic, and bell pepper in olive oil.
2. Add rice, stirring to coat with oil.
3. Pour in white wine and let it simmer until absorbed.
4. Add fish stock and saffron, bring to a boil.
5. Reduce heat, add seafood, cover, and simmer for 20-30 minutes.
6. Serve with lemon wedges.g.

# *Beef Wellington served with Baked Potato and Roasted Brussell Sprouts*

Prep Time: 30 minutes
Cooking Time: 45 minutes
Total Time: 1 hour 15 minutes

Servings:
6 people

Beef Wellington

Ingredients:

- 1 beef tenderloin (about 2-3 pounds)
- 2 tbsp olive oil
- Salt and freshly ground black pepper
- 4 tbsp Dijon mustard
- 1 package puff pastry, thawed
- 1 egg, beaten (for egg wash)
- 8 oz mushrooms, finely chopped
- 2 shallots, finely chopped
- 2 cloves garlic, minced
- 2 tbsp butter

- 2 tbsp fresh thyme, chopped

Instructions:

1. Preheat oven to 400°F (200°C).

2. Season & Sear Beef: Season the beef tenderloin with salt and pepper. In a skillet, heat olive oil and sear the beef on all sides until browned. Remove and let cool. Once cooled, brush all over with Dijon mustard.

3. Mushroom Duxelles: In the same skillet, melt butter. Add shallots, garlic, and mushrooms, cooking until all the moisture evaporates. Stir in thyme, season with salt and pepper, and let cool.

4. Wrap Beef: Roll out the puff pastry. Spread the mushroom mixture over it, place the beef in the center, and wrap it tightly. Seal the edges and brush with egg wash.

5. Bake: Place the wrapped beef seam-side down on a baking sheet. Bake for 25-30 minutes or until the pastry is golden brown. Let rest for 10 minutes before slicing.

### Baked Potato Recipe

Serving Size: 6

Prep Time: 10 minutes

Cook Time: 1 hour

Total Time: 1 hour 10 minutes

Ingredients:

- 4 large russet potatoes
- 2-3 tablespoons olive oil
- Salt, to taste
- Freshly ground black pepper, to taste
- Optional toppings: butter, sour cream, shredded cheddar cheese, chopped chives, bacon bits, broccoli, or any other favorite toppings

Instructions:

1. Preheat the Oven: Preheat your oven to 425°F (220°C).

2. Prepare the Potatoes: Wash and scrub the potatoes thoroughly under running water. Pat them dry with a kitchen towel or paper towel.

3. Pierce the Potatoes: Using a fork, pierce the potatoes several times on all sides. This allows steam to escape during the baking process.

4. Oil and Season: Rub each potato with olive oil, ensuring they are well coated. Season generously with salt and pepper.

5. Bake the Potatoes: Place the potatoes directly on the middle rack of the oven (you can place a baking sheet on the lower rack to catch any drippings). Bake for about 1 hour, or until the skin is crispy and the inside is soft when pierced with a fork.

6. Serve: Remove the potatoes from the oven. Make a slit down the middle of each potato, then use a fork to open them up. Fluff the inside with a fork.

7. Add Toppings: Serve the baked potatoes with your choice of toppings, such as butter, sour cream, shredded cheese, chopped chives, bacon bits, or steamed broccoli.

Enjoy your baked potatoes as a comforting and filling dish that's both simple and versatile. The crispy skin and fluffy interior make it a perfect canvas for a variety of delicious toppings.

### Roasted Brussel Sprouts

Ingredients:

- 1 lb Brussels sprouts, trimmed and halved
- 2 tbsp olive oil
- Salt and pepper to taste

Instructions:

1. Preheat oven to 400°F (200°C).

2. Prepare Brussels Sprouts: Toss Brussels sprouts with olive oil, salt, and pepper.

3. Roast: Spread on a baking sheet and roast for 20-25 minutes, until crispy on the outside and tender on the inside.

Serve the Beef Wellington slices alongside the creamy Scalloped Potatoes and the crispy Roasted Brussels Sprouts for a complete and exquisite meal. Enjoy!

# Lobster Thermidor served with Mixed Green Salad with Vinaigrette

Mixed Green Prep Time: 15 minutes

Lobster Prep Time: 1 hour and 30 minutes

Ingredients:

- Mixed greens (like arugula, spinach, and romaine) - 8 cups
- Cherry tomatoes, halved - 1 cup
- Cucumber, thinly sliced - 1
- Red onion, thinly sliced - 1/2

For the vinaigrette:

- Olive oil
- 1/2 cup, Balsamic vinegar
- 1/4 cup, Dijon mustard
- 1 tbsp, Honey
- 1 tsp, Salt and pepper to taste

Instructions:

1. Prepare Salad: In a large bowl, combine mixed greens, cherry tomatoes, cucumber, and red onion.

2. Make Vinaigrette: In a small bowl, whisk together olive oil, balsamic vinegar, Dijon mustard, honey, salt, and pepper.

3. Dress Salad: Drizzle the vinaigrette over the salad and toss gently to coat.

Lobster Thermidor

Ingredients:

- 4 whole lobsters (about 1 lb each)
- 4 tbsp butter
- 1 small onion, finely chopped
- 2 cloves garlic, minced
- 1/4 cup dry white wine
- 1 tbsp all-purpose flour
- 1 cup heavy cream
- 2 tsp Dijon mustard
- 1/2 cup grated Parmesan cheese
- Salt and pepper to taste
- Fresh parsley, chopped for garnish

Instructions:

1. Cook Lobsters: Boil lobsters in a large pot of salted water for about 8-10 minutes. Remove and let cool. Cut lobsters in half lengthwise; remove the meat and chop. Set aside shells.

2. Make Sauce: In a skillet, melt butter over medium heat. Add onion and garlic, sauté until soft. Stir in flour, then slowly add wine and cream, stirring continuously. Add mustard, half of the Parmesan, lobster meat, salt, and pepper. Cook until thickened.

3. Assemble: Spoon the mixture into lobster shells. Sprinkle with remaining Parmesan.

4. Broil: Broil for 3-5 minutes or until golden and bubbly. Garnish with parsley.

# Duck à l'Orange with Garlic Asparagus and Creamy Potato Gratin

Duck Prep Time: 45 minutes, Cook Time: 1 hour, Total Time: 1 hour 45 minutes

Asparagus Prep Time: 10 minutes, Cook Time: 10 minutes, Total Time: 20 minutes

Potato Prep Time: 20 minutes, Cook Time: 1 hour, Total Time: 1 hour 20 minutes

Servings:
4

### Ingredients:

- 2 whole ducks, about 5 lbs each
- Salt and pepper, to taste
- 1 orange, quartered
- 4 tbsp sugar
- 1/2 cup white vinegar
- 1 1/2 cups chicken stock
- Juice of 2 oranges (about 1/2 cup)
- Zest of 1 orange
- 2 tbsp Grand Marnier or other orange liqueur
- 2 tbsp unsalted butter

### Instructions:

1. Preheat oven to 350°F (175°C).
2. Prepare Ducks: Season ducks inside and out with salt and pepper. Stuff each duck with orange quarters. Place ducks breast side up on a rack in a roasting pan.
3. Roast Ducks: Roast for about 1 hour, or until skin is golden and crisp, and the internal temperature reaches 165°F (75°C).
4. Make Sauce: In a saucepan, dissolve sugar in vinegar over low heat. Increase heat and cook until it becomes a caramel color. Carefully add chicken stock, orange juice, and zest. Reduce heat and simmer until thickened, about 15 minutes. Stir in Grand Marnier and butter until smooth.
5. Serve: Carve the ducks and serve with the orange sauce.

### Garlic Asparagus

Ingredients:

- 1 lb asparagus, trimmed
- 3 tbsp olive oil
- 3 cloves garlic, minced
- Salt and pepper, to taste

### Instructions:

1. Blanch Asparagus: Boil a pot of salted water. Add asparagus and cook for 3-4 minutes until bright green and tender-crisp. Drain and plunge into ice water to stop cooking.
2. Sauté Garlic: In a skillet, heat olive oil. Add garlic and sauté for 1 minute.
3. Finish Asparagus: Add drained green beans to the skillet. Sauté for another 2-3 minutes. Season with salt and pepper.

### Creamy Potato Gratin

Ingredients:

- 2 lbs potatoes, thinly sliced
- 1 cup heavy cream
- 2 cloves garlic, minced
- 1 cup grated Gruyère cheese
- Salt and pepper, to taste
- Nutmeg, a pinch

### Instructions:

1. Preheat oven to 375°F (190°C).
2. Layer Potatoes: In a greased baking dish, layer half of the potatoes. Season with salt, pepper, and nutmeg. Sprinkle half of the garlic and cheese.
3. Add Cream: Pour half of the cream over the potatoes. Repeat layers with remaining ingredients.
4. Bake: Cover with foil and bake for 30 minutes. Remove foil and bake for another 30 minutes or until golden and bubbly.

Serve the Duck à l'Orange with a side of Garlic Green Beans and Creamy Potato Gratin for a truly delightful meal. Enjoy!

# Mushroom Risotto with Arugula and Parmesan Salad, and Roasted Cherry Tomatoes

Risoto Prep Time: 20 minutes, Cook Time: 30 minutes,
Total Time: 50 minutes

Salad Prep Time: 10 minutes

Tomatoes Prep Time: 5 minutes, Cook Time: 20 minutes,
Total Time: 25 minutes

Servings:
4

## Mushroom Risotto

Ingredients:

- 1 lb mixed mushrooms (like cremini, shiitake, and portobello), sliced
- 1 large onion, finely chopped
- 2 cloves garlic, minced
- 1 1/2 cups Arborio rice
- 1/2 cup dry white wine
- 4-5 cups chicken or vegetable broth, warmed
- 1/2 cup grated Parmesan cheese
- 4 tbsp unsalted butter
- 2 tbsp olive oil
- Salt and pepper, to taste
- Fresh parsley, chopped for garnish

Instructions:

1. Cook Mushrooms: In a large pan, heat 2 tbsp of olive oil. Add mushrooms and sauté until golden. Season with salt and pepper. Set aside.
2. Sauté Aromatics: In the same pan, melt 2 tbsp of butter. Add onion and garlic, cooking until soft.
3. Toast Rice: Add Arborio rice and stir to coat in the butter. Cook for 2 minutes. Pour in wine and simmer until evaporated.
4. Add Broth: Gradually add warm broth, one ladle at a time, stirring continuously until each ladle of broth is absorbed before adding the next.
5. Combine: Once the rice is al dente and creamy, stir in the cooked mushrooms, remaining butter, and Parmesan cheese. Season to taste.
6. Serve: Garnish with parsley and additional Parmesan if desired.

## Arugula and Parmesan Salad

Ingredients:

- 4 cups arugula
- 1/4 cup shaved Parmesan cheese
- 2 tbsp olive oil
- 1 tbsp lemon juice
- 5. Salt and pepper, to taste

Instructions:

1. Dress Salad: In a large bowl, whisk together olive oil, lemon juice, salt, and pepper.
2. Toss: Add arugula to the bowl and toss to coat with the dressing.
3. Serve: Top with shaved Parmesan cheese.

## Roasted Cherry Tomatoes

Ingredients:

- 2 cups cherry tomatoes
- 2 tbsp olive oil
- 1 clove garlic, minced
- Salt and pepper, to taste

Instructions:

1. Preheat oven to 400°F (200°C).
2. Prepare Tomatoes: In a baking dish, toss cherry tomatoes with olive oil, garlic, salt, and pepper.
3. Roast: Roast for 20 minutes, or until tomatoes are blistered and tender.

Serve the creamy Mushroom Risotto with a side of fresh Arugula and Parmesan Salad and Roasted Cherry Tomatoes for a well-rounded and delicious meal. Enjoy!

# Coq au Vin served with Creamy Mashed Potatoes and Sauteed Green Beans with Almonds

Coq au Vin Prep Time: 20 minutes, Cook Time: 2 hours, Total Time: 2 hours 20 minutes

Mashed Potatoes Prep Time: 15 minutes, Cook Time: 20 minutes, Total Time: 35 minutes

Green Beans Prep Time: 10 minutes, Cook Time: 10 minutes, Total Time: 20 minutes

Servings:
4-6

Ingredients:

- whole chicken, cut into pieces (or about 3 lbs chicken pieces)
- 4 slices of bacon, chopped
- 2 cups red wine (Burgundy or Pinot Noir)
- 1 cup chicken stock
- 2 tbsp tomato paste
- 2 onions, chopped
- 2 carrots, sliced
- 3 cloves garlic, minced
- 8 oz mushrooms, quartered
- 2 tbsp flour
- 2 tbsp butter
- Fresh thyme
- Salt and pepper, to taste
- Fresh parsley, chopped (for garnish)

Instructions:

1. 1. Brown Chicken: Season chicken with salt and pepper. In a large pot, cook bacon until crisp. Remove bacon and set aside. Brown chicken pieces in bacon fat and set aside.

2. Sauté Vegetables: In the same pot, add onions, carrots, and garlic. Cook until onions are translucent.

3. Make Sauce: Stir in flour, then add tomato paste, wine, and chicken stock. Bring to a simmer.

4. Cook Chicken: Add chicken and bacon back to the pot. Add thyme. Cover and simmer on low heat for about 1.5 hours.

5. Mushrooms: In a separate pan, sauté mushrooms in butter until golden. Add to the pot in the last 10 minutes of cooking.

6. Serve: Garnish with fresh parsley before serving.

Creamy Mashed Potatoes

Ingredients:

- 2 lbs potatoes, peeled and quartered
- 1/2 cup milk
- 4 tbsp butter
- Salt and pepper, to taste

Instructions:

1. Boil Potatoes: In a large pot, cover potatoes with water and bring to a boil. Cook until tender, about 15-20 minutes.

2. Mash: Drain potatoes and return to the pot. Add milk and butter. Mash until smooth. Season with salt and pepper.

Sautéed Green Beans with Almonds

Ingredients:

- 1 lb green beans, trimmed
- 2 tbsp butter
- 1/4 cup sliced almonds
- Salt and pepper, to taste

Instructions:

1. Blanch Green Beans: Boil a pot of salted water. Add green beans and cook for 3-4 minutes until bright green and tender-crisp. Drain and rinse with cold water.

2. Sauté: In a skillet, melt butter. Add almonds and cook until golden. Add green beans and sauté for 2-3 minutes. Season with salt and pepper.

Serve the Coq au Vin with Creamy Mashed Potatoes and Sautéed Green Beans with Almonds on the side for a truly satisfying and flavorful meal. Enjoy!

# *Vegetarian Mushroom and Spinach Stuffed Shells with a Roasted Beet and Goat Cheese Salad and Garlic Parmesan Roasted Broccoli*

Mushroom Prep Time: 30 minutes, Cook Time: 30 minutes, Total Time: 1 hour

Roasted Beet Prep Time: 10 minutes, Cook Time: 4 5 minutes, Total Time: 55 minutes

Broccoli Prep Time: 10 minutes, Cook Time: 20 minutes, Total Time: 30 minutes

Servings: 4-6

## Mushroom and Spinach Stuffed Shells

Ingredients:

- 24 jumbo pasta shells
- 2 tbsp olive oil
- 1 onion, finely chopped
- 3 cloves garlic, minced
- 8 oz mushrooms, chopped
- 4 cups fresh spinach, roughly chopped
- 15 oz ricotta cheese
- 1 cup grated Parmesan cheese
- 2 cups marinara sauce
- Salt and pepper, to taste
- 1 cup shredded mozzarella cheese

Instructions:

1. Preheat Oven: Preheat oven to 375°F (190°C).
2. Cook Shells: Cook pasta shells according to package instructions until al dente. Drain and set aside.
3. Sauté Vegetables: In a pan, heat olive oil. Sauté onion and garlic until translucent. Add mushrooms and cook until soft. Stir in spinach until wilted.
4. Make Filling: In a bowl, mix together ricotta, Parmesan, salt, and pepper. Add the cooked vegetables and mix well.
5. Assemble Shells: Spread marinara sauce in the bottom of a baking dish. Stuff each shell with the cheese and vegetable mixture and place in the dish.
6. Bake: Top with mozzarella cheese. Bake for 25-30 minutes or until cheese is bubbly and golden.

## Roasted Beet and Goat Cheese Salad

Ingredients:

- 4 medium beets, peeled and diced
- 2 tbsp olive oil
- Salt and pepper, to taste
- Mixed greens

- 1/2 cup goat cheese, crumbled
- 1/4 cup walnuts, chopped
- Balsamic vinaigrette

Instructions:

1. Roast Beets: Toss beets with olive oil, salt, and pepper. Roast in a 400°F (200°C) oven for 45 minutes, or until tender.
2. Assemble Salad: Arrange mixed greens on a platter. Top with roasted beets, goat cheese, and walnuts.
3. Dress: Drizzle with balsamic vinaigrette before serving.

## Garlic Parmesan Roasted Broccoli

Ingredients:

- 1 large head of broccoli, cut into florets
- 3 tbsp olive oil
- 4 cloves garlic, minced
- 1/2 cup grated Parmesan cheese
- Salt and pepper, to taste
- Lemon zest, for garnish

Instructions

1. Preheat Oven: Preheat your oven to 425°F (220°C).
2. Prepare Broccoli: Toss broccoli florets with olive oil, garlic, salt, and pepper.
3. Roast: Spread on a baking sheet and roast for 15-20 minutes or until crisp-tender and slightly charred.
4. Finish: Sprinkle with Parmesan cheese and roast for another 2-3 minutes.
5. Serve: Garnish with lemon zest before serving.

Serve the Mushroom and Spinach Stuffed Shells with a side of Roasted Beet and Goat Cheese Salad and Garlic Parmesan Roasted Broccoli for a complete, nutritious, and delicious vegetarian meal. Enjoy!

# Cocktails and Mocktails

# Midnight Sparkler Cocktail Recipe

Ingredients:

- Champagne or Sparkling Wine: 5 oz
- Blackberry Liqueur (like Crème de Mûre): 1 oz
- Fresh Blackberries: 3-4 berries
- Optional: A twist of lemon peel for garnish

Instructions:

1. Chill the Champagne: Ensure your champagne or sparkling wine is chilled beforehand for the best taste.

2. Prepare the Glass: Choose a flute or a champagne glass for serving. If you'd like, you can run a lemon peel around the rim of the glass for an extra zing.

3. Add Blackberry Liqueur: Pour 1 oz of blackberry liqueur into the glass. The liqueur will give a lovely sweet and tart flavor that complements the champagne.

4. Top with Champagne: Gently pour 5 oz of champagne into the glass. Pour slowly to avoid too much fizz and to keep the layers somewhat separate.

5. Garnish: Add fresh blackberries either directly into the glass or on a skewer placed atop the glass. The berries add a beautiful visual element and a touch of fruity flavor.

6. 6. Serve Immediately: The Midnight Sparkler is best served immediately while the champagne is bubbly and fresh.

Tips:

- For a non-alcoholic version, substitute sparkling grape juice or a nonalcoholic sparkling wine for the champagne.

- Adjust the amount of blackberry liqueur according to your taste preference.

- More liqueur will give a sweeter, fruitier flavor.

Enjoy your Midnight Sparkler, a sophisticated and bubbly cocktail that's perfect for ringing in the new year!

# Frosty Mint Julep

Ingredients:

- Bourbon: 2 oz
- Fresh Mint Leaves: 6-8 leaves, plus more for garnish
- Sugar: 1/2 teaspoon (or to taste)
- Crushed Ice
- Mint Syrup: 1/2 oz (optional, for extra minty flavor)
- Powdered Sugar (optional, for garnish)

Instructions:

1. Prepare the Mint Syrup (if using):

- In a small saucepan, combine equal parts water and sugar with some mint leaves. Heat until sugar dissolves, then let it cool. Strain out the mint leaves.

2. Muddle the Mint:

- In a julep cup or a cocktail glass, gently muddle the mint leaves with sugar. The goal is to bruise the leaves to release their oils, not to shred them.

3. Add Bourbon and Mint Syrup:

- Pour the bourbon over the muddled mint. Add mint syrup if you're using it for an extra minty kick.

4. Add Crushed Ice:

- Fill the glass to the top with crushed ice, stirring briefly to mix and chill the drink.

5. Garnish:

- Garnish with a sprig of fresh mint. Optionally, you can sprinkle powdered sugar over the mint for a "frosty" appearance.

6. Serve with a Straw:

- Serve immediately with a straw. The straw should be short enough so you get the aroma of the mint as you sip.

Tips:

- For a non-alcoholic version, substitute sparkling grape juice or a nonalcoholic sparkling wine for the champagne.
- Adjust the amount of blackberry liqueur according to your taste preference.
- More liqueur will give a sweeter, fruitier flavor.

Enjoy your Midnight Sparkler, a sophisticated and bubbly cocktail that's perfect for ringing in the new year!

# French 75 Recipe

Ingredients:

- Gin: 1.5 oz
- Fresh Lemon Juice: 1/2 oz
- Simple Syrup: 2 teaspoons (adjust to taste)
- Champagne or Sparkling Wine: 3 oz
- Ice
- Lemon Twist, for garnish

Instructions:

1. Combine Gin, Lemon Juice, and Simple Syrup:

- In a cocktail shaker, combine the gin, fresh lemon juice, and simple syrup.
- Add ice to the shaker.

2. Shake:

- Shake the mixture vigorously for about 10-15 seconds. This chills the ingredients and ensures they're well mixed.

3. Strain:

- Strain the mixture into a champagne flute. Make sure to leave enough room at the top for the champagne.

4. Top with Champagne:

- Gently top the drink with champagne or sparkling wine. Pour slowly to prevent it from bubbling over.

5. Garnish:

- Garnish with a lemon twist. To make a lemon twist, use a peeler or a knife to cut a thin strip of lemon peel, and twist it over the drink to release the oils, then drop it in.

Tips:

- The quality of the gin and champagne will greatly affect the taste, so use good quality brands.
- You can adjust the amount of simple syrup based on how sweet you like your cocktail.
- The French 75 is known for its balance of tartness, sweetness, and a bubbly finish, making it both refreshing and festive.

Enjoy your French 75, a delightful cocktail that's perfect for toasting the New Year!

# *Blueberry Gin Fizz*

Ingredients:

- Gin: 2 oz
- Fresh Blueberries: 1/4 cup (plus extra for garnish)
- Fresh Lemon Juice: 1 oz
- Simple Syrup: 1/2 oz (adjust to taste)
- Club Soda: To top
- Ice
- Optional: A sprig of mint for garnish

Instructions:

1. Muddle the Blueberries:
- In a shaker, muddle the blueberries with the simple syrup. You want to extract the juice and flavor from the berries.
2. Add Gin and Lemon Juice:
- Add the gin and fresh lemon juice to the shaker.
3. Shake:
- Fill the shaker with ice and shake the mixture well. This will chill the ingredients and mix them thoroughly.
4. Strain into Glass:
- Strain the mixture into a highball glass filled with ice. The straining will keep the blueberry skins and pulp out of the drink.
5. Top with Club Soda:
- Gently top the drink with club soda. This will add fizz and lighten the drink.
6. Garnish:
- Garnish with a few fresh blueberries and a sprig of mint. The mint adds a fresh aroma and an extra touch of color.

Tips:

- Adjust the amount of simple syrup depending on the sweetness of your blueberries and your personal taste preference.
- You can also use frozen blueberries if fresh ones aren't available. Thaw them before using.
- The Blueberry Gin Fizz is a perfect balance of fruity, tart, and refreshing flavors, making it a delightful cocktail for celebrations.

Enjoy your Blueberry Gin Fizz, a beautifully colorful and tasty cocktail that's sure to be a hit at your New Year's Eve party!

# Spiced Rum Punch

Ingredients:

- Spiced Rum: 2 cups
- Pineapple Juice: 2 cups
- Orange Juice: 1 cup
- Ginger Beer: 1 cup
- Lime Juice: 1/4 cup
- Simple Syrup: 1/2 cup (adjust to taste)
- Cinnamon Sticks: 2-3 for flavor
- Star Anise: 2-3 for flavor
- Orange Slices: for garnish
- Pineapple Chunks: for garnish
- Ice

Instructions:

1. Combine Liquids:

- In a large punch bowl or pitcher, combine the spiced rum, pineapple juice, orange juice, lime juice, and simple syrup.

2. Add Spices:

- Add cinnamon sticks and star anise to the mixture. These spices will infuse the punch with a warm, aromatic flavor.

3. Chill:

- Refrigerate the mixture for at least 1 hour to allow the flavors to meld together. The longer it sits, the more pronounced the flavors will become.

4. Add Ginger Beer:

- Just before serving, stir in the ginger beer. This adds a spicy and slightly effervescent element to the punch.

5. Serve:

- Serve the punch over ice in punch cups or glasses.
- Garnish each serving with a slice of orange and a chunk of pineapple.

Tips:

- Adjust the sweetness by varying the amount of simple syrup. You can also add a bit of honey for a different flavor profile.
- If you prefer a non-alcoholic version, replace the spiced rum with a mixture of apple juice and a few drops of rum extract.
- The combination of spiced rum and tropical juices, balanced with the zing of ginger beer, makes this punch a delightful treat for festive occasions.

Enjoy your Spiced Rum Punch, a perfect drink to keep your guests warm and cheerful as you ring in the New Year!

# Whiskey Sour Recipe

Ingredients:

- Whiskey (Bourbon or Rye): 2 oz
- Fresh Lemon Juice: 3/4 oz
- Simple Syrup: 1/2 oz (adjust to taste)
- Egg White: 1 (optional, for a frothier texture)
- Ice
- Cherry and/or Lemon Twist, for garnish

Instructions:

1. Combine Ingredients:

- In a shaker, combine the whiskey, fresh lemon juice, and simple syrup.
- If you're using an egg white, add it to the shaker at this stage. The egg white is optional but adds a smooth, frothy texture to the drink.

2. Dry Shake (If Using Egg White):

- If you added egg white, first do a dry shake (shake without ice) for about 15 seconds. This helps to emulsify the egg white.

3. Add Ice and Shake Again:

- Add ice to the shaker and shake again vigorously for about 10-15 seconds. This chills and dilutes the drink to a perfect balance.

4. Strain:

- Strain the cocktail into a rocks glass filled with ice. If you've used egg white, you'll get a nice frothy layer on top.

5. Garnish:

- Garnish with a cherry, a lemon twist, or both. The garnish adds a touch of elegance and a hint of additional flavor.

Tips:

- Adjust the sweetness by altering the amount of simple syrup.
- For a stronger sour flavor, increase the amount of lemon juice slightly.
- Always use fresh lemon juice for the best flavor.
- The classic Whiskey Sour is a perfect blend of sweet, sour, and whiskey flavors, making it a favorite for many cocktail enthusiasts.

Enjoy your Whiskey Sour, a classic cocktail that's both refreshing and satisfying, ideal for a New Year's Eve toast!

# Cranberry Mimosa Recipe

Ingredients:

- Cranberry Juice: 1 part (chilled)
- Champagne or Sparkling Wine: 2 parts (chilled)
- Triple Sec (Orange-flavored liqueur): A splash (optional)
- Fresh Cranberries: for garnish
- Orange Twist: for garnish

Instructions:

1. Prepare the Glasses:
- Chill champagne flutes in advance to keep the drink cold.
2. Add Cranberry Juice:
- Pour cranberry juice into each flute, filling about one-third of the glass.
3. Add Triple Sec (Optional):
- Add a splash of triple sec to each glass for a hint of citrus sweetness. This step is optional but adds a nice depth of flavor.
4. Top with Champagne or Sparkling Wine:
- Gently fill the rest of the glass with champagne or sparkling wine. Pour slowly to prevent it from bubbling over and to maintain the layered effect.
5. Garnish:
- Garnish with a few fresh cranberries in the glass and an orange twist on the rim.

Tips:

- Choose a dry or brut champagne or sparkling wine to balance the sweetness of the cranberry juice.
- For a non-alcoholic version, substitute the champagne with sparkling white grape juice or non-alcoholic sparkling wine.
- Adjust the proportions to your taste. More cranberry juice will result in a sweeter, fruitier drink.

Enjoy your Cranberry Mimosa, a delightful and visually appealing cocktail that's perfect for toasting in the New Year!

# Espresso Martini

Ingredients:

- Vodka: 2 oz
- Freshly Brewed Espresso: 1 oz (cooled)
- Coffee Liqueur (like Kahlúa): 1/2 oz
- Simple Syrup: 1/2 oz (optional, adjust to taste)
- Ice
- Coffee Beans: for garnish (typically three)

Instructions:

1. Brew Espresso:
- Brew a shot of espresso and allow it to cool. The quality of the espresso will greatly influence the flavor of the cocktail.
2. Combine Ingredients:
- In a shaker, combine the vodka, cooled espresso, coffee liqueur, and simple syrup (if using).
3. Shake:
- Fill the shaker with ice and shake vigorously for about 15-20 seconds. This not only chills the drink but also helps to create a frothy top.
4. Strain:
- Strain the mixture into a chilled martini glass. A fine strainer can be used to ensure a smooth texture.
5. Garnish:
- Garnish with three coffee beans placed on top of the foam. The beans are not only decorative but also add a subtle aroma.

Tips:

- If you want a stronger coffee flavor, increase the amount of espresso or coffee liqueur.
- The simple syrup is optional and can be adjusted depending on how sweet you like your cocktail.
- Ensure that the espresso is cool before adding it to the shaker to maintain the integrity of the flavors.

Enjoy your Espresso Martini, a rich and delightful cocktail that's perfect for a festive evening!

# Blood Orange Negroni

Ingredients:

- Gin: 1 oz
- Sweet Vermouth: 1 oz
- Campari: 1 oz
- Fresh Blood Orange Juice: 1 oz
- Ice
- Blood Orange Slice: for garnish
- Optional: A sprig of rosemary for garnish

Instructions:

1. Combine Ingredients:
- In a mixing glass, combine the gin, sweet vermouth, Campari, and fresh blood orange juice.
2. Stir:
- Add ice to the mixing glass. Stir the mixture for about 30 seconds to chill and dilute the drink slightly.
3. Strain into Glass:
- Strain the cocktail into a rocks glass filled with ice. A large ice cube is preferable as it melts slower, keeping the drink cold without overly diluting it.
4. Garnish:
- Garnish with a slice of blood orange. Optionally, you can also add a sprig of rosemary for an aromatic touch.

Tips:

- The quality of the ingredients, especially the gin and vermouth, will significantly affect the drink's flavor, so choose them wisely.
- Freshly squeezed blood orange juice is preferred for the best flavor and vibrant color.
- Blood orange has a distinct, slightly tart flavor, which adds a unique twist to the traditional Negroni profile.

Enjoy your Blood Orange Negroni, a stylish and flavorful cocktail that's sure to add a special touch to your New Year's Eve festivities!

# Cucumber Cooler

Ingredients:

- Vodka: 2 oz
- Fresh Cucumber Slices: 4-5, plus extra for garnish
- Fresh Lime Juice: 1 oz
- Simple Syrup: 1/2 oz (adjust to taste)
- Soda Water: To top
- Ice
- Optional: A sprig of mint or a slice of lime for garnish

Instructions:

1. Muddle the Cucumber:
- In a shaker, muddle the cucumber slices with the simple syrup. You want to extract the juice and release the cucumber flavor.
2. Add Vodka and Lime Juice:
- Add the vodka and fresh lime juice to the shaker.
3. Shake:
- Fill the shaker with ice and shake the mixture well. This combines the ingredients and chills the drink.
4. Strain into Glass:
- Strain the mixture into a highball glass filled with ice.
5. Top with Soda Water:
- Gently top the drink with soda water. This adds a light fizz and dilutes the drink to a pleasant strength.
6. Garnish:
- Garnish with additional cucumber slices, a sprig of mint, or a lime slice.

Tips:

- Adjust the sweetness by varying the amount of simple syrup. You can make it less sweet or omit the syrup altogether for a more natural cucumber flavor.
- For an alcoholic-free version, simply omit the vodka. It will still be a delightful and refreshing drink.
- The Cucumber Cooler is an excellent choice for those who prefer lighter, less sweet cocktails.

Enjoy your Cucumber Cooler, a refreshing and hydrating cocktail that's perfect for a celebratory yet relaxed New Year's Eve!

# Pear and Rosemary Cocktail

Ingredients:

- Pear Vodka: 2 oz
- Fresh Lemon Juice: 1/2 oz
- Rosemary Simple Syrup: 1 oz (recipe below)
- Sparkling Water: To top
- Ice
- Pear Slices and Rosemary Sprig: for garnish

Rosemary Simple Syrup:

- Water: 1 cup
- Sugar: 1 cup
- Fresh Rosemary Sprigs: 2-3

Instructions:

1. Prepare Rosemary Simple Syrup:
- Combine water and sugar in a saucepan over medium heat. Stir until sugar dissolves.
- Add rosemary sprigs and simmer for about 5 minutes.
- Remove from heat and let it cool. Strain out the rosemary.

2. Mix the Cocktail:
- In a shaker, combine the pear vodka, fresh lemon juice, and rosemary simple syrup.
- Add ice and shake well.

3. Serve:
- Strain the mixture into a glass filled with ice.
- Top with sparkling water for a light fizz.

4. Garnish:
- Garnish with a slice of pear and a sprig of rosemary for an aromatic and visual appeal.

Tips:

- The amount of rosemary syrup can be adjusted according to your taste preference. More syrup will make the cocktail sweeter and more aromatic.
- If you don't have pear vodka, you can use regular vodka and a splash of pear juice.
- The combination of pear and rosemary creates a unique flavor profile, making this cocktail both refreshing and sophisticated.

Enjoy your Pear and Rosemary Cocktail, a delightful drink that's sure to impress your guests and add a touch of elegance to your New Year's Eve celebration!

# Mocktail Recipes

# Sparkling Apple Cider Mocktail

Ingredients:

- Sparkling apple cider
- Fresh apple slices
- Cinnamon sticks
- Ice cubes
- Optional: a dash of cinnamon or nutmeg powder for garnish
- Optional: a splash of ginger ale or club soda for extra fizz

Instructions:

1. 1. Prepare the Glassware:
- Chill your serving glasses in the refrigerator for about 15-30 minutes before preparation.
2. Add Ice:
- Fill the glasses about halfway with ice cubes.
3. Pour the Sparkling Cider:
- Slowly pour the sparkling apple cider over the ice, filling the glass about three-quarters of the way.
4. Add a Splash of Fizz:
- For an extra fizzy touch, add a splash of ginger ale or club soda.
5. Garnish:
- Add a few fresh apple slices to each glass. For a hint of warmth and spice, insert a cinnamon stick into each glass. Optionally, sprinkle a dash of cinnamon or nutmeg powder on top for garnish.
6. Serve Immediately:
- Serve the mocktails immediately to enjoy the fizz and fresh flavors.

Tips:

- For a more intense apple flavor, you can mix in a bit of apple juice concentrate.
- If you want a slightly sweeter drink, rim the glasses with a mix of sugar and cinnamon before adding the ingredients.
- This recipe is versatile; feel free to add other fruits like orange slices or pomegranate seeds for a colorful twist.

Enjoy your Sparkling Apple Cider Mocktail as a refreshing and elegant drink perfect for any celebration or gathering!

# Midnight Blue Lemonade Recipe

Ingredients:

- Blue curaçao syrup: 2 tablespoons
- Freshly squeezed lemonade: 1 cup
- Club soda: ½ cup
- Ice cubes
- Lemon slice, for garnish
- Optional: Edible glitter or blueberries for an extra decorative touch

Instructions:

1. Prepare the Lemonade:
- If you're making your lemonade from scratch, mix freshly squeezed lemon juice with water and a sweetener of your choice (like sugar or honey) to taste. Chill the lemonade in the refrigerator.
2. Chill the Glasses:
- Place your serving glasses in the fridge for about 15 minutes to get them nicely chilled. This step is optional but adds a nice touch.
3. Mix the Drink:
- In a cocktail shaker or a jug, combine the blue curaçao syrup with the chilled lemonade. Stir well to ensure the color is evenly
- distributed.
4. Add Ice:
- Fill the chilled glasses with ice cubes.
5. Pour the Lemonade Mixture:
- Gently pour the blue lemonade mixture over the ice in each glass, filling them about two-thirds of the way.
6. Top with Club Soda:
- Slowly add club soda to each glass to create a layered effect. The soda will add a nice fizz to your mocktail.
7. Garnish:
- Add a slice of lemon on the rim of each glass for a citrusy garnish. If using, sprinkle a tiny bit of edible glitter on top or drop in a few blueberries for an extra festive look.
8. Serve Immediately:
- Serve the mocktails right away while the fizz is fresh and the drink is chilled.

Tips:

- For a sweeter taste, you can rim the glasses with sugar before adding the drink.
- Adjust the amount of blue curaçao syrup to achieve your desired color intensity. More syrup will result in a deeper blue color.

Enjoy your Midnight Blue Lemonade Mocktail – a non-alcoholic drink that's as delightful to look at as it is to sip!

# Pomegranate Mojito Mocktail

Ingredients:

- 1/2 cup fresh pomegranate seeds
- Fresh mint leaves (about 10-12 leaves)
- 2 tablespoons lime juice (freshly squeezed)
- 1-2 teaspoons sugar (adjust to taste)
- Ice cubes
- Sparkling water or club soda
- Optional: lime slices or wedges for garnish
- Optional: extra mint sprigs for garnish

Instructions:

1. Muddle the Pomegranate and Mint:

- In a sturdy glass, combine the pomegranate seeds, mint leaves, and sugar. Use a muddler or the back of a spoon to gently crush them together, releasing the mint oils and pomegranate juice.

2. Add Lime Juice:

- Pour in the freshly squeezed lime juice and stir the mixture.

3. Prepare the Glasses:

- Fill the glasses with ice cubes to the top.

4. Assemble the Mocktail:

- Pour the pomegranate-mint mixture over the ice, dividing it evenly between the glasses.

5. Top with Sparkling Water:

- Fill the rest of the glass with sparkling water or club soda. Gently stir to combine all the flavors.

6. Garnish:

- Add a slice of lime on the rim of each glass and a sprig of mint for a fresh look.

7. Serve Immediately:

- Serve the mocktails immediately to enjoy the refreshing and tangy flavors.

Tips:

- For a sweeter mocktail, you can add more sugar or use a splash of simple syrup.
- If pomegranate seeds are not available, pomegranate juice can be a good substitute.
- Adjust the amount of lime juice according to your taste preference for more or less tanginess.
- This recipe is easily scalable to serve more people, making it perfect for parties or gatherings.

Enjoy your Pomegranate Mojito Mocktail, a delicious and elegant drink ideal for any festive occasion or a relaxing day at home!

# Virgin Mary

Ingredients:

- Tomato juice – 1 cup (240 ml)
- Lemon juice – 1 tablespoon (freshly squeezed)
- Worcestershire sauce – 1 teaspoon
- Tabasco sauce (or any hot sauce) – a few drops, adjust to taste
- Horseradish (optional) – ½ teaspoon
- Celery salt – a pinch
- Ground black pepper – a pinch
- Ice cubes
- Optional garnishes: celery stick, lemon wedge, pickled vegetables, olives

Instructions:

1. Prepare the Glass:

- If you like, you can rim the glass with salt. To do this, rub a lemon wedge around the rim and dip it in coarse salt.

2. Mix Ingredients:

- In a shaker or a large glass, combine the tomato juice, lemon juice, Worcestershire sauce, Tabasco, horseradish (if using), celery salt, and black pepper. If you don't have a shaker, you can simply stir the ingredients together in a glass.

3. Add Ice:

- Fill the glass with ice cubes.

4. Shake or Stir:

- If using a shaker, shake the mixture well. If you're stirring, mix thoroughly until the ingredients are well combined.

5. Garnish:

- Pour the mixture into the prepared glass. Garnish with a celery stick, a wedge of lemon, or other garnishes like pickled vegetables or olives.

6. Serve:

- Serve immediately and enjoy the spicy, savory flavors of your Virgin Mary.

Tips:

- Adjust the amount of Tabasco and horseradish to suit your taste for spiciness.
- For a deeper flavor, you can add a small amount of smoked paprika or a splash of pickle juice.
- This drink is highly customizable, so feel free to experiment with different garnishes or additional spices to find your perfect mix.

The Virgin Mary is a great choice for brunches, as a hangover cure, or simply as a refreshing and savory non-alcoholic drink option. Enjoy!

# *Peach Bellini Mocktail*

**Ingredients:**

- Peach nectar or peach puree – 1 cup
- Sparkling white grape juice or non-alcoholic sparkling wine – 2 cups
- Fresh peach slices – for garnish
- Optional: a splash of lemon juice for added tartness
- Optional: a small amount of sugar or simple syrup, if more sweetness is desired

**Instructions:**

1. Chill Ingredients: Ensure both the peach nectar/puree and the sparkling white grape juice/non-alcoholic sparkling wine are chilled.

2. Prepare the Glasses: Chill your serving glasses in the refrigerator for about 15-30 minutes for an extra refreshing experience.

3. Mix Peach Nectar and Sparkling Juice: In a pitcher or large glass, mix the peach nectar or puree with the sparkling white grape juice or non alcoholic sparkling wine. Stir gently to combine. If you're using lemon juice or sugar/simple syrup, add it now.

4. Assemble the Drink: Pour the peach and sparkling juice mixture into the chilled glasses, filling them about two-thirds of the way.

5. Garnish: Add a slice or two of fresh peach to each glass for garnish.

6. Serve Immediately: Serve the mocktails right away while the mix is bubbly and fresh.

**Tips:**

- • If you prefer a smoother texture, you can blend the peach nectar or puree
- until smooth before mixing it with the sparkling juice.
- • Adjust the sweetness to your liking by adding more or less sugar/simple syrup.
- • For a fun twist, you can freeze peach nectar into ice cubes and use them instead of regular ice cubes to keep the drink cold without diluting it.

Enjoy your Peach Bellini Mocktail, a sophisticated and delicious drink that's perfect for any special occasion or just a relaxing day!

# Raspberry Fizz Mocktail

Ingredients:

- Fresh raspberries – 1/2 cup
- Lemon juice – 2 tablespoons (freshly squeezed)
- Simple syrup – 2 tablespoons (adjust according to taste)
- Soda water or club soda – 1 cup
- Ice cubes
- Optional: mint leaves for garnish
- Optional: extra raspberries or lemon slices for garnish

Instructions:

1. Muddle the Raspberries: In a glass, add the fresh raspberries and simple syrup. Use a muddler or the back of a spoon to gently crush the raspberries, releasing their juice and flavor.

2. Add Lemon Juice: Pour in the freshly squeezed lemon juice. This adds a nice tangy flavor that complements the sweetness of the raspberries.

3. Prepare the Glass: Fill the glass with ice cubes.

4. Add Soda Water: Slowly pour the soda water or club soda over the ice, filling up the glass. Stir gently to mix the raspberry and lemon mixture with the soda.

5. Garnish and Serve: Garnish with a few mint leaves, extra raspberries, or a lemon slice on the rim for a decorative touch.

6. Enjoy: Serve immediately to enjoy the fizz and fresh flavors of your Raspberry Fizz Mocktail.

Tips:

- If you prefer a sweeter drink, you can increase the amount of simple syrup.
- For an alternative flavor profile, try using lime juice instead of lemon juice.
- This mocktail can be made in larger quantities for parties or gatherings.

Just multiply the ingredients by the number of servings you need and mix in a large pitcher.

Enjoy your Raspberry Fizz Mocktail, a delightful and effervescent drink perfect for any occasion!

# Mango Mule Mocktail

Ingredients:

- Mango juice or puree – 1/2 cup
- Fresh lime juice – 2 tablespoons (from about 1 lime)
- Ginger beer (non-alcoholic) – 1 cup
- Ice cubes
- Fresh mint leaves – for garnish
- Optional: simple syrup or honey, if more sweetness is desired
- Optional: a slice of lime and mango for garnish

Instructions:

1. Chill Ingredients: Ensure that the mango juice/puree and ginger beer are chilled.

2. Prepare the Glass: Traditionally, Moscow Mules are served in copper mugs, but any glass will work. Fill the glass with ice cubes.

3. Mix Mango and Lime: In the glass, combine the mango juice or puree and freshly squeezed lime juice. If you prefer a sweeter drink, add a bit of simple syrup or honey.

4. Add Ginger Beer: Pour the ginger beer over the mango and lime mixture. Stir gently to combine the flavors.

5. Garnish: Add a sprig of fresh mint to the glass. You can also garnish with a slice of lime and a small wedge of mango on the rim of the glass.

6. Serve Immediately: Enjoy your Mango Mule Mocktail right away while it's cold and fizzy.

Tips:

- Adjust the proportions of mango juice and ginger beer to your taste. More mango juice will make it sweeter and fruitier, while more ginger beer will add zest and fizz.

- For an extra kick, you can muddle a small piece of fresh ginger at the bottom of the glass before adding the other ingredients.

- This recipe is easily scalable for a crowd. Just multiply the ingredients by the number of servings and mix in a large pitcher.

Enjoy your Mango Mule Mocktail, a delightful and exotic drink that's perfect for any occasion!

# Non-Alcoholic Sangria

Ingredients:

- Grape juice – 3 cups (as a substitute for red wine, preferably 100% juice)
- Orange juice – 1 cup (freshly squeezed is best)
- Lemon juice – 1/4 cup (freshly squeezed)
- Fresh fruits – oranges, lemons, limes, berries, apples, and peaches, sliced or chopped
- Sparkling water or club soda – 1-2 cups (for fizz)
- Optional: Cinnamon sticks for added spice
- Optional: A few tablespoons of honey or sugar, if additional sweetness is desired
- Ice cubes

Instructions:

1. Prepare the Fruit: Slice or chop your chosen fruits into bite-sized pieces.

2. Traditional fruits used in sangria include oranges, lemons, and apples, but feel free to use whatever you like or have on hand.

3. Mix Juices: In a large pitcher, combine the grape juice, orange juice, and lemon juice. If you're using honey or sugar, add it now and stir well until it's completely dissolved.

4. Add Fruits and Cinnamon: Add the prepared fruits and cinnamon sticks (if using) to the juice mixture. Stir gently to combine.

5. Chill: Allow the mixture to chill in the refrigerator for at least 1-2 hours, but preferably overnight. This helps the flavors to meld together and intensifies the fruity essence of the sangria.

6. Before Serving: Just before serving, add ice cubes to the pitcher and pour in the sparkling water or club soda. Stir gently to mix.

7. Serve: Serve the non-alcoholic sangria in glasses filled with more ice. Make sure to get some of the fruit pieces into each glass.

Tips:

- The longer the sangria sits, the more the flavors will develop, so don't hesitate to prepare it a day in advance.
- Feel free to adjust the proportions of the juices or add other fruit juices like pomegranate or berry for different flavors.
- For a more adult-like flavor, a splash of non-alcoholic wine can be a great addition.
- To keep the sangria from becoming diluted, serve it over ice rather than adding ice directly to the pitcher (unless you're serving it immediately)

Enjoy your Non-Alcoholic Sangria, a perfect drink for sunny days, family gatherings, or any occasion where you want a festive, fruity beverage!

# Super Bowl Party Time

*Welcome to the Ultimate Super Bowl Feast! In this chapter, we dive into a culinary celebration that's as thrilling as the game itself. Get ready to elevate your game day with a spectacular array of appetizers, hearty main dishes, and playful desserts, each themed around the excitement of the Super Bowl. From classic finger foods that keep the crowd cheering to innovative main courses that are a touchdown in flavor, and finally, to desserts that capture the spirit of the game in every bite, we've got your Super Bowl party covered. Whether you're hosting a large gathering or enjoying the game with a few friends, these recipes are designed to delight fans of all ages and tastes, ensuring your Super Bowl celebration is as memorable as the game itself. Let's gear up for a day of fun, flavor, and football!*

# Game Day Snacks and Appetizers

# Stuffed Jalapeño Poppers Recipe

Prep Time: 20 minutes
Cook Time: 10 minutes
Total Time: 30 minutes

Servings:
Makes about 20 poppers

Ingredients:

- 10 fresh jalapeños, halved lengthwise and seeds removed
- 8 oz cream cheese, softened
- 1 cup shredded sharp cheddar cheese
- 1/2 teaspoon garlic powder
- 1/2 teaspoon onion powder
- Salt and pepper, to taste
- 1 cup milk
- 1 cup all-purpose flour
- 1 cup breadcrumbs
- 2 eggs, beaten
- Oil for frying (if deep frying) or cooking spray (if baking)

Instructions:

1. Prepare the Jalapeños: Slice the jalapeños in half lengthwise and remove the seeds. If you're sensitive to spice, wear gloves to avoid irritation.

2. Make the Filling: In a mixing bowl, combine the softened cream cheese, shredded cheddar cheese, garlic powder, onion powder, salt, and pepper. Mix until well blended.

3. Stuff the Jalapeños: Spoon the cheese mixture into each jalapeño half, filling them generously.

4. Coat the Poppers: Pour the milk, flour, and breadcrumbs into separate, shallow dishes. Dip each stuffed jalapeño first into the milk, then flour, back into the milk, and finally into the breadcrumbs, ensuring they are well coated.

5. Prepare for Cooking: If frying, heat oil in a deep fryer or large skillet to 365°F (185°C). If baking, preheat your oven to 400°F (200°C) and line a baking sheet with parchment paper.

6. Cook the Poppers: For frying, carefully place a few poppers at a time into the hot oil, frying them for about 2-3 minutes or until golden brown. Place the poppers on the prepared baking sheet, spray lightly with cooking spray, and bake for 10 minutes or until the breadcrumbs are golden and crisp.

7. Cool and Serve: Let the jalapeño poppers cool slightly on a paper towellined plate to drain excess oil (if fried). Serve warm with your favorite dipping sauce.

Enjoy these delicious Stuffed Jalapeño Poppers as a spicy and crowd-pleasing appetizer!

# Classic Buffalo Wings Recipe

Prep Time: 15 minutes
Cook Time: 45 minutes
Total Time: 1 hour

Servings:
4-6

Ingredients:

- 2 lbs chicken wings, tips removed, drumettes and flats separated
- 1 tablespoon vegetable oil
- 1 tsp garlic powder
- Salt and pepper, to taste
- 1/2 cup hot sauce (like Frank's RedHot)
- 1/4 cup unsalted butter, melted
- 1 tablespoon white vinegar
- 1/4 teaspoon Worcestershire sauce
- Celery sticks and blue cheese dressing, for serving

Instructions:

1. Preheat the Oven: Preheat your oven to 400°F (205°C).

2. Prepare the Wings: In a large bowl, toss the chicken wings with vegetable oil, garlic powder, salt, and pepper. Ensure each wing is well coated.

3. Bake the Wings: Arrange the wings in a single layer on a baking rack set over a baking sheet. Bake in the preheated oven for 40-45 minutes, or until the wings are golden brown and crispy, turning them halfway through.

4. Make the Buffalo Sauce: While the wings are baking, whisk together hot sauce, melted butter, white vinegar, and Worcestershire sauce in a bowl.

5. Toss the Wings in Sauce: Remove them from the oven and place them in a large bowl once the wings are cooked. Pour the buffalo sauce over the wings and toss to coat evenly.

6. Serve: Serve the wings hot with celery sticks and blue cheese or ranch dressing on the side.

Enjoy your Classic Buffalo Wings, the perfect spicy and tangy treat for any sports gathering or casual get-together!

# *Buffalo Cauliflower Bites Recipe*

Prep Time: 15 minutes
Cook Time: 20 minutes
Total Time: 35 minutes

Servings:
4-6

Ingredients:

- 1 head of cauliflower, cut into bite-sized florets
- 1 cup all-purpose flour
- 1 cup water
- 1/2 teaspoon garlic powder
- Salt and pepper, to taste
- 1 cup buffalo sauce
- 2 tablespoons unsalted butter, melted
- Ranch or blue cheese dressing, for dipping
- Celery sticks, for serving

Instructions:

1. Preheat the Oven: Preheat your oven to 450°F (230°C). Line a baking sheet with parchment paper or lightly grease it.

2. Prepare the Batter: In a large bowl, whisk together the flour, water, garlic powder, salt, and pepper until smooth. The batter should be thick enough to coat the cauliflower pieces but not too thick.

3. Coat the Cauliflower: Dip each cauliflower floret into the batter, shaking off any excess. Place the coated cauliflower on the prepared baking sheet in a single layer.

4. Bake the Cauliflower: Bake in the preheated oven for 15-20 minutes, or until the cauliflower is golden and crispy.

5. Prepare the Buffalo Sauce: While the cauliflower is baking, combine the buffalo sauce and melted butter in a small bowl.

6. Toss with Sauce: Once the cauliflower is done, remove it from the oven and toss it in the buffalo sauce mixture until evenly coated. Return the cauliflower to the baking sheet and bake for an additional 5 minutes to set the sauce.

7. Serve: Serve the Buffalo Cauliflower Bites warm with ranch or blue cheese dressing and celery sticks on the side.Enjoy your Classic Buffalo Wings, the perfect spicy and tangy treat for any sports gathering or casual get-together!

Enjoy these Buffalo Cauliflower Bites as a flavorful and vegetarian-friendly alternative to traditional buffalo wings, perfect for game days, parties, or as a tasty snack!

# *Nachos Supreme*

30-35 minutes

Prep Time: 15 minutes
Cook Time: 15-20 minutes
Total Time:

Servings:
4-6

## Ingredients:

- 1 bag (about 13 oz) of tortilla chips
- 1 lb ground beef or ground turkey
- 1 packet taco seasoning
- 1 cup shredded cheddar cheese
- 1 cup shredded Monterey Jack cheese
- 1 can (15 oz) black beans, drained and rinsed
- 1 large tomato, diced
- 1/2 red onion, finely chopped
- 1 jalapeño, thinly sliced
- 1/2 cup black olives, sliced
- 1/4 cup green onions, chopped
- 1/2 cup sour cream
- 1/2 cup guacamole
- 1/2 cup salsa

## Instructions:

1. Preheat the Oven: Preheat your oven to 375°F (190°C).

2. Cook the Meat: In a skillet over medium heat, cook the ground beef or turkey until browned. Drain the excess fat, then stir in the taco seasoning and cook according to the package instructions.

3. Layer the Chips and Cheese: Spread half of the tortilla chips in a large, oven-safe dish or baking sheet. Sprinkle half of both types of cheese over the chips. Repeat with the remaining chips and cheese.

4. Add Meat and Beans: Evenly distribute the cooked meat over the cheesetopped chips. Then, scatter the black beans on top.

5. Bake: Place the dish in the oven and bake for 10-15 minutes, or until the cheese is melted and bubbly.

6. Add Fresh Toppings: Remove the nachos from the oven. Sprinkle the diced tomato, red onion, jalapeño slices, black olives, and green onions over the top.

7. Serve with Sides: Serve immediately with sides of sour cream, guacamole, and salsa.

Chef's Note: You can customize your Nachos Supreme with additional toppings like corn, diced bell peppers, or lettuce. Feel free to adjust the amount of jalapeño or omit it for a milder version.

# Spinach and Artichoke Dip Recipe

Prep Time: 10 minutes
Cook Time: 25 minutes
Total Time: 35 minutes

Servings:
6-8

Ingredients:

- 1 (10 oz) package frozen chopped spinach, thawed and drained
- 1 (14 oz) can artichoke hearts, drained and chopped
- 1/2 cup mayonnaise
- 1/2 cup sour cream
- 1 cup cream cheese, softened
- 1 cup grated Parmesan cheese
- 1 cup grated mozzarella cheese
- 2 cloves garlic, minced
- Salt and pepper, to taste
- Bread, crackers, or vegetables for serving

Instructions:

1. Preheat the Oven: Preheat your oven to 375°F (190°C).

2. Prepare the Spinach: Squeeze the thawed spinach in a clean dishcloth or paper towel to remove excess moisture.

3. Mix the Ingredients: In a large bowl, combine the drained spinach, chopped artichoke hearts, mayonnaise, sour cream, cream cheese, Parmesan cheese, mozzarella cheese, and minced garlic. Stir well until all ingredients are thoroughly mixed. Season with salt and pepper to taste.

4. Transfer to Baking Dish: Spread the mixture into an 8x8 inch baking dish or a similar sized ovenproof dish.

5. Bake the Dip: Bake in the preheated oven for 20-25 minutes, or until the dip is hot and bubbly, and the cheese is melted and slightly golden on top.

6. Serve: Remove the dip from the oven and let it cool for a few minutes. Serve warm with bread, crackers, or your choice of vegetables for dipping.

This Spinach and Artichoke Dip is sure to be a hit at your next party, offering a delicious blend of creamy cheese, tender artichokes, and nutritious spinach. Enjoy!

# Guacamole with Tortilla Chips Recipe

Prep Time: 15 minutes
Total Time: 15 minutes
Total Time: 30 minutes

Servings:
4-6

Ingredients:

- 3 ripe avocados, peeled, pitted, and mashed
- 1 lime, juiced
- 1/2 teaspoon salt
- 1/2 cup onion, finely diced
- 3 tablespoons fresh cilantro, chopped
- 2 Roma tomatoes, diced
- 1 teaspoon minced garlic
- 1 pinch ground cayenne pepper (optional)
- Tortilla chips, for serving

Instructions:

1. Prepare the Avocados: In a medium bowl, mash the avocados with a fork or potato masher until you reach your desired consistency.

2. Add Flavor: Stir in the lime juice and salt. This not only adds flavor but also helps prevent the avocado from browning.

3. Mix in Other Ingredients: Add the diced onion, chopped cilantro, diced tomatoes, minced garlic, and cayenne pepper (if using). Mix well to ensure all ingredients are evenly distributed.

4. Adjust Seasonings: Taste and adjust the seasoning as necessary. Depending on your preference, you might want to add more salt, lime juice, or cayenne pepper.

5. Serve: Transfer the guacamole to a serving bowl and serve immediately with tortilla chips for dipping.

6. Storage Tip: If you need to store the guacamole before serving, place plastic wrap directly on the surface of the guacamole to prevent oxidation

Enjoy your homemade Guacamole with Tortilla Chips, a simple yet delicious treat that's always a hit at parties and get-togethers!

# *Pigs in a Blanket Recipe*

Prep Time: 15 minutes

Cook Time: 15 minutes

Total Time: 30 minutes

Servings:
Makes about 24 pieces

Ingredients:

- 1 package (8 oz) refrigerated crescent roll dough
- 24 mini sausages or cocktail franks
- 1 egg, beaten (for egg wash, optional)
- Mustard or ketchup, for serving

Instructions:

1. Preheat the Oven: Preheat your oven to 375°F (190°C). Line a baking sheet with parchment paper.

2. Prepare the Dough: Unroll the crescent roll dough and separate it into triangles along the perforated lines. Cut each triangle into 3 smaller triangles.

3. Wrap the Sausages: Place a mini sausage on the wider end of each dough triangle and roll up towards the pointed end. Place the wrapped sausages on the prepared baking sheet.

4. Apply Egg Wash (Optional): If you want a golden finish, lightly brush each pig in a blanket with beaten egg.

5. Bake: Bake in the preheated oven for about 12-15 minutes, or until the dough is golden brown and puffed up.

6. Serve: Remove from the oven and let them cool for a few minutes. Serve with mustard, ketchup, or your favorite dipping sauce.

Enjoy your Pigs in a Blanket, the perfect bite-sized treat for any gathering, party, or as a fun snack!

# *Veggie Platter with Dip Recipe*

Prep Time: 20 minutes

Servings:
6-8

Ingredients for Veggie Platter:

- 1 red bell pepper, sliced
- 1 yellow bell pepper, sliced
- 1 cucumber, sliced
- 2 carrots, peeled and cut into sticks
- 1 celery stalk, cut into sticks
- 1 cup cherry tomatoes
- 1 cup broccoli florets
- 1 cup cauliflower florets
- Any other favorite vegetables of your choice

For the Dips
Hummus:

- 1 can (15 oz) chickpeas, drained and rinsed
- 1/4 cup tahini
- 1/4 cup lemon juice
- 2 garlic cloves, minced
- 2 tablespoons olive oil
- Salt, to taste
- Paprika, for garnish (optional)

Ranch Dip:

- 1 cup sour cream
- 1/4 cup mayonnaise
- 1 tablespoon dried parsley
- 1 teaspoon dried dill
- 1 teaspoon garlic powder
- 1 teaspoon onion powder
- Salt and pepper, to taste

Instructions for Veggie Platter:

1. Prepare the Vegetables: Wash all the vegetables thoroughly. Slice the bell peppers, cucumber, carrots, and celery into sticks or slices that are easy to grab and dip.

2. Arrange the Platter: Arrange the prepared vegetables on a large serving platter or tray. Create a colorful and appealing display by grouping different colored vegetables together.

Instructions for Hummus Dip:

1. Blend the Ingredients: In a food processor, combine the chickpeas, tahini, lemon juice, garlic, and olive oil. Blend until smooth. Add a little water if the hummus is too thick.

2. Season and Serve: Season with salt to taste. Transfer to a serving bowl and sprinkle with paprika for garnish if desired.

Instructions for Ranch Dip:

1. Mix the Ingredients: In a bowl, combine sour cream, mayonnaise, parsley, dill, garlic powder, and onion powder. Stir until well mixed.

2. Season and Chill: Season with salt and pepper to taste. For the best flavor, refrigerate for at least 30 minutes before serving to allow the flavors to meld.

Serve:

Place the bowl of your chosen dip in the center of the veggie platter and serve.

Enjoy this Veggie Platter with Dip as a healthy and delicious appetizer or snack, perfect for any occasion!

# BBQ Meatballs Recipe

Prep Time: 15 minutes
Cook Time: 25 minutes
Total Time: 40 minutes

Servings:
6-8

Ingredients for Meatballs:

- 1 lb ground beef
- 1/4 cup breadcrumbs
- 1 egg
- 1/4 cup onion, finely chopped
- 1 clove garlic, minced
- 1/2 teaspoon salt
- 1/4 teaspoon black pepper

Ingredients for BBQ Sauce:

- 1 cup barbecue sauce (store-bought or homemade)
- 2 tablespoons honey (optional for extra sweetness)
- 1 tablespoon Worcestershire sauce
- 1 teaspoon smoked paprika (optional for a smoky flavor)

Instructions:

1. Prepare the Vegetables: Wash all the vegetables thoPreheat the Oven: Preheat your oven to 375°F (190°C).

2. Make the Meatball Mixture: In a large bowl, combine the ground beef, breadcrumbs, egg, chopped onion, minced garlic, salt, and pepper. Mix until well combined but avoid overmixing.

3. Form the Meatballs: Shape the mixture into small, bite-sized meatballs, about 1 inch in diameter. Place them on a baking sheet lined with parchment paper or lightly greased.

4. Bake the Meatballs: Bake the meatballs in the preheated oven for about 15-20 minutes, or until they are cooked through.

5. Prepare the BBQ Sauce: While the meatballs are baking, combine the barbecue sauce, honey, Worcestershire sauce, and smoked paprika (if using) in a small saucepan. Heat over medium heat until the sauce is warmed through.

6. Glaze the Meatballs: Once the meatballs are cooked, remove them from the oven and transfer them to a bowl. Pour the warm BBQ sauce over the meatballs and gently toss to coat them evenly.

7. Serve: Serve the BBQ meatballs warm. They can be skewered with toothpicks for easy serving as an appetizer.

Enjoy these BBQ Meatballs, a simple yet flavorful dish that's sure to be a hit at your next party or gathering!

# Cheese and Charcuterie Board Recipe

Prep Time: 20 minutes

Servings:
6-8

Ingredients:

- A variety of cheeses (about 3-5 types), such as Brie, Cheddar, Gouda, Blue Cheese, and Goat Cheese
- A selection of cured meats (about 2-4 types), like Prosciutto, Salami, Soppressata, and Chorizo
- Assorted nuts, such as almonds, walnuts, and cashews
- A variety of fruits, like grapes, figs, apple slices, and berries
- Crackers and/or slices of baguette
- Olives, pickles, and/or other pickled vegetables
- Optional extras: Honey, fruit preserves, mustard, dried fruits

Instructions:

1. Select the Cheeses: Choose a variety of cheeses, aiming for different textures and flavors. Aim for a mix of soft, semi-soft, and hard cheeses.

2. Choose the Meats: Select a range of cured meats. Thinly sliced options are typically preferred.

3. Prepare Fruits and Nuts: Wash and dry fresh fruits, and slice them if necessary. Gather your selection of nuts.

4. Assemble the Board: Begin by placing the cheeses on the board. Arrange them spaced out, so there's room to slice and pick them up. Add the cured meats, folding or rolling slices for a pleasant presentation.

5. Add Fruits and Nuts: Fill in the gaps with clusters of grapes, figs, apple slices, and berries. Add small piles of nuts around the board.

6. Include Crackers and Bread: Arrange crackers and/or baguette slices around the edges of the board or in a separate basket or plate.

7. Add Condiments and Extras: Place small bowls of olives, pickles, honey, or fruit preserves on the board. These can be used to complement the flavors of the cheeses and meats.

8. Serve: Provide cheese knives, spreaders, and small forks or toothpicks for easy serving. Invite your guests to mix and match their favorite combinations.

Enjoy creating and serving this Cheese and Charcuterie Board, a luxurious and inviting centerpiece that encourages casual dining and conversation. Perfect for any social gathering!

# Fried Mac and Cheese Balls Recipe

Prep Time: 30 minutes (plus chilling time)
Cook Time: 15 minutes
Total Time: 45 minutes (plus chilling time)

Servings:
Makes about 20 balls

Ingredients:

- 2 cups leftover macaroni and cheese, chilled
- 2 eggs, beaten
- 1 cup all-purpose flour
- 1 cup breadcrumbs
- 1/2 teaspoon paprika (optional)
- Salt and pepper, to taste
- Oil for frying

Instructions:

1. Prepare the Mac and Cheese: If you don't have leftover macaroni and cheese, prepare a batch and let it cool in the fridge until it's firm (preferably overnight).
2. Form the Balls: Scoop and roll the chilled mac and cheese into balls, about the size of a golf ball.
3. Set Up a Breading Station: In three separate bowls, place the beaten eggs, flour, and breadcrumbs mixed with paprika, salt, and pepper.
4. Coat the Balls: Roll each mac and cheese ball first in flour, then dip in egg, and finally roll in breadcrumbs until well coated.
5. Chill Again: Place the coated balls on a baking sheet and chill in the refrigerator for at least 1 hour. This step helps them hold together when frying.
6. Heat the Oil: Heat oil in a deep fryer or large pot to 350°F (175°C).
7. Fry the Balls: Fry the mac and cheese balls in batches, being careful not to overcrowd the pot. Cook for about 3-4 minutes or until they are golden brown and crispy.
8. Drain and Serve: Remove the balls from the oil and drain on paper towels. Serve hot, optionally with dipping sauces like marinara or ranch dressing.

Enjoy these Fried Mac and Cheese Balls as a decadent and satisfying treat that's sure to be a hit with guests of all ages!

# Quesadilla Appetizer Recipe

Prep Time: 10 minutes
Cook Time: 10 minutes
Total Time: 20 minutes

Servings:
Makes 4 servings (8 pieces)

Ingredients:

- 4 large flour tortillas
- 2 cups shredded cheese (such as cheddar, Monterey Jack, or a blend)
- 1/2 cup onion, finely chopped
- 1/2 cup bell pepper, diced (any color)
- 1/2 cup black beans, rinsed and drained
- 1/2 cup corn kernels (canned, fresh, or frozen)
- 2 tablespoons olive oil or butter
- Salt and pepper, to taste
- Optional: cooked chicken, beef, or shrimp
- For serving: sour cream, salsa, and guacamole

Instructions:

1. Prepare the Fillings: If you're using any optional meat, cook it ahead of time and set aside. Chop the onions and bell peppers, and prepare the black beans and corn.
2. Assemble the Quesadillas: Lay out the flour tortillas on a flat surface. Sprinkle half of each tortilla with cheese, followed by onions, bell peppers, black beans, corn, and optional meat. Season with a little salt and pepper. Fold the other half of the tortilla over the filling to create a half-moon shape.
3. Cook the Quesadillas: Heat a teaspoon of olive oil or butter in a large skillet over medium heat. Place one quesadilla in the skillet and cook for about 2-3 minutes on each side, or until the tortilla is golden brown and the cheese is melted. Repeat with the remaining quesadillas, adding more oil or butter as needed.
4. Cut and Serve: Remove the quesadilla from the skillet, let it cool for a minute, and then cut each into 4 pieces. Serve warm with sour cream, salsa, and guacamole on the side.

These Quesadillas are a fantastic appetizer for any gathering, offering a combination of melty cheese and flavorful fillings in a crispy tortilla. They're sure to be a crowd-pleaser!

# *Pretzel Bites with Cheese Sauce Recipe*

Prep Time: 30 minutes
Cook Time: 15 minutes
Total Time: 45 minutes

Servings:
Makes about 40 bites

Ingredients for Pretzel Bites:

- 1 1/2 cups warm water (110°F to 115°F)
- 1 tablespoon sugar
- 2 teaspoons kosher salt
- 1 package active dry yeast (2 1/4 teaspoons)
- 4 1/2 cups all-purpose flour
- 4 tablespoons unsalted butter, melted
- Vegetable oil, for pan
- 10 cups water
- 2/3 cup baking soda
- 1 large egg yolk beaten with 1 tablespoon water (for egg wash)
- Coarse sea salt, for sprinkling

Ingredients for Cheese Sauce:

- 2 tablespoons butter
- 2 tablespoons all-purpose flour
- 1 cup milk
- 1 cup cheddar cheese, shredded
- Salt and pepper to taste

Instructions:

1. Prepare the Dough: In the bowl of a stand mixer, combine the warm water, sugar, and kosher salt. Sprinkle the yeast on top and let it sit for 5 minutes until it begins to foam. Add the flour and melted butter, and using the dough hook attachment, mix on low speed until well combined. Increase to medium speed and knead until the dough is smooth and pulls away from the side of the bowl, about 4 to 5 minutes. Remove the dough from the bowl, clean the bowl and then oil it well. Return the dough to the bowl, cover with plastic wrap, and let sit in a warm place for approximately 50 to 55 minutes, or until the dough has doubled in size.

2. Preheat the Oven and Prepare Baking Sheets: Preheat the oven to 450°F (232°C). Line 2 baking sheets with parchment paper and lightly oil them. Set aside.

3. Boil the Pretzels: In a large pot, bring the 10 cups of water and the baking soda to a rolling boil. Meanwhile, turn the dough out onto a slightly oiled work surface and divide into 8 equal pieces. Roll out each piece of dough into a 20-inch rope. Cut the dough into 1-inch pieces to make the pretzel bites. Boil the pretzel bites in the baking soda water in batches, for about 30 seconds each, then remove with a slotted spoon and place onto the prepared baking sheets.

4. Bake the Pretzel Bites: Brush the top of each pretzel bite with the egg wash and sprinkle with coarse sea salt. Bake in preheated oven until dark golden brown in color, approximately 12 to 14 minutes. Transfer to a cooling rack for at least 5 minutes before serving.

5. Make the Cheese Sauce: While the pretzel bites are baking, melt the butter in a small saucepan over medium heat. Add the flour and cook for 1 minute. Whisk in the milk and continue to cook until slightly thickened. Remove from heat and stir in the shredded cheese until smooth. Season with salt and pepper to taste.

6. Serve: Serve the warm pretzel bites alongside the cheese sauce for dipping.

Enjoy these Pretzel Bites with Cheese Sauce, a wonderfully satisfying snack with a soft, chewy interior and a golden, crispy exterior, paired with a creamy, cheesy dip!

# Bacon-Wrapped Dates Recipe

Prep Time: 15 minutes
Cook Time: 20-25 minutes
Total Time: 35-40 minutes

Servings:
Makes about 24 pieces

**Ingredients:**

- 24 Medjool dates
- 12 slices of bacon, cut in half
- 1/2 cup soft cheese (such as goat cheese or cream cheese)
- Toothpicks, for securing

**Instructions:**

1. Preheat the Oven: Preheat your oven to 400°F (200°C). Line a baking sheet with parchment paper or aluminum foil for easy cleanup.

2. Prepare the Dates: Slice each date along one side and remove the pit. Be careful not to cut all the way through the date.

3. Stuff the Dates: Fill the cavity of each date with a small amount of cheese. You can use a teaspoon or a small piping bag for this step.

4. Wrap with Bacon: Wrap each stuffed date with a half slice of bacon. Secure the bacon with a toothpick, ensuring it's wrapped tightly around the date.

5. Arrange on Baking Sheet: Place the bacon-wrapped dates on the prepared baking sheet, with the seam side of the bacon down.

6. Bake: Bake in the preheated oven for 20-25 minutes, or until the bacon is crispy to your liking. You may want to turn the dates halfway through the cooking time for even crispness.

7. Serve: Remove from the oven and let them cool slightly. Serve warm.

Enjoy your Bacon-Wrapped Dates, a perfect combination of sweet, salty, and creamy flavors that make for an irresistible appetizer!

# Mozzarella Sticks Recipe

Prep Time: 15 minutes (plus 2 hours for freezing)
Cook Time: 5 minutes
Total Time: 20 minutes (plus 2 hours for freezing)

Servings:
Makes 12 sticks

Ingredients:

- 12 mozzarella cheese sticks
- 1 cup all-purpose flour
- 2 large eggs, beaten
- 2 cups Italian seasoned breadcrumbs
- 1 teaspoon garlic powder
- 1 teaspoon onion powder
- Salt and pepper, to taste
- Vegetable oil, for frying
- Marinara sauce, for serving

Instructions:

1. Freeze the Cheese Sticks: Begin by freezing the mozzarella sticks. Open the package and place the sticks on a tray or plate. Freeze for at least 2 hours. This step is crucial to maintain their shape during frying.

2. Prepare the Dredging Stations: Set up three shallow bowls for the dredging process. In the first bowl, place the all-purpose flour. In the second, beat the eggs. In the third, mix together the breadcrumbs, garlic powder, onion powder, salt, and pepper.

3. Bread the Mozzarella Sticks: Take the mozzarella sticks out of the freezer. Dip each stick in the flour, shaking off the excess, then dip in the beaten egg, and finally coat thoroughly with the breadcrumb mixture. Repeat this process twice for each stick to ensure a thick coating.

4. Refreeze the Breaded Sticks: Place the breaded sticks back on the tray and freeze again for at least 30 minutes. This helps the coating stick to the cheese when fried.

5. Heat the Oil: In a large frying pan or deep fryer, heat the vegetable oil to 350°F (175°C).

6. Fry the Mozzarella Sticks: Fry the mozzarella sticks in batches, being careful not to overcrowd the pan. Cook for about 1 minute or until they are golden brown, then carefully flip and fry for another minute on the other side.

7. Drain and Serve: Remove the sticks from the oil and drain on paper towels. Serve hot with marinara sauce for dipping.

Enjoy your homemade Mozzarella Sticks, a crunchy and cheesy delight that's always a hit at parties, as a snack, or as part of a fun meal!

# Classic Deviled Eggs Recipe

Prep Time: 20 minutes
Cook Time: 10 minutes
Total Time: 30 minutes

Servings:
Makes 24 halves

Ingredients:

- 12 large eggs
- 1/2 cup mayonnaise
- 2 teaspoons Dijon mustard
- 1 teaspoon white vinegar
- Salt and pepper, to taste
- Paprika, for garnish

Optional Fillings:

- Crumbled cooked bacon
- Finely diced avocado
- Chopped fresh herbs (like chives or parsley)

Instructions:

1. Boil the Eggs: Place the eggs in a single layer in a saucepan and cover with enough water that there's 1-2 inches of water above them. Bring the water to a boil, then cover, turn off the heat, and let sit for 10 minutes. Transfer the eggs to a bowl of ice water to cool.

2. Peel the Eggs: Once cooled, gently peel the eggs and slice them in half lengthwise.

3. Prepare the Filling: Remove the yolks and place them in a bowl. Add mayonnaise, Dijon mustard, white vinegar, salt, and pepper to the yolks and mash until smooth.

4. Optional Variations: For bacon deviled eggs, mix in crumbled cooked bacon. For avocado deviled eggs, mix in finely diced avocado and a bit of lime juice to prevent browning. You can also add chopped herbs for additional flavor.

5. Fill the Egg Whites: Spoon or pipe the yolk mixture back into the egg whites.

6. Garnish and Serve: Sprinkle with paprika for a classic look. Arrange the eggs on a platter and serve.Enjoy your homemade Mozzarella Sticks, a crunchy and cheesy delight that's always a hit at parties, as a snack, or as part of a fun meal!

Enjoy these Deviled Eggs, either classic or with your choice of creative fillings, as a delicious and elegant addition to any menu!

# *Potato Skins Recipe*

Prep Time:15 minutes
Cook Time: 1 hour 15 minutes
Total Time: 1 hour 30 minutes

Servings:
Makes 8 skins

Ingredients:

- 4 medium russet potatoes
- 2 tablespoons olive oil
- Salt and pepper, to taste
- 1 cup shredded cheddar cheese
- 4 slices bacon, cooked and crumbled
- 1/4 cup green onions, chopped
- Sour cream, for serving

Instructions:

1. Preheat the Oven: Preheat your oven to 400°F (200°C).

2. Prepare the Potatoes: Wash the potatoes and prick them several times with a fork. Bake directly on the oven rack for 1 hour, or until they are tender.

3. Cool and Slice the Potatoes: Remove the potatoes from the oven and let them cool until they can be handled. Cut each potato in half lengthwise.

4. Scoop Out the Flesh: Using a spoon, scoop out the inside of the potatoes, leaving about a 1/4 inch of potato on the skin. Reserve the scooped potato for another use.

5. Season and Oil: Brush the inside and outside of the potato skins with olive oil and season with salt and pepper.

6. Bake the Skins: Place the skins cut-side down on a baking sheet and bake for about 10 minutes. Flip the skins over and bake for another 5 minutes until they start to crisp.

7. Add Fillings: Remove the skins from the oven. Sprinkle the inside of each skin with shredded cheese and crumbled bacon. Return to the oven and bake until the cheese is melted, about 2-3 minutes.

8. Serve: Top the potato skins with green onions and serve with sour cream on the side.arties, as a snack, or as part of a fun meal!

Enjoy these Potato Skins as a deliciously hearty appetizer, perfect for sharing and customizable with various toppings to suit your taste!

# 7 Layer Dip Recipe

Prep Time: 20 minutes
Cook Time: 0 minutes (No cooking required)
Total Time: 20 minutes

Servings:
8-10

Ingredients:

- 1 (16 oz) can refried beans
- 1 (1 oz) packet taco seasoning
- 1 cup guacamole (store-bought or homemade)
- 1 cup sour cream
- 1 cup salsa
- 1 cup shredded lettuce
- 1 cup shredded cheddar or Mexican blend cheese
- 1/2 cup chopped tomatoes
- 1/4 cup sliced black olives
- 1/4 cup chopped green onions
- Tortilla chips, for serving

Instructions:

1. Prepare the Bean Layer: In a bowl, mix the refried beans with taco seasoning. Spread this mixture evenly as the first layer in a large serving dish or a 9x13 inch baking dish.

2. Add the Guacamole Layer: Carefully spread the guacamole over the bean layer.

3. Add the Sour Cream Layer: Spread the sour cream over the guacamole layer.

4. Add the Salsa Layer: Gently spread the salsa over the sour cream layer.

5. Add the Lettuce: Sprinkle shredded lettuce evenly over the salsa.

6. Add the Cheese: Sprinkle the shredded cheese over the lettuce layer.

7. Add the Final Toppings: Sprinkle the chopped tomatoes, black olives, and green onions on top.

8. Chill (Optional): For the best flavor, you can cover and chill the dip in the refrigerator for about an hour before serving, but it's also great served immediately.

9. Serve: Serve the 7 Layer Dip with tortilla chips for dipping.

Enjoy this 7 Layer Dip at your next party or gathering, a simple yet flavorful dish that's always a hit!

# Super Bowl Meals

# Pizza Bar

Prep Time: 30 minutes
Cook Time: 10-15 minutes per pizza
Total Time: Varies depending on the number of pizzas

Servings:
Varies (adjust based on the number of guests)

Ingredients:

For the Pizza Dough:

- Store-bought pizza dough or pre-made pizza crusts (estimate 1 per 3-4 guests)

Sauces:

- Marinara sauce
- Pesto
- Alfredo sauce
- BBQ sauce

Cheeses:

- Mozzarella, shredded
- Parmesan, grated
- Cheddar, shredded
- Feta, crumbled

Meats:

- Pepperoni slices
- Cooked sausage, crumbled
- Cooked bacon, crumbled
- Grilled chicken, diced

Vegetables:

- Bell peppers, sliced
- Onions, sliced
- Mushrooms, sliced
- Spinach leaves
- Olives, sliced
- Tomatoes, sliced
- Pineapple chunks
- Jalapeños, sliced

Extras:

- Fresh basil
- Red pepper flakes
- Garlic powder
- Olive oil

Equipment:

- Pizza cutter
- Baking sheets or pizza stones
- Oven

Instructions:

1. Preheat the Oven: Preheat your oven to its highest setting, usually between 450°F and 500°F (230°C - 260°C). If you have pizza stones, place them in the oven to preheat as well.

2. Prepare the Ingredients: Arrange all the toppings in separate bowls. You can put the sauces in squeeze bottles for easy use. Place the cheeses in bowls with spoons or tongs for serving.

3. Set Up the Pizza Dough Station: If using store-bought dough, divide it into smaller balls for individual-sized pizzas. Flatten the dough into thin rounds and place them on parchment paper for easy transfer to the oven.

4. Create Your Pizza Bar: Set up a table or counter space with all the ingredients laid out in order. Start with the pizza dough, followed by sauces, cheeses, meats, vegetables, and extras.

5. Bake the Pizzas: As guests create their pizza masterpieces, transfer each pizza to the oven. Bake for 10-15 minutes or until the crust is golden and the cheese is bubbly and slightly browned.

6. Serve and Enjoy: Once a pizza is done, let it cool for a few minutes, then slice and serve. Continue the process until all guests have made their pizzas.

A Pizza Bar is not only a fun interactive food station but also allows everyone to enjoy their personalized pizza just the way they like it, making your Super Bowl party a memorable event!

# Taco Bar

Prep Time: 1 hour
Cook Time: Varies
Total Time: Varies based on the number of guests

Servings:
Adjust based on the number of guests

Ingredients:

- Proteins:
- Ground beef or turkey, seasoned with taco seasoning
- Shredded chicken, seasoned with taco seasoning or salsa
- Cooked and flaked fish or shrimp for seafood tacos (optional)

Taco Shells and Tortillas:

- Hard taco shells
- Soft flour tortillas
- Soft corn tortillas

Toppings:

- Shredded lettuce
- Diced tomatoes
- Sliced jalapeños
- Chopped onions
- Chopped cilantro
- Shredded cheese (cheddar, Monterey Jack, etc.)
- Sour cream
- Guacamole
- Salsa (various types, e.g., pico de gallo, salsa verde)
- Black beans or refried beans
- Corn kernels
- Lime wedges

Extras:

- Rice (Mexican rice or plain)
- Tortilla chips
- Queso dip

Equipment:

- Serving bowls and spoons for toppings
- Plates and napkins
- Skillets for warming tortillas (optional)

Instructions:

1. Cook the Proteins: Prepare the ground beef or turkey, shredded chicken, and any other proteins. Cook them with appropriate seasonings or salsa. Keep them warm in slow cookers or on the stove.
2. Prepare Toppings: Chop and prepare all the toppings, placing them in separate serving bowls. Include a variety of options to cater to different tastes and dietary preferences.
3. Warm the Tortillas: If desired, warm the tortillas in a skillet or in the oven wrapped in foil to keep them soft and pliable.
4. Set Up the Taco Bar: Arrange the cooked proteins, warm tortillas, and all the toppings on a long table or counter in an order that makes sense for building tacos.
5. Include Extras: Set up a side station for extras like Mexican rice, tortilla chips, and queso dip.
6. Serve and Enjoy: Invite your guests to assemble their tacos to their liking. You can provide plates and napkins nearby.

A Taco Bar allows your guests to customize their tacos exactly how they like them, making your Super Bowl party interactive and enjoyable for everyone!

# *Fajita Bar*

Prep Time: 45 minutes
Cook Time: 30 minutes
Total Time: 1 hour 15 minutes

Servings:
Adjust based on the number of guests

Ingredients:

Proteins:

- 2 lbs boneless chicken breasts or thighs, sliced
- 2 lbs flank steak or skirt steak, sliced
- 2 lbs shrimp (optional), peeled and deveined

Vegetables:

- 3 bell peppers (various colors), sliced
- 2 large onions, sliced
- 1 jalapeño, sliced (optional)

Fajita Marinade:

- 1/2 cup olive oil
- 1/3 cup soy sauce
- Juice of 2 limes
- 2 garlic cloves, minced
- 1 tablespoon chili powder
- 1 teaspoon cumin
- 1 teaspoon paprika
- Salt and pepper to taste

Tortillas:

- Flour tortillas
- Corn tortillas

Toppings:

- Shredded lettuce
- Diced tomatoes
- Sour cream
- Guacamole
- Shredded cheese (cheddar, Monterey Jack, etc.)
- Salsa (various types)
- Chopped cilantro
- Lime wedges

Equipment:

- Grilling pan or skillet
- Serving bowls and utensils
- Plates and napkins

Instructions:

1. Marinate the Proteins: Combine all the marinade ingredients in a bowl. Divide the marinade among the chicken, steak, and shrimp (if using) in separate bowls or plastic bags. Marinate for at least 30 minutes in the refrigerator.

2. Cook the Proteins: Heat a grill pan or skillet over medium-high heat. Cook the chicken, steak, and shrimp in batches, making sure not to overcrowd the pan. Cook until the meats are well-seared and fully cooked. Once cooked, transfer to serving plates and keep warm.

3. Sauté the Vegetables: In the same pan, add a bit more oil if needed, and sauté the bell peppers, onions, and jalapeño until they are soft and slightly caramelized.

4. Warm the Tortillas: Warm the tortillas in a dry skillet, oven, or microwave. Keep them warm in a tortilla keeper or wrapped in a cloth.

5. Set Up the Fajita Bar: Arrange the cooked meats, sautéed vegetables, warm tortillas, and all the toppings on a long table. Organize everything in a way that makes it easy to assemble the fajitas.

6. Serve: Let your guests build their fajitas to their liking, choosing from the variety of fillings and toppings.

Enjoy the game while your guests enjoy customizing their fajitas at your Super Bowl Fajita Bar!

# *Burger and Hot Dog Bar*

Prep Time: 1 hour
Cook Time: Varies
Total Time: Varies based on the number of guests

Servings:
Adjust based on the number of guests

Ingredients:

For the Burgers:

- Ground beef patties (estimate 1 per guest)
- Burger buns
- Cheese slices (e.g., cheddar, Swiss, American)

For the Hot Dogs:

- Hot dogs or sausages (estimate 1 per guest)
- Hot dog buns

Toppings and Condiments:

- Lettuce
- Tomato slices
- Onion slices (raw or caramelized)
- Pickles
- Relish
- Jalapeños
- Sauerkraut
- Ketchup
- Mustard
- Mayonnaise
- BBQ sauce
- Hot sauce

Additional Toppings:

- Bacon strips
- Avocado slices
- Sautéed mushrooms
- Chili (for chili dogs or burgers)
- Coleslaw

Extras:

- Potato chips
- French fries or onion rings (optional)
- Sliced watermelon or other fruit (for a fresh side)

Equipment:

- Grill or large skillet
- Serving plates and utensils
- Napkins and disposable plates

Instructions:

1. Prep the Ingredients: Prepare all the toppings and condiments. Place them in separate bowls or containers with serving utensils.

2. Prepare the Grill: Preheat your grill or skillet to medium-high heat. Make sure it's hot before you start cooking the burgers and hot dogs.

3. Cook the Burgers and Hot Dogs: Grill the burgers to the desired doneness, typically about 4-5 minutes per side for medium. Grill the hot dogs until they are nicely browned and heated through.

4. Toast the Buns: Lightly toast the burger and hot dog buns on the grill for a minute or two.

5. Set Up the Burger and Hot Dog Bar: Arrange the cooked burgers and hot dogs, buns, and all the toppings and condiments on a large table. Include serving utensils for the condiments and toppings.

6. Serve the Extras: Serve potato chips, French fries, onion rings, and sliced fruit on the side.

7. Enjoy: Let your guests assemble their burgers and hot dogs just the way they like them.

This Burger and Hot Dog Bar is perfect for a Super Bowl party, offering a casual and customizable dining experience for all your guests!

# Meatball Sandwich Recipe

Prep Time: 30 minutes
Cook Time: 30 minutes
Total Time: 1 hour

Servings:
Makes about 8 sandwiches

Ingredients:

For the Meatballs:

- 1 lb ground beef
- 1 lb ground pork (or additional beef)
- 1/2 cup breadcrumbs
- 1/4 cup grated Parmesan cheese
- 2 garlic cloves, minced
- 2 eggs
- 1/4 cup milk
- 1 teaspoon salt
- 1/2 teaspoon black pepper
- 1 teaspoon dried Italian herbs (oregano, basil, thyme)

For the Sandwich:

- 8 hoagie rolls or sub buns
- 2 cups marinara sauce (store-bought or homemade)
- 2 cups shredded mozzarella cheese
- Fresh basil leaves (optional)
- Olive oil for cooking

Instructions:

1. Make the Meatballs: In a large bowl, combine ground beef, ground pork, breadcrumbs, Parmesan, minced garlic, eggs, milk, salt, pepper, and Italian herbs. Mix until just combined, being careful not to overwork the meat.

2. Form the Meatballs: Shape the mixture into meatballs, about 1.5 inches in diameter.

3. Cook the Meatballs: Heat a bit of olive oil in a large skillet over medium heat. Brown the meatballs on all sides, then add marinara sauce to the pan. Cover and simmer for about 20 minutes, or until the meatballs are cooked through.

4. Prepare the Sandwiches: Preheat your oven to 350°F (175°C). Slice the hoagie rolls in half, but not all the way through, so they can hold the meatballs and sauce.

5. Assemble the Sandwiches: Place a few meatballs and a generous amount of sauce in each roll. Sprinkle with shredded mozzarella cheese.

6. Bake the Sandwiches: Place the assembled sandwiches on a baking sheet and bake in the preheated oven for about 10 minutes, or until the cheese is melted and bubbly.

7. Garnish and Serve: Garnish with fresh basil leaves if desired and serve hot.

These Meatball Sandwiches are sure to be a hit at your Super Bowl party, offering a delicious and filling option that guests can grab and enjoy while watching the game!

# *Air Fryer Chicken Drums with Apricot Sticky Sauce*

Prep Time: 15 minutes
Cook Time: 25 minutes for chicken,
20 minutes for macaroni and cheese, 10 minutes for corn
Total Time: ~30 minutes
(some preparations can be done simultaneously)

Servings:
4

Ingredients:

For the Chicken Drums:

- 8 chicken drumsticks
- 2 tablespoons olive oil
- Salt and pepper, to taste
- 1 teaspoon garlic powder
- 1 teaspoon paprika

For the Apricot Sticky Sauce:

- 1/2 cup apricot jam
- 2 tablespoons soy sauce
- 2 tablespoons Dijon mustard
- 1 tablespoon apple cider vinegar
- 1 garlic clove, minced
- 1 teaspoon ginger, grated

For the Macaroni and Cheese:

- 2 cups elbow macaroni
- 2 tablespoons butter
- 2 tablespoons all-purpose flour
- 2 cups milk
- 2 cups shredded sharp cheddar cheese
- Salt and pepper, to taste

For the Corn on the Cob:

- 4 ears of corn, husked
- Butter (for serving)
- Salt (for serving)

Instructions:

Chicken Drums:

1. Preheat the air fryer to 380°F (190°C).
2. Rub the chicken drums with olive oil, and season with salt, pepper, garlic powder, and paprika.
3. Place the chicken in the air fryer basket and cook for 25 minutes, turning halfway through, until crispy and cooked through.

Apricot Sticky Sauce:

1. While the chicken is cooking, combine apricot jam, soy sauce, Dijon mustard, apple cider vinegar, minced garlic, and grated ginger in a saucepan.
2. Simmer on low heat for 10 minutes, stirring occasionally, until the sauce thickens.

Macaroni and Cheese:

1. Cook the macaroni according to package instructions. Drain and set aside.
2. In a pot, melt butter over medium heat. Stir in flour and cook for 1-2 minutes to create a roux.
3. Gradually add milk, whisking continuously to avoid lumps. Cook until the sauce thickens.
4. Remove from heat and stir in shredded cheese until melted. Season with salt and pepper.
5. Add the cooked macaroni to the cheese sauce and stir to combine.

Corn on the Cob:

1. Boil the corn in a large pot of salted water for 7-10 minutes until tender.
2. Serve with butter and a pinch of salt.

To Serve:

1. Once the chicken is done, brush the drums with the apricot sticky sauce.
2. Serve the glazed chicken with a side of creamy macaroni and cheese and buttered corn on the cob.

Enjoy this delicious meal that combines the sweet and savory flavors of apricot glazed chicken with the classic comfort of homemade macaroni and cheese and the simplicity of corn on the cob.

# Sausage and Pepper Hoagies with Pasta Salad

Prep Time: 15 minutes
Cook Time: 25 minutes
Total Time: 40 minutes

Servings:
4 hoagies

## Ingredients:

- 4 Italian sausages (about 1 pound)
- 2 tablespoons olive oil
- 1 large bell pepper, sliced
- 1 large onion, sliced
- 2 cloves garlic, minced
- 1 teaspoon dried oregano
- Salt and pepper, to taste
- 2 cups marinara sauce (store-bought or homemade)
- 4 hoagie rolls
- 1 cup shredded mozzarella cheese (optional)

## Instructions:

1. Cook the Sausages: In a large skillet over medium heat, cook the sausages, turning occasionally, until they're browned and cooked through, about 10-12 minutes. Remove from the skillet and set aside.

2. Sauté the Vegetables: In the same skillet, add the olive oil, sliced bell pepper, and onion. Cook over medium heat until the vegetables are soft and slightly caramelized, about 10 minutes. Add the minced garlic, dried oregano, salt, and pepper, and cook for an additional 2 minutes.

3. Slice the Sausages: Once the sausages have cooled slightly, slice them lengthwise without cutting all the way through, so they can be opened flat.

4. Combine Sausages and Vegetables: Return the sausages to the skillet with the vegetables. Pour the marinara sauce over the sausage and vegetables, and simmer everything together for about 5 minutes, or until the sauce is heated through.

5. Prepare the Hoagie Rolls: If desired, lightly toast the hoagie rolls in the oven.

6. Assemble the Hoagies: Open each hoagie roll and place a sausage inside. Top with the pepper, onion, and marinara sauce mixture. If using cheese, sprinkle the shredded mozzarella on top.

7. Broil (Optional): For melted cheese, place the assembled hoagies on a baking sheet and broil in the oven for a couple of minutes until the cheese is melted and bubbly.

8. Serve: Serve the hoagies hot, with additional marinara sauce on the side if desired.

Enjoy these Sausage and Pepper Hoagies with the rich flavors of Italian sausage, sweet peppers, onions, and savory marinara sauce - a true crowdpleaser!

Mediterranean-Style Pasta Salad

Ingredients:

- 8 oz pasta (such as rotini, penne, or farfalle)
- 1 cup artichoke hearts, chopped
- 1/2 cup Kalamata olives, pitted and sliced
- 1/2 cup sun-dried tomatoes, chopped
- 1/2 cup feta cheese, crumbled
- 1 cup shredded carrots
- 1/4 cup balsamic vinaigrette or Italian dressing
- Salt and pepper, to taste
- Fresh basil or parsley, chopped (for garnish)

Instructions:

9. 1. Cook the Pasta: Bring a large pot of salted water to a boil. Add the pasta and cook according to package instructions until al dente. Drain and rinse under cold water to cool.

10. 2. Prepare the Ingredients: While the pasta is cooking, prepare the artichoke hearts, Kalamata olives, sun-dried tomatoes, and shredded carrots. Place them in a large mixing bowl.

11. 3. Combine Ingredients: Add the cooled pasta to the bowl with the prepared vegetables. Add the crumbled feta cheese.

12. 4. Dress the Salad: Pour the balsamic vinaigrette or Italian dressing over the salad. Toss gently to coat everything evenly. Season with salt and pepper to taste.

13. 5. Chill (Optional): For the best flavor, cover and refrigerate the salad for at least 30 minutes to allow the flavors to meld together.

14. 6. Serve: Before serving, give the salad a quick toss and garnish with chopped fresh basil or parsley.

This Mediterranean-Style Pasta Salad is a colorful and delicious side that pairs wonderfully with the robust flavors of the Sausage and Pepper Hoagies, creating a balanced and satisfying meal. Enjoy!

# Slider Bar

# Spicy Whiskey BBQ Chicken Sliders Recipe

Prep Time: 15 minutes (plus marinating time)

Cook Time: 20 minutes

Total Time: 35 minutes (plus marinating time)

Servings:
8 Sliders

Certainly! Here's a recipe for Spicy Whiskey BBQ Chicken Sliders, a flavorful and slightly fiery dish perfect for a Super Bowl party or any casual gathering.

Ingredients:

For the Chicken:

- 2 large chicken breasts
- 1 cup whiskey BBQ sauce (below)
- 1 teaspoon cayenne pepper (adjust to taste)
- 1 teaspoon garlic powder
- 1 teaspoon onion powder
- Salt and pepper to taste
- 8 slider buns
- 1 tablespoon olive oil

For the Slaw:

- 2 cups shredded cabbage
- 1 carrot, shredded
- 1/2 cup mayonnaise
- 1 tablespoon apple cider vinegar
- 1 teaspoon sugar
- Salt and pepper to taste

Additional Toppings:

- Sliced pickles
- Extra whiskey BBQ sauce for drizzling

Instructions:

1. Marinate the Chicken: In a bowl, combine the whiskey BBQ sauce, cayenne pepper, garlic powder, and onion powder. Season the chicken breasts with salt and pepper and then coat them in the marinade. Refrigerate for at least 1 hour, or overnight for more flavor.

2. Prepare the Slaw: In a separate bowl, mix together the shredded cabbage, carrot, mayonnaise, apple cider vinegar, sugar, salt, and pepper. Set aside in the refrigerator.

3. Cook the Chicken: Heat olive oil in a skillet over medium heat. Remove the chicken from the marinade (reserving the marinade) and cook for about 5-7 minutes on each side or until fully cooked through. During the last few minutes of cooking, brush the chicken with the reserved marinade for extra flavor.

4. Slice the Chicken: Once cooked, let the chicken rest for a few minutes, then slice it into thin pieces.

5. Assemble the Sliders: Toast the slider buns if desired. Place a generous amount of the sliced chicken on each bun. Top with the prepared slaw and a few slices of pickles. Drizzle with additional whiskey BBQ sauce if desired.

6. Serve: Serve the sliders immediately while the chicken is warm and juicy.

These Spicy Whiskey BBQ Chicken Sliders are packed with flavor and have a delightful balance of sweet, smoky, and spicy. They're sure to be a hit at your Super Bowl party!

Whiskey BBQ Sauce Recipe

Ingredients:

- 1 cup ketchup
- 1/2 cup whiskey (choose a brand you like the flavor of)
- 1/4 cup apple cider vinegar
- 1/4 cup brown sugar, packed
- 2 tablespoons honey
- 1 tablespoon Worcestershire sauce
- 1 tablespoon lemon juice
- 2 cloves garlic, minced
- 1/2 teaspoon smoked paprika
- 1/2 teaspoon onion powder
- 1/2 teaspoon ground black pepper
- 1/4 teaspoon cayenne pepper (adjust to taste for spiciness)
- Salt to taste

Instructions:

7. Combine Ingredients: In a medium saucepan, combine the ketchup, whiskey, apple cider vinegar, brown sugar, honey, Worcestershire sauce, lemon juice, minced garlic, smoked paprika, onion powder, black pepper, and cayenne pepper.

8. Simmer the Sauce: Bring the mixture to a simmer over medium heat, stirring occasionally.

9. Reduce and Thicken: Reduce the heat to low and let the sauce simmer for about 20 minutes, or until it has thickened to your desired consistency. Stir the sauce occasionally as it simmers to prevent sticking and burning.

10. Adjust Seasonings: Taste the sauce and adjust the salt and spices as needed. If you prefer a sweeter sauce, you can add a little more honey.

11. Cool and Store: Remove the sauce from the heat and let it cool. The sauce can be used immediately or stored in an airtight container in the refrigerator for up to a week.

This Whiskey BBQ Sauce is versatile and can be used as a glaze for grilled meats, a flavorful addition to pulled pork, or as a dipping sauce. Enjoy its rich, smoky flavor with a hint of whiskey for a gourmet touch to your BBQ dishes!

# Classic Cheeseburger Sliders

Prep Time: 15 minutes

Cook Time: 30 minutes

Total Time: 45 minutes

Servings:
Makes 12 sliders

Ingredients:

- 12 Hawaiian rolls, sliced in half
- 1 lb ground beef
- Salt and pepper, to taste
- 12 slices cheddar cheese
- Lettuce, tomato slices, and pickles for topping
- Ketchup and mustard, for serving

Instructions:

1. Preheat the Oven: Preheat your oven to 350°F (175°C).

2. Form Hamburger: In a 9x13 baking dish spread the ground beef evenly in the dish. Salt and pepper the beef.

3. Cook the Hamburger: Cook the beef in the oven until cooked through, approx. 10 minutes.

4. Assemble the Sliders: Place the bottom halves of the Hawaiian rolls on a baking sheet. Using a spatula place the cooked beef on the rolls. Top with cheese.

5. Bake: Cover with the top halves of the rolls. Bake in the preheated oven for about 10 minutes, or until the cheese is melted and the rolls are slightly toasted.

6. Serve: Serve warm with Veggies, ketchup and mustard on the side.

# BBQ Pulled Pork Sliders

Prep Time: 20 minutes (plus slow cooking time)

Cook Time: 6 hours

Total Time: 6 hours 20 minutes

Servings:
Makes 12 sliders

Ingredients:

- 12 Hawaiian rolls, sliced in half
- 2 lbs pork shoulder
- 1 bottle BBQ sauce
- 1 onion, chopped
- 1/2 cup chicken broth
- Coleslaw, for serving

Instructions:

1. Slow Cook the Pork: Place the pork shoulder, BBQ sauce, onion, and chicken broth in a slow cooker. Cook on low for 6 hours or until the pork is tender and shreds easily.

2. Shred the Pork: Remove the pork from the slow cooker and shred it using two forks. Return it to the slow cooker and mix with the sauce.

3. Assemble the Sliders: Place the bottom halves of the Hawaiian rolls on a baking sheet. Top each with a generous amount of pulled pork.

4. Serve: Top with coleslaw and cover with the top halves of the rolls. Serve immediately.

Classic Coleslaw Recipe

Ingredients:

- 1 medium green cabbage, finely shredded (about 6 cups)
- 2 medium carrots, grated
- 1 small onion, finely chopped (optional)
- 1/2 cup mayonnaise
- 2 tablespoons white vinegar
- 1 tablespoon Dijon mustard
- 1 tablespoon sugar
- 1/2 teaspoon salt
- 1/4 teaspoon black pepper
- 1/2 teaspoon celery seed (optional)

Instructions:

5. Prepare the Vegetables: In a large bowl, combine the shredded cabbage, grated carrots, and chopped onion (if using).

6. Make the Dressing: In a separate bowl, whisk together the mayonnaise, white vinegar, Dijon mustard, sugar, salt, pepper, and celery seed (if using) until smooth and well blended.

7. Combine and Mix: Pour the dressing over the cabbage mixture. Toss well to ensure all the vegetables are evenly coated with the dressing.

8. Chill (Optional): For the best flavor, cover and refrigerate the coleslaw for at least 1 hour before serving. This allows the flavors to meld and the cabbage to soften slightly.

9. Serve: Toss the coleslaw again before serving. Adjust seasoning if necessary.

# Cooked Ham and Cheese Sliders

Ingredients:

- Sliced cooked ham
- Sliced Swiss cheese
- Slider buns
- Dijon mustard

Instructions:

1. Spread Dijon mustard on slider buns.
2. Layer with a slice of ham and a slice of Swiss cheese.
3. Warm in the oven until the cheese melts slightly, then serve.

# Veggie Slider Option

Ingredients:

- 1 can black beans, drained and mashed
- 1/2 cup breadcrumbs
- 1/4 cup finely chopped bell peppers
- 1 egg
- 1 teaspoon cumin
- Salt and pepper, to taste
- Slider buns
- Lettuce and tomato slices for garnish
- Avocado or vegan mayo (optional)

Instructions:

1. Combine mashed black beans, breadcrumbs, bell peppers, egg, cumin, salt, and pepper. Form into small patties.
2. Fry patties in a skillet with a little oil until crispy on both sides.
3. Serve on slider buns with lettuce, tomato, and avocado or vegan mayo.

These slider options offer something for everyone, from the rich and hearty to the light and healthy. Don't forget to check out more appetizer recipes in the Appetizer section to complement your Slider Bar at your Super Bowl party!

# Chicken Parmesan Sliders

Prep Time: 20 minutes
Cook Time: 20 minutes
Total Time: 40 minutes

Servings:
Makes 12 sliders

Ingredients:

- 12 Hawaiian rolls, sliced in half
- 2 cups cooked, shredded chicken
- 1 cup marinara sauce
- 1 cup shredded mozzarella cheese
- 1/2 cup grated Parmesan cheese
- Fresh basil leaves for garnish

Instructions:

1. Preheat the Oven: Preheat your oven to 375°F (190°C).
2. Prepare Chicken Mixture: In a bowl, mix together the shredded chicken and marinara sauce.
3. Assemble the Sliders: Place the bottom halves of the Hawaiian rolls on a baking sheet. Top each with the chicken mixture, then sprinkle mozzarella and Parmesan cheese over the top.
4. Bake: Cover with the top halves of the rolls. Bake in the preheated oven for about 15-20 minutes, or until the cheese is melted and bubbly.
5. Garnish and Serve: Garnish with fresh basil leaves and serve warm.

Each of these slider recipes offers a unique flavor profile, ensuring there's something for everyone to enjoy!

# Hearty Chili Recipe with Cornbread (below)

Prep Time: 20 minutes
Cook Time: 1 hour 30 minutes
Total Time: 1 hour 50 minutes

Servings:

6-8

**Ingredients:**

- 2 tablespoons olive oil
- 1 large onion, chopped
- 2 cloves garlic, minced
- 1 bell pepper, chopped (any color)
- 1 lb ground beef or turkey
- 1 (28 oz) can crushed tomatoes
- 1 (15 oz) can kidney beans, drained and rinsed
- 1 (15 oz) can black beans, drained and rinsed
- 2 tablespoons tomato paste
- 1 cup beef or chicken broth
- 2 tablespoons chili powder
- 1 teaspoon cumin
- 1 teaspoon paprika
- Salt and pepper, to taste
- Optional: 1 teaspoon cayenne pepper (for extra heat)

**Toppings:**

- Shredded cheddar cheese
- Chopped green onions or red onions
- Sour cream
- Additional optional toppings: diced avocados, chopped cilantro, lime wedges

**Instructions:**

1. Cook the Aromatics: Heat the olive oil in a large pot over medium heat. Add the chopped onion, bell pepper, and garlic, and sauté until softened, about 5 minutes.

2. Brown the Meat: Add the ground beef or turkey to the pot. Cook, breaking it apart with a spoon, until browned and no longer pink.

3. Add Tomatoes and Beans: Stir in the crushed tomatoes, kidney beans, black beans, and tomato paste. Mix well.

4. Add Liquids and Seasonings: Pour in the broth. Add chili powder, cumin, paprika, salt, and pepper. If you like your chili spicy, add the cayenne pepper.

5. Simmer the Chili: Bring the mixture to a boil, then reduce the heat to low. Cover and simmer, stirring occasionally, for about 1 hour to let the flavors meld. If the chili is too thick, add more broth as needed.

6. Serve: Ladle the chili into bowls. Top with shredded cheese, chopped onions, and a dollop of sour cream. Add any other toppings of your choice.

Enjoy this Hearty Chili, a warm and filling dish that's great for a cozy dinner, game day, or any time you're in the mood for something satisfying and delicious!

# *Slow Cooker White Chicken Chili with Cornbread*

Prep Time: 15 minutes

Cook Time: 4 hours on high or 7-8 hours on low

Total Time: 4 hours 15 minutes (for high setting) or 7-8 hours 15 minutes (for low setting)

Servings:

6-8

Ingredients:

*   2 lbs boneless, skinless chicken breasts
*   1 large onion, chopped
*   2 cloves garlic, minced
*   2 cans (15 oz each) Great Northern beans, drained and rinsed
*   1 can (4 oz) diced green chiles
*   2 teaspoons ground cumin
*   1 teaspoon chili powder
*   1/2 teaspoon oregano
*   4 cups chicken broth
*   Salt and pepper, to taste
*   1 cup sour cream
*   1/2 cup fresh cilantro, chopped
*   Juice of 1 lime
*   Avocado for serving
*   Shredded Monterey Jack cheese, for serving

Instructions:

1.  Combine Ingredients in Slow Cooker: Place the chicken breasts, onion, garlic, Great Northern beans, green chiles, cumin, chili powder, oregano, and chicken broth in the slow cooker. Season with salt and pepper.

2.  Cook: Cover and cook on high for 4 hours or on low for 7-8 hours, until the chicken is tender and cooked through.

3.  Shred Chicken: Remove the chicken from the slow cooker and shred it using two forks. Return the shredded chicken to the slow cooker.

4.  Add Final Touches: Stir in the sour cream, chopped cilantro, and lime juice. Adjust seasoning if necessary.

5.  Serve: Serve the chili hot with chopped avocado, shredded Monterey Jack cheese and a side of cornbread.

# *Sour Cream and Cheddar Cornbread Recipe*

Prep Time: 10 minutes
Cook Time: 25-30 minutes
Total Time: 35-40 minutes

Servings:
9-12 servings

Ingredients:

- 1 cup cornmeal
- 1 cup all-purpose flour
- 1/4 cup granulated sugar
- 1 tablespoon baking powder
- 1/2 teaspoon salt
- 1 cup sour cream
- 1/3 cup milk
- 1/3 cup vegetable oil or melted butter
- 2 large eggs
- 1 cup shredded sharp cheddar cheese
- 1/4 cup chopped green onions or chives (optional)

Instructions:

1. Preheat the Oven and Prepare the Pan: Preheat your oven to 400°F (200°C). Grease an 8x8 inch baking dish or a 9-inch round cake pan.

2. Mix Dry Ingredients: In a large bowl, combine the cornmeal, flour, sugar, baking powder, and salt.

3. Combine Wet Ingredients: In another bowl, whisk together the sour cream, milk, vegetable oil (or melted butter), and eggs until well blended.

4. Combine Wet and Dry Ingredients: Add the wet ingredients to the dry ingredients and mix until just combined. Be careful not to overmix.

5. Add Cheese and Optional Green Onions: Fold in the shredded cheddar cheese and green onions (if using) into the batter.

6. Pour the Batter into the Pan: Transfer the batter to the prepared baking dish, spreading it out evenly.

7. Bake: Bake for 25-30 minutes, or until the top is golden brown and a toothpick inserted into the center of the cornbread comes out clean.

8. Cool and Serve: Let the cornbread cool for a few minutes in the pan, then cut it into squares or wedges. Serve warm.

This Sour Cream and Cheddar Cornbread is delightfully moist and flavorful, making it a perfect accompaniment to chili, soups, or as a tasty snack on its own. Enjoy!

# Valentine's Day Delights

*Ah, love is in the air, and the world is painted in shades of pink and red as Valentine's Day approaches. It's that special time of year when hearts skip a beat, roses bloom with added vibrancy, and couples everywhere celebrate the beauty of romance. In our culinary journey through the pages of this cookbook, there's no better occasion to explore the art of creating unforgettable moments through food than Valentine's Day. Welcome to the enchanting chapter of "Valentine's Day Delights," where we embrace the magic of this romantic holiday and indulge in the pleasure of sharing exceptional dishes with the ones we cherish. Planning a candlelit dinner for two? Our carefully curated recipes are designed to ignite the flames of passion and make your Valentine's Day celebration truly unforgettable.*

# Creative heart-themed appetizers and drinks

# Beet and Goat Cheese Napoleons

## Ingredients

- 2-3 medium-sized red beets
- Olive oil
- Salt and freshly ground black pepper
- 8 ounces goat cheese, softened
- Honey, for drizzling
- 1/2 cup chopped walnuts, toasted
- Fresh herbs such as thyme or parsley for garnish (optional)

## Instructions

Roasting the Beets:

1. Preheat Oven: Preheat your oven to 400°F (200°C).

2. Prepare Beets: Trim the beets and wash them thoroughly. Wrap each beet in foil and place them on a baking sheet.

3. Roast: Roast in the oven until tender, about 45-60 minutes depending on their size. You can check for doneness by inserting a fork into a beet; it should slide in easily.

4. Cool and Slice: Once cool enough to handle, peel the beets and slice them into even, round slices about 1/4 inch thick.

Assembling the Napoleons:

1. Cut Heart Shapes: Using a heart-shaped cookie cutter, cut out heart shapes from the beet slices. Do the same with the goat cheese. If the goat cheese is too soft to cut, place it in the freezer for a few minutes to firm up.

2. Layer: Start with a beet slice, add a layer of goat cheese, and then another beet slice. Repeat until you have a stack of 2-3 layers, ending with a beet on top.

3. Drizzle with Honey: Drizzle each Napoleon with honey.

4. Add Walnuts: Sprinkle the chopped walnuts over the top.

5. Garnish: Garnish with fresh herbs if desired.

Serving:

- Serve the Beet and Goat Cheese Napoleons immediately, arranged on a platter or individual plates.

- They can be served as an elegant starter or as part of a salad course.

These Beet and Goat Cheese Napoleons are not only delicious but also a feast for the eyes, making them a perfect dish for special occasions or when you want to impress your guests with something both beautiful and flavorful.

# *Heart-Shaped Bruschetta*

### Ingredients

- 1 baguette
- 2-3 ripe tomatoes, diced
- 2 cloves of garlic, minced
- A handful of fresh basil leaves, finely chopped
- 2-3 tablespoons extra virgin olive oil, plus extra for brushing
- Salt and freshly ground black pepper
- Balsamic glaze (optional, for drizzling)

### Instructions

**Preparing the Bread:**

1. Cut Baguette: Slice the baguette diagonally to create oval slices. Use a heart-shaped cookie cutter to cut each slice into a heart shape.

2. Toast the Bread: Preheat your oven to 375°F (190°C). Brush both sides of each heart-shaped bread slice with olive oil and place them on a baking sheet.

3. Bake: Toast in the oven until the bread is golden and crisp, about 10-15 minutes. Flip them halfway through to ensure even toasting.

**Making the Tomato Topping:**

1. Combine Ingredients: In a mixing bowl, combine the diced tomatoes, minced garlic, chopped basil, and olive oil. Season with salt and pepper to taste. Mix well.

2. Marinate: Let the tomato mixture sit for about 10-15 minutes to allow the flavors to meld.

**Assembling the Bruschetta:**

1. Top the Bread: Once the bread is toasted, remove it from the oven. Spoon a generous amount of the tomato mixture onto each heart-shaped toast.

2. Drizzle: If desired, drizzle a little balsamic glaze over each bruschetta for added sweetness and depth of flavor.

### Serving:

- Serve the Heart-Shaped Bruschetta immediately while the bread is still warm and crisp.

- These are perfect as a starter for a romantic meal, part of a brunch spread, or as a delightful snack for any occasion.

Enjoy your Heart-Shaped Bruschetta, a simple yet elegant dish that's sure to win the hearts of your guests with its lovely presentation and classic flavors!

# Valentine's Sushi Hearts

Ingredients:

- Pink soy wrappers (available at specialty Asian markets)
- 2 cups sushi rice
- 3 tablespoons rice vinegar
- 2 tablespoons sugar
- 1/2 teaspoon salt
- Sashimi-grade tuna, thinly sliced
- 1 avocado, thinly sliced
- 1 cucumber, peeled and cut into thin strips
- Optional: cream cheese, for added creaminess
- Soy sauce, for serving
- Pickled ginger, for serving
- Wasabi, for serving

Instructions

Preparing the Sushi Rice:

1. Cook Rice: Rinse the sushi rice under cold water until the water runs clear. Cook the rice according to package instructions.
2. Season Rice: While the rice is still warm, gently fold in rice vinegar, sugar, and salt. Let the rice cool to room temperature.

Assembling the Sushi Hearts:

1. Prepare Fillings: Ensure the tuna, avocado, and cucumber are cut into thin strips that will fit easily into your sushi hearts.
2. Shape the Sushi: Lay out a pink soy wrapper on a clean, dry surface. Place a heart-shaped cookie cutter or sushi mold on the wrapper.
3. Fill the Mold: Press a thin layer of sushi rice into the bottom of the mold. Add a layer of tuna, followed by layers of avocado and cucumber. You can also add a strip of cream cheese if desired.
4. Top with Rice: Add another thin layer of sushi rice on top of the fillings.
5. Wrap the Sushi: Carefully remove the mold and fold the soy wrapper over the top of the rice, trimming any excess wrapper. If needed, dampen the edges of the wrapper slightly to seal them.
6. Repeat: Continue this process until all ingredients are used.

Serving:

1. Cut into Hearts: If you have not used a heart-shaped mold, you can cut the rolls into heart shapes using a sharp knife.
2. Presentation: Arrange the sushi hearts on a platter. Serve with soy sauce, pickled ginger, and wasabi.

Enjoy your Valentine's Sushi Hearts, a special and romantic take on sushi that's perfect for celebrating love and impressing your significant other with your culinary creativity!

# Heart-Shaped Mini Pizzas

Ingredients

- Mini pizza bases or a large pizza dough
- Tomato sauce (pizza sauce or marinara sauce)
- Shredded mozzarella cheese
- Your favorite pizza toppings (such as pepperoni, sliced olives, mushrooms,
- bell peppers, etc.)
- Fresh basil leaves for garnish
- Olive oil (optional)
- Salt and pepper to taste

Instructions

Preparing the Pizza Bases:

1. Preheat Oven: Preheat your oven to 425°F (220°C). If you have a pizza stone, place it in the oven to preheat as well.
2. Shape the Bases: If using a large pizza dough, roll it out on a floured surface and use a heart-shaped cookie cutter to cut out mini pizza bases. If using pre-made mini pizza bases, simply cut them into heart shapes.
3. Place on Baking Sheet: Arrange the heart-shaped pizza bases on a baking sheet lined with parchment paper.

Adding Toppings:

1. Add Sauce: Spread a thin layer of tomato sauce over each pizza base, leaving a small border around the edges.
2. Add Cheese: Sprinkle a generous amount of shredded mozzarella cheese over the sauce.
3. Add Toppings: Place your chosen toppings on the pizzas. Remember not to overload the mini pizzas as it can make them soggy.

Baking the Pizzas:

1. Bake: Place the baking sheet in the preheated oven (or transfer the pizzas to the preheated pizza stone using a pizza peel). Bake for 10-12 minutes or until the cheese is bubbly and golden brown, and the edges are crisp.

Garnishing and Serving:

1. Garnish: Once out of the oven, garnish each pizza with fresh basil leaves. For an extra touch of flavor, you can drizzle a little olive oil over the top and season with salt and pepper.
2. Serve: Serve the heart-shaped mini pizzas hot and enjoy!

These Heart-Shaped Mini Pizzas are not only adorable but also customizable to suit any taste preference. They make a great meal for a cozy night in, a family dinner, or even a party where everyone can choose their own toppings.

# Cucumber and Smoked Salmon Hearts

Ingredients:

- 1-2 large cucumbers
- Smoked salmon, sliced
- Cream cheese, softened
- Fresh dill for garnish
- Thin lemon slices or lemon zest, for garnish
- Salt and pepper to taste
- Heart-shaped cookie cutter

Instructions

Preparing the Cucumbers:

1. Slice Cucumbers: Wash the cucumbers and slice them into thick rounds, about 1/2 inch thick.

2. Cut Heart Shapes: Use a heart-shaped cookie cutter to cut each cucumber slice into a heart shape. If desired, lightly season the cucumber hearts with salt and pepper.

Assembling the Appetizers:

1. Add Cream Cheese: Place a small dollop of cream cheese on eachncucumber heart. You can use a small spoon, a piping bag, or a plastic bagnwith a corner cut off for more precise application.

2. Add Smoked Salmon: Cut the smoked salmon into pieces that will fit nicely on the cucumber hearts. Place a piece of smoked salmon on top of each cream cheese dollop.

3. Garnish: Garnish each appetizer with a small sprig of dill or a tiny slice of lemon. Alternatively, you can use lemon zest for a burst of citrus flavor without the extra liquid.

Serving:

- Arrange the Cucumber and Smoked Salmon Hearts on a platter.
- Serve immediately, or refrigerate until ready to serve. They are best enjoyed fresh.

These Cucumber and Smoked Salmon Hearts are not only visually appealing but also offer a burst of refreshing and savory flavors. They're perfect for a romantic dinner, a special brunch, or as a part of a festive appetizer spread.

# Love Potion Cocktail

Ingredients:

- 1 1/2 ounces vodka
- 1 ounce cranberry juice
- 1/2 ounce triple sec
- Ice cubes
- Heart-shaped ice cube tray
- Fresh raspberries
- Optional: a small amount of simple syrup or sugar, to taste
- Optional garnish: a twist of lemon or lime peel

Instructions

Preparing the Heart-Shaped Ice Cubes:

1. Fill Ice Cube Tray: Place a raspberry in each compartment of a heartshaped ice cube tray.

2. Add Water and Freeze: Fill the tray with water and freeze until solid.

Making the Love Potion Cocktail:

1. Chill the Glass: Chill a cocktail glass by placing it in the freezer for a few minutes.

2. Combine Ingredients: In a shaker, combine the vodka, cranberry juice, and triple sec. If you prefer a sweeter cocktail, add a small amount of simple syrup or sugar.

3. Shake: Add regular ice cubes to the shaker. Shake well until the mixture is chilled.

4. Strain and Serve: Strain the mixture into the chilled cocktail glass.

Garnishing and Serving:

1. Add Heart-Shaped Ice Cube: Carefully add a heart-shaped ice cube with a raspberry inside to the cocktail.

2. Optional Garnish: Garnish with a twist of lemon or lime peel for an extra touch of elegance and a hint of citrus aroma.

3. Serve: Serve immediately and enjoy the romantic and refreshing flavors of your Love Potion Cocktail.

This cocktail is not only visually appealing but also has a delightful balance of flavors, making it an excellent choice for celebrating love and special moments.

# Strawberry Heart Bellinis

Ingredients:

- 1 cup fresh strawberries, hulled
- Prosecco or another sparkling wine, chilled
- Fresh strawberries for garnish
- Sugar (optional, for sweetening)
- Heart-shaped cookie cutter or knife

Instructions

Preparing the Strawberry Puree:

1. Puree Strawberries: In a blender, puree the fresh strawberries until smooth. If your strawberries aren't very sweet, you can add a bit of sugar to the puree.
2. Strain: For a smoother texture, strain the puree through a fine-mesh sieve to remove seeds.

Preparing the Strawberry Garnish:

1. Slice Strawberries: Cut fresh strawberries into thin slices.
2. Cut Heart Shapes: Use a small heart-shaped cookie cutter or a knife to cut each strawberry slice into a heart shape.

Assembling the Bellinis:

1. Add Strawberry Puree: Pour about 2 tablespoons of strawberry puree into each champagne flute.
2. Top with Prosecco: Gently pour Prosecco over the strawberry puree. The puree will mix with the Prosecco as you pour, creating a layered effect.
3. Garnish: Place a strawberry heart on the rim of each flute or let it float on top of the drink.

Serving:

- Serve the Strawberry Heart Bellinis immediately to enjoy the fizz and freshness.
- These bellinis are perfect for brunch, as a welcome drink at a party, or as a romantic gesture.

Enjoy your Strawberry Heart Bellinis, a simple yet elegant cocktail that's sure to add a touch of romance and festivity to your occasion!

# Cupid's Arrow Smoothie

Ingredients

For the Smoothie:

- 1 cup frozen strawberries
- 1 ripe banana
- 1/2 cup Greek yogurt (plain or vanilla)
- 1/2 cup milk (dairy or plant-based)
- 1 tablespoon honey or to taste (optional)

For the Cupid's Arrow Skewer:

- Assorted fruits such as strawberries, watermelon, and pineapple
- Wooden skewers
- Heart-shaped cookie cutter

Instructions

Preparing the Cupid's Arrow Skewer:

1. Cut Heart Shapes: Use the heart-shaped cookie cutter to cut heart shapes from slices of watermelon, pineapple, and whole strawberries.
2. Assemble Skewer: Thread the heart-shaped fruit pieces onto a wooden skewer, alternating the types of fruit.

Making the Smoothie:

1. Blend Ingredients: In a blender, combine the frozen strawberries, banana, Greek yogurt, milk, and honey (if using). Blend until smooth and creamy. Add more milk if needed to reach your desired consistency.
2. Taste and Adjust: Taste the smoothie and adjust the sweetness with additional honey if needed.

Serving:

1. Pour Smoothie: Pour the smoothie into a tall glass.
2. Add Skewer: Garnish with the Cupid's Arrow skewer of heart-shaped fruit.
3. Serve Immediately: Enjoy the smoothie right away for the best flavor and texture.

Cupid's Arrow Smoothie is not only visually appealing but also packed with nutrients, making it a wonderful choice for a wholesome and charming treat. It's especially perfect for a Valentine's Day breakfast, a romantic brunch, or anytime you want to show a little extra love.

# Raspberry Rose Fizz

## Ingredients

For the Raspberry Rose Fizz:

- 1 cup fresh raspberries, plus more for garnish
- 1-2 teaspoons rose water (adjust to taste)
- 2 teaspoons honey or simple syrup, or to taste (optional)
- Sparkling water or club soda, chilled
- Ice cubes

For the Heart-Shaped Raspberry Ice Cubes:

- Water
- Small fresh raspberries
- Heart-shaped ice cube tray

## Instructions

Preparing the Heart-Shaped Raspberry Ice Cubes:

1. Prepare Ice Cube Tray: Place one small raspberry in each compartment of a heart-shaped ice cube tray.
2. Fill and Freeze: Fill the tray with water and freeze until the ice cubes are solid.

Making the Raspberry Puree:

1. Puree Raspberries: In a blender, puree the 1 cup of fresh raspberries until smooth. For a smoother texture, strain the puree through a fine mesh sieve to remove seeds.
2. Sweeten: If desired, sweeten the raspberry puree with honey or simple syrup to taste.

Assembling the Raspberry Rose Fizz:

1. Add Raspberry Puree: In a glass, add about 2 tablespoons of raspberry puree.
2. Add Rose Water: Stir in the rose water. Start with a small amount and adjust according to your preference.
3. Add Ice: Add regular ice cubes or the heart-shaped raspberry ice cubes to the glass.
4. Top with Sparkling Water: Fill the glass with sparkling water or clubnsoda, and gently stir to combine.

Garnishing and Serving:

1. Garnish: Garnish with a few fresh raspberries or a sprig of mint for an extra touch of elegance.
2. Serve: Serve the Raspberry Rose Fizz immediately to enjoy its fizzy and refreshing qualities.

Raspberry Rose Fizz is a delightful drink that's perfect for any celebration, offering a unique and sophisticated flavor profile. Its beautiful presentation, complete with heart-shaped ice cubes, makes it a standout choice for occasions like Valentine's Day, anniversaries, or elegant gatherings.

# *Heart's Delight Hot Chocolate*

Ingredients

For the Hot Chocolate:

- 2 cups milk (dairy or plant-based)
- 1/2 cup heavy cream
- 4 ounces high-quality dark or milk chocolate, chopped
- 2 tablespoons cocoa powder
- 2 tablespoons sugar (adjust to taste)
- 1/2 teaspoon vanilla extract
- A pinch of salt

For the Toppings:

- Whipped cream
- Ground cinnamon
- Heart-shaped marshmallows (store-bought or homemade)

Instructions

Making the Hot Chocolate:

1. Heat Milk and Cream: In a saucepan, gently heat the milk and cream over medium heat until hot but not boiling.

2. Melt Chocolate: Add the chopped chocolate, cocoa powder, and sugar to the saucepan. Whisk continuously until the chocolate is fully melted and the mixture is smooth.

3. Flavor: Stir in the vanilla extract and a pinch of salt.

4. Simmer: Let the mixture simmer for a few minutes, stirring occasionally. Be careful not to let it boil.

Preparing the Toppings:

1. Whip Cream: If using homemade whipped cream, whip the cream until it forms soft peaks.

2. Prepare Marshmallows: If you're using store-bought heart-shaped marshmallows, have them ready. If making your own, use a heart-shaped cookie cutter to cut out marshmallows from a sheet of homemade or store-bought marshmallow.

Assembling the Hot Chocolate:

1. Pour Hot Chocolate: Carefully pour the hot chocolate into mugs.

2. Add Whipped Cream: Top each mug with a generous dollop of whipped cream.

3. Add Marshmallows: Place a few heart-shaped marshmallows on top of the whipped cream.

4. Sprinkle Cinnamon: Sprinkle a dash of ground cinnamon over the whipped cream.

Serving:

- Serve the Heart's Delight Hot Chocolate immediately while it's warm and comforting.

- This drink is perfect for a cozy night in, a romantic evening, or as a special treat during the colder months.

Enjoy your Heart's Delight Hot Chocolate, a rich and creamy concoction that not only warms the body but also delights the heart with its charming presentation and decadent flavors!

# Dinner for Two

# Caprese Salad with Balsamic Reduction followed by Garlic Butter Shrimp Pasta finished with Chocolate Fondue Romantic Dinner for two

Appetizer: Caprese Salad with Balsamic Reduction

Ingredients:

- 2 large ripe tomatoes
- 1 ball of fresh mozzarella cheese
- Fresh basil leaves
- Salt and black pepper, to taste
- Extra virgin olive oil
- Balsamic vinegar (for reduction)
- Optional: pine nuts or olives for garnish

Instructions:

1. Balsamic Reduction: Pour about a cup of balsamic vinegar into a small saucepan. Heat over low heat, simmering until it thickens and reduces to about a quarter of its original volume. Let it cool.

2. Salad Preparation: Slice the tomatoes and mozzarella into 1/4 inch slices.

3. Assembly: Arrange tomato and mozzarella slices and basil leaves alternately on a plate, slightly overlapping each other.

4. Seasoning: Drizzle with olive oil, then add salt and pepper to taste.

5. Finishing Touch: Drizzle the balsamic reduction over the arranged salad. Garnish with pine nuts or olives if desired.

Main Course: Garlic Butter Shrimp Pasta

Ingredients:

- 200g of your preferred pasta (like spaghetti or linguine)
- 200g large shrimp, peeled and deveined
- 4 cloves garlic, minced
- 1/2 cup unsalted butter
- 1/4 cup grated Parmesan cheese
- 1 tablespoon fresh lemon juice
- Salt and pepper, to taste
- Fresh parsley, chopped (for garnish)

Instructions:

1. Pasta: Cook the pasta according to package instructions until al dente. Drain and set aside.

2. Shrimp: In a large skillet, melt half the butter over medium heat. Add the shrimp, season with salt and pepper, and cook until they turn pink, about 2-3 minutes per side. Remove shrimp and set aside.

3. Garlic Butter Sauce: In the same skillet, add the remaining butter and minced garlic. Sauté for about 1 minute.

4. Combining: Return the shrimp to the skillet, add lemon juice, and stir well.

5. Finishing the Dish: Add the cooked pasta to the skillet and toss until well coated with the garlic butter sauce. Sprinkle with Parmesan cheese and mix.

6. Serve: Garnish with fresh parsley and serve immediately.

Dessert: Chocolate Fondue

Ingredients:

- 200g dark chocolate, chopped
- 1/2 cup heavy cream
- Assorted fruits for dipping (like strawberries, banana slices, and pineapple chunks)
- Marshmallows, biscotti, or pound cake for dipping

Instructions:

1. Chocolate Fondue: In a fondue pot or a small saucepan, heat the cream over low heat until warm. Add the chopped chocolate and stir until melted and smooth.

2. Serving: Arrange the fruits, marshmallows, and cake pieces on a platter.

3. Enjoy: Dip the fruits and other items into the chocolate fondue and enjoy.

With a bottle of your favorite wine, this dinner is sure to create a romantic and memorable Valentine's Day experience.

# *Bruschetta al Pomodoro followed by Homemade Spinach and Ricotta Ravioli finished with Tiramisu Dinner for two*

Starter: Bruschetta al Pomodoro

Ingredients:

- 4 slices of Italian bread or baguette
- 2 ripe tomatoes, finely chopped
- 1 clove garlic, minced
- Fresh basil leaves, chopped
- Extra virgin olive oil
- Salt and pepper, to taste
- Optional: Balsamic glaze

Instructions:

1. Preparation: Preheat your oven to 180°C (350°F).
2. Tomato Topping: Mix chopped tomatoes, minced garlic, chopped basil, salt, and pepper in a bowl. Drizzle with olive oil and mix well.
3. Toasting Bread: Place the bread slices on a baking sheet and toast in the oven until slightly golden, about 5-6 minutes.
4. Assembly: Spoon the tomato mixture onto the toasted bread. Drizzle with a bit more olive oil or balsamic glaze if desired.

Main Course: Homemade Spinach and Ricotta Ravioli

Ingredients:

- For the Pasta: 200g all-purpose flour, 2 eggs
- For the Filling: 1 cup ricotta cheese, 1/2 cup cooked spinach (drained and chopped), 1/4 cup grated Parmesan cheese, salt and pepper, nutmeg (optional)
- For the Sauce: Your choice of marinara sauce or sage butter sauce

Instructions:

1. Pasta Dough: Mix flour and eggs to form a dough. Knead until smooth. Let it rest for 30 minutes.
2. Filling: Combine ricotta, spinach, Parmesan, salt, pepper, and a pinch of nutmeg.
3. Assembling Ravioli: Roll out the pasta dough thinly. Place small spoonfuls of filling at intervals. Cover with another layer of rolled-out dough. Press around the filling to seal and cut into individual ravioli.
4. Cooking: Boil the ravioli in salted water for about 4 minutes or until they float to the surface.
5. Sauce: Heat your chosen sauce in a pan. Add cooked ravioli to the sauce and gently coat.

Dessert: Tiramisu

Ingredients:

- 1 cup espresso or strong coffee, cooled
- 1 tablespoon rum or coffee liqueur
- 12 ladyfingers
- 1 cup mascarpone cheese
- 1/2 cup powdered sugar
- Cocoa powder for dusting

Instructions:

1. Coffee Mixture: Mix the espresso and rum in a shallow dish.
2. Cream Mixture: Whisk together mascarpone and powdered sugar until smooth.
3. Assembly: Briefly dip each ladyfinger in the coffee mixture and lay them in a layer in a serving dish. Spread half of the mascarpone mixture over the ladyfingers. Repeat with another layer of ladyfingers and mascarpone.
4. Chill and Serve: Dust with cocoa powder. Refrigerate for at least 2 hours before serving.

Pair this meal with a bottle of Italian wine, such as Chianti or Prosecco, to enhance the flavors and add to the romantic ambiance. This carefully crafted Italian dinner is sure to provide a memorable and intimate Valentine's Day experience.

# Mixed Greens Salad with Balsamic Vinaigrette followed by Grilled Filet Mignon with Creamy Mashed Potatoes and Sauteed Green Beans finished with Raspberry Cheesecake

Starter: Mixed Greens Salad with Balsamic Vinaigrette

Ingredients:

- Mixed salad greens (like arugula, spinach, and romaine)
- Cherry tomatoes, halved
- Cucumber, sliced
- Red onion, thinly sliced
- Crumbled goat cheese or feta
- Balsamic vinaigrette dressing
- Optional: toasted nuts or seeds for crunch

Instructions:

1. Salad Assembly: In a large bowl, combine salad greens, cherry tomatoes, cucumber, and red onion.
2. Dressing: Drizzle with balsamic vinaigrette and toss gently to coat.
3. Finishing Touches: Top with crumbled goat cheese or feta and toasted nuts or seeds if desired.

Main Course: Grilled Filet Mignon

Ingredients:

- 2 filet mignon steaks (about 1 1/2 inches thick)
- Salt and freshly ground black pepper
- 2 tablespoons olive oil
- Optional: a knob of butter, fresh rosemary, or thyme

Instructions:

1. Steak Preparation: Season the steaks with salt and pepper and let them sit at room temperature for about 20-30 minutes.
2. Grilling: Preheat your grill or grill pan over medium-high heat. Brush the steaks with olive oil and grill them for about 4-5 minutes per side for medium-rare, or until they reach your desired level of doneness.
3. Resting: Let the steaks rest for a few minutes before serving. Optionally, top with a knob of butter and a sprig of rosemary or thyme for added flavor.

Side Dish 1: Creamy Mashed Potatoes

Ingredients:

- 4 large potatoes, peeled and cubed
- 4 tablespoons butter
- 1/2 cup heavy cream or milk
- Salt and pepper, to taste

Instructions:

1. Potatoes: Boil the potatoes in salted water until tender, about 15-20 minutes. Drain.
2. Mashing: Add butter and cream to the potatoes. Mash until smooth and creamy. Season with salt and pepper.

Side Dish 2: Sautéed Green Beans

Ingredients:

- Green beans, trimmed
- 2 tablespoons olive oil
- 2 cloves garlic, minced
- Salt and pepper, to taste
- Lemon zest or juice (optional)

Instructions:

1. Green Beans: Blanch the green beans in boiling water for 3-4 minutes, then plunge them into ice water.
2. Sautéing: Heat olive oil in a pan. Add minced garlic and sauté for a minute. Add green beans, and cook for another 3-4 minutes. Season with salt and pepper.
3. Finish: Add a touch of lemon zest or juice for a fresh twist.

Dessert: Raspberry Cheesecake

This meal, paired with a bottle of your favorite wine, creates a perfectly balanced and romantic dinner. The combination of flavors, from the starter to the dessert, is sure to make your Valentine's Day special and memorable.

Ingredients:

For the Crust:

- 1 1/2 cups graham cracker crumbs
- 1/4 cup granulated sugar
- 1/2 cup unsalted butter, melted

For the Filling:

- 4 (8-ounce) packages cream cheese, softened
- 1 1/4 cups granulated sugar
- 1 teaspoon vanilla extract
- 4 large eggs
- 2 tablespoons all-purpose flour
- 1/2 cup sour cream

For the Raspberry Sauce:

- 2 cups fresh raspberries (or frozen, thawed)
- 1/2 cup granulated sugar
- 1 tablespoon cornstarch
- Juice of half a lemon

For Topping:

- Fresh raspberries for garnish

Instructions:

Crust:

1. Preheat the Oven: Preheat your oven to 325°F (163°C).

2. Making the Crust: Combine graham cracker crumbs, sugar, and melted butter in a bowl. Press the mixture firmly into the bottom of a 9-inch springform pan.

3. Baking: Bake the crust for about 10 minutes. Remove from the oven and let it cool.

Filling:

1. Cream Cheese Mixture: In a large bowl, beat the cream cheese, sugar, and vanilla extract until smooth and creamy.

2. Adding Eggs: Add eggs one at a time, beating well after each addition. Mix in the flour and sour cream until just combined.

3. Baking the Cheesecake: Pour the filling over the crust in the springform pan. Smooth the top with a spatula.

4. Water Bath (Optional): For a smoother cheesecake, place the springform pan in a larger pan filled with about an inch of water (this is called a water bath).

5. Baking: Bake in the preheated oven for 55-60 minutes. The center should be set, but still slightly wobbly.

6. Cooling: Turn off the oven, slightly open the door, and let the cheesecake cool inside for about an hour. This helps prevent cracking.

Raspberry Sauce:

1. Making the Sauce: Combine raspberries, sugar, cornstarch, and lemon juice in a saucepan over medium heat. Cook until the berries break down and the sauce thickens.

2. Straining: Strain the sauce through a fine-mesh sieve to remove seeds, then let it cool.

Finishing Touches:

1. Chilling the Cheesecake: Refrigerate the cheesecake for at least 4 hours, preferably overnight.

2. Adding Raspberry Sauce: Before serving, spoon the raspberry sauce over the cheesecake.

3. Garnish: Decorate with fresh raspberries. This raspberry cheesecake, with its creamy filling and vibrant sauce, is not only a visual delight but also a delicious end to a special meal.

Enjoy the rich flavors and the sweet, tart raspberry topping that makes this dessert truly unforgettable

# *Pear and Walnut Salad with Honey Vinaigrette followed by Seared Scallops with Lemon Butter Sauce and Garlic Parmesan Risotto finished with Fresh Berry Parfait*

Main Course: Seared Scallops with Lemon Butter Sauce

Ingredients:

- 6 large sea scallops, cleaned and pat dry
- Salt and pepper, to taste
- 2 tablespoons olive oil
- 2 tablespoons unsalted butter
- Juice of 1 lemon
- 1 tablespoon fresh parsley, chopped
- Optional: Garlic, minced

Instructions:

1. Prepping Scallops: Season the scallops with salt and pepper.
2. Cooking Scallops: Heat olive oil in a pan over medium-high heat. Sear the scallops for about 2 minutes on each side, until they have a golden crust.
3. Making Lemon Butter Sauce: In the same pan, reduce heat to low and add butter, lemon juice, and garlic (if using). Stir to combine and coat the scallops in the sauce.
4. Serving: Place the scallops on plates and drizzle with the lemon butter sauce. Garnish with chopped parsley.

Side Dish: Garlic Parmesan Risotto

Ingredients:

- 1 cup Arborio rice
- 1/2 cup white wine
- 3-4 cups chicken or vegetable broth, warmed
- 1/2 cup Parmesan cheese, grated
- 2 tablespoons unsalted butter
- 2 cloves garlic, minced
- Salt and pepper, to taste

Instructions:

1. Cooking Rice: In a pan, melt butter over medium heat. Add garlic and rice, stirring until the rice is lightly toasted.
2. Adding Liquid: Pour in the wine and cook until absorbed. Then gradually add the warm broth, one cup at a time, allowing each addition to be absorbed before adding the next.
3. Finishing the Risotto: Once the rice is tender, stir in the Parmesan cheese. Season with salt and pepper.

Light Dessert: Fresh Berry Parfait

Ingredients:

- Mixed berries (strawberries, blueberries, raspberries)
- Greek yogurt or whipped cream
- Honey or agave nectar
- Optional: Granola or crushed nuts for texture

Instructions:

1. Layering the Parfait: In two glasses, layer Greek yogurt or whipped cream with fresh berries.
2. Sweetening: Drizzle with honey or agave nectar between layers.
3. Finishing Touches: Top with a final layer of berries and a sprinkle of granola or crushed nuts if desired.

This menu balances rich flavors with light and refreshing elements, creating an unforgettable dining experience. The creamy risotto complements the delicate scallops, and the berry parfait provides a sweet yet light ending to the meal. Pair this menu with a bottle of chilled white wine or a sparkling beverage to elevate the experience further.

# French Baguette with Olive Tapenade followed by Classic Bouillabaisse finished with Chocolate Mousse

Appetizer: French Baguette with Olive Tapenade

Ingredients for Olive Tapenade:

- 1 cup mixed olives, pitted
- 2 tablespoons capers, rinsed
- 1-2 cloves garlic
- 2 tablespoons olive oil
- 1 teaspoon lemon juice
- Fresh herbs (like thyme or parsley)

Instructions:

1. Tapenade: In a food processor, blend olives, capers, garlic, olive oil, and lemon juice until combined but still chunky.
2. Serving: Serve the tapenade with slices of a fresh French baguette.

Main Course: Classic Bouillabaisse

Ingredients:

- Assorted seafood (like shrimp, mussels, clams, and firm white fish)
- 1 onion, chopped
- 2 cloves garlic, minced
- 1 fennel bulb, thinly sliced
- 1 can diced tomatoes
- 4 cups fish stock
- 1/2 cup white wine
- Saffron, a pinch
- Orange zest
- Olive oil
- Salt and pepper, to taste
- Rouille sauce (optional, for serving)
- Extra baguette slices, for serving

Instructions:

1. Sauté Vegetables: In a large pot, heat olive oil over medium heat. Add onion, garlic, and fennel. Sauté until softened.
2. Adding Tomatoes and Stock: Stir in the diced tomatoes, fish stock, white wine, saffron, and orange zest. Bring to a simmer.
3. Cooking Seafood: Add the seafood, starting with what takes longest to cook. Simmer gently until all the seafood is cooked.
4. Seasoning: Season with salt and pepper to taste.

Dessert: Chocolate Mousse

Ingredients:

- 4 ounces dark chocolate, chopped
- 2 tablespoons unsalted butter
- 2 eggs, separated
- 2 tablespoons sugar
- 1/2 cup heavy cream
- Fresh berries, for garnish

Instructions:

1. Melting Chocolate: Melt the chocolate and butter together. Let cool slightly.
2. Egg Yolks: Stir egg yolks into the chocolate mixture.
3. Whipping Egg Whites: In a separate bowl, beat egg whites until soft peaks form. Gradually add sugar and beat until stiff peaks form.
4. Whipping Cream: In another bowl, whip the heavy cream until it holds soft peaks.
5. Combining: Gently fold the egg whites and then the whipped cream into the chocolate mixture.
6. Chilling: Divide the mousse into two serving dishes and chill for at least 1 hour.
7. Serving: Garnish with fresh berries before serving.

This meal, paired with a bottle of good French wine, perhaps a Rosé or a light-bodied red wine, would wonderfully complement the rich flavors of the Bouillabaisse and the simplicity of the appetizer and dessert, creating an elegant and romantic dining experience.

# *Spinach and Strawberry Salad followed by Honey Mustard Pork Tenderloin and Garlic Mashed Potatoes and Roasted Asparagus finished with Classic Crème Brûlée*

Appetizer: Spinach and Strawberry Salad

Ingredients:

- Fresh spinach leaves
- Sliced strawberries
- Sliced almonds or pecans
- Crumbled goat cheese or feta
- Balsamic vinaigrette or poppy seed dressing

Instructions:

1. Salad Assembly: In a large bowl, combine spinach leaves, sliced strawberries, and nuts.
2. Dressing: Drizzle with your choice of balsamic vinaigrette or poppy seed dressing.
3. Finish: Top with crumbled goat cheese or feta before serving.

Main Course: Honey Mustard Pork Tenderloin

Ingredients:

- 1 pork tenderloin (about 1 pound)
- Salt and pepper, to taste
- 2 tablespoons olive oil

For the Honey Mustard Glaze:

- 1/4 cup honey
- 1/4 cup Dijon mustard
- 1 tablespoon apple cider vinegar
- 1 clove garlic, minced
- 1 teaspoon fresh thyme or rosemary, chopped

Instructions:

1. Preheat the Oven: Preheat your oven to 375°F (190°C).
2. Seasoning the Pork: Season the pork tenderloin with salt and pepper.
3. Searing: In a skillet, heat olive oil over medium-high heat. Sear the pork on all sides until golden brown.
4. Glaze Preparation: In a bowl, mix together honey, Dijon mustard, apple cider vinegar, garlic, and herbs.

5. Glazing the Pork: Brush the pork tenderloin with the honey mustard glaze.
6. Baking: Place the pork in the oven and bake for 15-20 minutes or until it reaches an internal temperature of 145°F (63°C). Baste occasionally with the glaze.
7. Resting: Let the pork rest for a few minutes before slicing.

Side Dish 1: Roasted Asparagus

Ingredients:

- Asparagus spears, trimmed
- Olive oil
- Salt and pepper
- Lemon zest or juice

Instructions:

1. Preparation: Toss asparagus with olive oil, salt, and pepper.
2. Roasting: Roast in the oven alongside the pork for about 10-15 minutes.
3. Finish: Sprinkle with lemon zest or a squeeze of lemon juice before serving.

Side Dish 2: Garlic Mashed Potatoes

Ingredients:

- 4 large potatoes, peeled and cubed
- 4 tablespoons butter
- 1/2 cup milk
- 2 cloves garlic, minced
- Salt and pepper, to taste

Instructions:

1. Potatoes: Boil the potatoes until tender. Drain.
2. Mashing: Mash with butter, milk, and garlic. Season with salt and pepper.

Dessert: Classic Crème Brûlée

Ingredients:

- 2 cups heavy cream
- 1 vanilla bean, split lengthwise (or 1 teaspoon vanilla extract)

- 5 egg yolks
- 1/2 cup granulated sugar
- Additional sugar for the caramelized topping

Instructions:

1. Preheat the Oven: Preheat your oven to 325°F (163°C).

2. Infusing the Cream: In a saucepan, heat the cream and vanilla bean (scraping out the seeds into the cream) over low heat just until hot. If using vanilla extract, you can add it directly to the egg mixture later.

3. Egg Mixture: In a bowl, whisk together the egg yolks and 1/2 cup sugar until well blended.

4. Combining: Remove the vanilla bean from the cream. Gradually add the hot cream to the egg mixture, whisking constantly.

5. Pouring into Ramekins: Pour the mixture into ramekins. Place the ramekins in a large baking pan. Pour hot water into the pan to come halfway up the sides of the ramekins.

6. Baking: Bake until the centers are just set, about 40 to 45 minutes.

7. Cooling: Remove the ramekins from the water bath and refrigerate for at least 2 hours, or up to 2 days.

8. Caramelizing the Top: Before serving, sprinkle the top of each custard with a thin layer

Enjoy this Crème Brûlée as a sophisticated and indulgent end to your Valentine's Day dinner. Its creamy texture and rich vanilla flavor, topped with a delightfully crisp caramelized sugar layer, make it an irresistible dessert choice for a special occasion.

# Grilled Polenta with Tomato and Basil followed by Eggplant Parmesan and Garlic Bread finished with Lemon Sorbet with Fresh Berries

Starter: Grilled Polenta with Tomato and Basil

Ingredients:

- Polenta, prepared and cooled in a sheet
- Olive oil
- Cherry tomatoes, halved
- Fresh basil, chopped
- Balsamic glaze
- Salt and pepper
- Parmesan cheese, grated (optional)

Instructions:

1. Prepare Polenta: Slice the cooled polenta into squares or rectangles.
2. Grilling Polenta: Brush each side with olive oil and grill until each side is golden and has grill marks.
3. Topping: Top with halved cherry tomatoes, a sprinkle of fresh basil, and a drizzle of balsamic glaze.
4. Seasoning: Season with salt and pepper, and sprinkle with grated Parmesan cheese if desired.

Main Course: Eggplant Parmesan

Ingredients:

- 1 large eggplant, sliced into 1/2 inch rounds
- Salt
- 2 eggs, beaten
- 1 cup breadcrumbs
- 1 cup grated Parmesan cheese, divided
- 1 teaspoon Italian seasoning
- Olive oil, for frying
- 2 cups marinara sauce
- 1 cup shredded mozzarella cheese
- Fresh basil, for garnish

Instructions:

1. Prep Eggplant: Sprinkle eggplant slices with salt and let them sit for about 20 minutes to draw out moisture. Pat dry with paper towels.
2. Breading: Dip eggplant slices in beaten eggs, then in a mixture of breadcrumbs, 1/2 cup Parmesan cheese, and Italian seasoning.
3. Frying: In a skillet, heat olive oil over medium heat. Fry eggplant slices until golden brown on both sides. Drain on paper towels.

4. Layering: In a baking dish, layer marinara sauce, fried eggplant, mozzarella, and the remaining Parmesan. Repeat layers.
5. Baking: Bake in a preheated oven at 375°F (190°C) for 20-25 minutes or until cheese is bubbly and golden.
6. Garnish: Garnish with fresh basil before serving. Seasoning: Season with salt and pepper to taste.

Side Dish: Garlic Bread

Ingredients:

- 1 small baguette
- 4 tablespoons butter, softened
- 2 cloves garlic, minced
- Parsley, chopped

Instructions:

1. Garlic Butter: Mix butter with minced garlic and parsley.
2. Prep Bread: Slice the baguette in half lengthwise. Spread garlic butter over each half.
3. Baking: Bake in the oven alongside the eggplant Parmesan until golden and crispy.

Dessert: Lemon Sorbet with Fresh Berries

Ingredients:

- Lemon sorbet
- Mixed fresh berries (such as strawberries, blueberries, and raspberries)
- Mint leaves for garnish
- Optional: a splash of champagne or prosecco

Instructions:

1. Serving Sorbet: Scoop lemon sorbet into serving bowls or glasses.
2. Adding Berries: Top with a mix of fresh berries.
3. Finishing Touch: Garnish with a mint leaf. For an extra special touch, add a splash of champagne or prosecco over the sorbet.

The richness of the Eggplant Parmesan, with the grilled polenta, provides a warm and savory beginning, and the lemon sorbet offers a light, refreshing finish to your romantic dinner.

# Roasted Red Pepper and Feta Dip followed by Salmon Croquettes with Dill Sauce with Lemon Herb Couscous finished with Chocolate Raspberry Tarts

Appetizer: Roasted Red Pepper and Feta Dip

Ingredients:

- 1 cup roasted red peppers, drained and chopped
- 1/2 cup feta cheese, crumbled
- 1 clove garlic, minced
- 2 tablespoons olive oil
- 1 teaspoon lemon juice
- Fresh parsley, chopped
- Salt and pepper, to taste
- Baguette slices or pita chips for serving

Instructions:

1. Dip Preparation: Blend roasted red peppers, feta cheese, garlic, olive oil, and lemon juice in a food processor until smooth.
2. Seasoning: Season with salt and pepper to taste.
3. Garnish and Serve: Transfer to a serving bowl, garnish with chopped parsley, and serve with baguette slices or pita chips.

Main Course: Salmon Croquettes with Dill Sauce

Ingredients for Salmon Croquettes:

- 2 cans salmon, drained and flaked
- 1/2 cup breadcrumbs
- 2 green onions, finely chopped
- 1 egg, beaten
- 1 tablespoon lemon juice
- Salt and pepper, to taste
- Olive oil, for frying

Ingredients for Dill Sauce:

- 1/2 cup mayonnaise
- 1 tablespoon fresh dill, chopped
- 1 teaspoon lemon juice
- 1 clove garlic, minced
- Salt and pepper, to taste

Instructions:

1. Croquettes: Combine salmon, breadcrumbs, green onions, egg, and lemon juice. Season with salt and pepper. Form into patties.
2. Frying: Heat olive oil in a pan and fry the croquettes until golden on both sides.
3. Dill Sauce: Mix mayonnaise, dill, lemon juice, and garlic. Season with salt and pepper.

Side Dish: Lemon Herb Couscous

Ingredients:

- 1 cup couscous
- 1 1/4 cups vegetable or chicken broth
- Zest of 1 lemon
- Juice of 1/2 lemon
- 2 tablespoons olive oil
- 1/4 cup fresh parsley, chopped
- 1/4 cup fresh dill, chopped (optional)
- Salt and pepper, to taste
- Optional: Cherry tomatoes, halved; cucumber, diced; green onions, sliced

Instructions:

1. Cooking Couscous: In a saucepan, bring the broth to a boil. Stir in the couscous, then cover and remove from heat. Let it stand for 5 minutes.
2. Flavoring: Fluff the couscous with a fork. Stir in lemon zest, lemon juice, olive oil, parsley, and dill. If using, add cherry tomatoes, cucumber, and green onions.
3. Seasoning: Season with salt and pepper to taste.

Dessert: Chocolate Raspberry Tarts

Ingredients:

- Pre-made mini tart shells
- Dark chocolate, chopped
- Heavy cream
- Fresh raspberries

Instructions:

1. Chocolate Ganache: Heat cream and pour over chopped chocolate. Stir until smooth.
2. Assembling Tarts: Spoon ganache into tart shells. Top each tart with fresh raspberries.
3. Chill: Refrigerate until the ganache is set.

This meal plan provides a delightful mix of flavors and textures, starting with a tangy and creamy appetizer, moving on to a heartier and satisfying main course, and finishing with a sweet and elegant dessert. Pair this meal with a light white wine, like a Sauvignon Blanc or Pinot Grigio, to complement the flavors of the salmon croquettes and risotto.

# *Baked Brie with Fig Jam and Crostini followed by Glazed Braised Duck Legs finished by Chocolate Lava Cakes*

Starter: Baked Brie with Fig Jam and Crostini

Ingredients:

- 1 small wheel of Brie cheese
- 2 tablespoons fig jam
- Crostini or sliced baguette
- Fresh thyme or rosemary for garnish

Instructions:

1. Baking Brie: Place the Brie in a small baking dish. Bake in a preheated oven at 350°F (175°C) until melted, about 10-15 minutes.
2. Serving: Top the warm Brie with fig jam and garnish with fresh thyme or rosemary. Serve with crostini or baguette slices.

Main Course: Glazed Braised Duck Legs

Ingredients for Duck:

- 2 duck legs
- Salt and pepper
- • 1 onion, chopped
- 2 cloves garlic, minced
- 1 cup chicken broth
- 1/2 cup red wine
- Fresh herbs (thyme, rosemary)

Ingredients for Glaze:

- 1/4 cup balsamic vinegar
- 1/4 cup honey
- 2 tablespoons soy sauce
- 1 clove garlic, minced
- 1 teaspoon ginger, grated

Instructions:

1. Prepare Duck: Season duck legs with salt and pepper.
2. Searing: In a heavy skillet or Dutch oven, sear the duck legs, skin-side down, until the skin is crisp and golden. Remove and set aside.
3. Sauté Aromatics: In the same skillet, sauté onion and minced garlic until translucent.
4. Deglazing: Add red wine to the skillet, scraping up any browned bits from the bottom.
5. Braising: Return the duck to the skillet. Add chicken broth and fresh herbs. Bring to a simmer.
6. Oven Cooking: Cover and transfer to a preheated oven at 325°F (163°C). Braise for about 1.5 to 2 hours, or until the duck is tender.

For the Glaze:

7. Combine Glaze Ingredients: In a saucepan, combine balsamic vinegar, honey, soy sauce, minced garlic, and ginger. Bring to a boil, then reduce heat and simmer until the mixture thickens and becomes syrupy.
8. Final Glazing: In the last 30 minutes of braising, brush the duck legs with the glaze every 10 minutes.

Side Dish: Roasted Brussels Sprouts

Ingredients:

- Brussels sprouts, halved
- Olive oil
- Salt and pepper
- Balsamic vinegar (optional)

Instructions:

1. Preparation: Toss Brussels sprouts with olive oil, salt, and pepper.
2. Roasting: Spread on a baking sheet and roast in the oven at 400°F (200°C) until caramelized, about 20-25 minutes.
3. Finishing Touch: Drizzle with balsamic vinegar if desired.

Dessert: Chocolate Lava Cakes

Ingredients:

- 4 ounces dark chocolate
- 1/2 cup unsalted butter
- 2 eggs plus 2 egg yolks
- 1/4 cup sugar
- 2 tablespoons flour
- Powdered sugar for dusting
- Fresh raspberries for garnish

Instructions:

1. Melting Chocolate: Melt chocolate and butter together.
2. Mixing Batter: Whisk eggs, yolks, and sugar until light. Fold in melted chocolate and flour.
3. Baking: Pour into greased ramekins. Bake at 425°F (220°C) for about 10-12 minutes.
4. Serving: Let stand for a minute, then invert onto plates. Dust with powdered sugar and garnish with raspberries.

Pair this meal with a bottle of Pinot Noir or a similar red wine that complements both the duck and the chocolate dessert. The combination of flavors, textures, and the luxurious feel of the dishes will make your Valentine's Day dinner both special and memorable.

# Goat Cheese and Herb Stuffed Tomatoes followed by Wild Mushroom and Parsnip Ragout with Cheesy Polenta finished with Avocado Chocolate Mousse (Vegetarian)

Appetizer: Goat Cheese and Herb Stuffed Tomatoes

Ingredients:

- 4 large ripe tomatoes
- 4 ounces goat cheese
- 2 tablespoons fresh herbs (such as basil, thyme, or parsley), finely chopped
- 1 clove garlic, minced
- Salt and pepper, to taste
- Olive oil, for drizzling

Instructions:

1. Prepare Tomatoes: Slice off the tops of the tomatoes and scoop out the seeds and inner pulp.
2. Filling Mixture: Mix goat cheese, herbs, garlic, salt, and pepper in a bowl.
3. Stuffing Tomatoes: Fill each tomato with the goat cheese mixture.
4. Drizzle: Drizzle with olive oil before serving.

Main Course: Wild Mushroom and Parsnip Ragout with Cheesy Polenta

Ingredients for Ragout:

- Assorted wild mushrooms, sliced (such as shiitake, oyster, and cremini)
- 2 parsnips, peeled and diced
- 1 onion, diced
- 2 cloves garlic, minced
- 1 cup vegetable broth
- 1/2 cup white wine
- Fresh thyme
- Salt and pepper, to taste
- Olive oil

Ingredients for Cheesy Polenta:

- 1 cup polenta (cornmeal)
- 4 cups water or vegetable broth
- 1/2 cup grated Parmesan cheese
- 2 tablespoons unsalted butter
- Salt, to taste

Instructions:

1. Cooking Ragout: In a large skillet, heat olive oil over medium heat. Sauté onion, garlic, mushrooms, and parsnips until tender. Add white wine and let it reduce slightly. Add vegetable broth and thyme. Simmer until the liquid is reduced and the ragout is thickened. Season with salt and pepper.
2. Making Polenta: In a saucepan, bring water or vegetable broth to a boil. Gradually whisk in polenta. Reduce heat and simmer, stirring frequently, until polenta is creamy and cooked through. Stir in Parmesan cheese and butter. Season with salt.
3. Serving: Spoon creamy polenta onto plates and top with the mushroom and parsnip ragout.

Dessert: Chocolate Avocado Mousse

Ingredients:

- 2 ripe avocados, peeled and pitted
- 1/4 cup cocoa powder
- 1/4 cup maple syrup or honey
- 1 teaspoon vanilla extract
- Pinch of salt
- Fresh berries for garnish

Instructions:

1. Blend Mousse Ingredients: In a food processor, blend avocados, cocoa
2. powder, maple syrup (or honey), vanilla extract, and a pinch of salt until smooth.
3. Chill: Refrigerate the mousse for at least 1 hour.
4. Serve: Garnish with fresh berries before serving.

This meal plan offers a variety of flavors and textures, from the fresh and creamy appetizer to the hearty and comforting main course, ending with a rich and healthy dessert. Pair this meal with a nice bottle of red or white wine that complements the earthy tones of the mushroom ragout and the richness of the chocolate mousse. Enjoy your vegetarian Valentine's Day dinner!

# Easter Feasts

*Classic and modern Easter brunch recipes*

*As the gentle breath of spring whispers through the air and nature awakens with the promise of new life, Easter arrives, bringing with it a sense of joy, renewal, and the perfect opportunity to gather around the table with loved ones. In this chapter of our cookbook, "Easter Feasts," we embark on a culinary journey that captures the essence of this vibrant and cherished holiday.*

*Easter is a time of celebration, a time to honor traditions old and new, and a time to savor the flavors of the season. Within these pages, you'll discover a treasure trove of recipes that are perfect for your Easter brunch, dinner, and dessert gatherings. Whether you're hosting a festive morning brunch, an elegant dinner, or simply indulging in the sweetest treats, we've curated a collection of dishes that will make your Easter celebration memorable and delicious.*

# *Classic French Toast Recipe*

Prep Time: 10 minutes
Cook Time: 20 minutes
Total Time: 30 minutes

Servings:
4

Ingredients:

- 8 slices of thick-cut bread (like brioche or challah)
- 4 large eggs
- 1 cup whole milk or heavy cream
- 1/4 cup granulated sugar
- 2 teaspoons pure vanilla extract
- 1 teaspoon ground cinnamon
- Pinch of salt
- Butter for frying
- Maple syrup, for serving
- Powdered sugar, for dusting
- Fresh berries (such as strawberries or blueberries), for garnish

Instructions:

1. Prep the Bread: If you have time, lay the bread slices out on a wire rack for a few hours to dry out slightly. This helps them soak up the egg mixture without getting too soggy.

2. Make the Egg Mixture: In a large bowl, whisk together the eggs, milk or cream, granulated sugar, vanilla extract, cinnamon, and a pinch of salt.

3. Soak the Bread: Dip each slice of bread into the egg mixture, allowing it to soak for about 20-30 seconds on each side. Transfer the soaked bread to a separate plate.

4. Cook the French Toast: Heat a large skillet or griddle over medium heat. Add a pat of butter to the skillet. Once the butter has melted, add a few slices of the soaked bread (do not overcrowd the skillet). Cook for 2-3 minutes on each side, or until golden brown and cooked through.

5. Serve: Serve the French toast hot, topped with maple syrup, a dusting of powdered sugar, and fresh berries.

Tips:

- For an extra rich French toast, use half-and-half or heavy cream instead of milk.

- You can add a splash of orange liqueur (like Grand Marnier) to the egg mixture for a citrusy twist.

- To keep the French toast warm while cooking in batches, preheat your oven to 200°F (95°C) and place the cooked slices on a baking sheet in the oven.

- This classic French Toast is a simple yet luxurious dish, perfect for an Easter brunch. The soft, custardy center and crisp, golden exterior, paired with the sweetness of maple syrup and fresh berries, make it a truly delightful treat.

# Eggs Benedict Recipe

Prep Time: 20 minutes
Cook Time: 20 minutes
Total Time: 40 minutes

Servings:
4

Ingredients:

For the Hollandaise Sauce:

- 3 egg yolks
- 1 tablespoon lemon juice
- 1/2 cup unsalted butter, melted
- Pinch of cayenne pepper
- Salt, to taste

For the Eggs Benedict:

- 4 English muffins, split and toasted
- 8 slices of ham or bacon, cooked
- 8 large eggs
- White vinegar (for poaching eggs)
- Fresh chives or parsley, chopped for garnish
- Paprika, for garnish (optional)

Instructions:

For the Hollandaise Sauce:

1. Whisk Egg Yolks and Lemon Juice: In a heatproof bowl, whisk together the egg yolks and lemon juice until the mixture is thickened and doubled in volume.

2. Double Boiler: Place the bowl over a pot of simmering water (double boiler), making sure the water doesn't touch the bottom of the bowl. Whisk continuously.

3. Add Melted Butter: Slowly drizzle in the melted butter and continue to whisk until the sauce is thickened and doubled in volume. Remove from heat.

4. Season: Add a pinch of cayenne pepper and salt. Keep the sauce warm by placing the bowl over a pot of warm water.

For the Eggs Benedict:

1. Poach Eggs: Fill a large saucepan with about 3 inches of water. Add a splash of white vinegar. Bring the water to a gentle simmer. Crack each egg into a small bowl and gently slide it into the simmering water. Poach the eggs for about 3-4 minutes until the

whites are set but the yolks are still runny. Remove with a slotted spoon and set on a warm plate.

2. Toast English Muffins: Toast the English muffins until golden brown.

3. Assemble the Eggs Benedict: Place a slice of ham or bacon on each English muffin half. Top with a poached egg.

4. Add Hollandaise Sauce: Spoon the hollandaise sauce over the poached eggs.

5. Garnish: Sprinkle with chopped chives or parsley and a dash of paprika for color.

6. Serve: Serve immediately while warm.

Eggs Benedict is a showstopper dish that's perfect for an Easter Brunch, offering a delightful mix of flavors and textures. Enjoy!

# *Hot Cross Buns Recipe*

Prep Time: 30 minutes (plus rising time)
Cook Time: 20-25 minutes
Total Time: About 2 hours 55 minutes
(including rising time)

Servings:
12 buns

## Ingredients:

### For the Buns:

- 4 cups all-purpose flour
- 1/4 cup granulated sugar
- 2 teaspoons active dry yeast
- 1 teaspoon salt
- 2 teaspoons ground cinnamon
- 1/2 teaspoon ground nutmeg
- 1/4 teaspoon ground cloves
- 1/4 cup unsalted butter, melted
- 1 cup warm milk
- 2 large eggs, beaten
- 1 cup currants or raisins
- Zest of 1 orange

### For the Cross:

- 1/2 cup all-purpose flour
- 4-5 tablespoons water

### For the Glaze:

- 1/4 cup apricot jam
- 1 tablespoon water

## Instructions:

1. Make the Dough: In a large mixing bowl, combine 4 cups flour, sugar, yeast, salt, cinnamon, nutmeg, and cloves. Add the melted butter, warm milk, and beaten eggs. Stir until a dough forms. Mix in the currants (or raisins) and orange zest.

2. Knead the Dough: Turn the dough onto a floured surface and knead for about 8-10 minutes until smooth and elastic. Add a little more flour if the dough is too sticky.

3. First Rise: Place the dough in a greased bowl, cover with a clean cloth, and let rise in a warm place for 1.5 hours, or until doubled in size.

4. Shape the Buns: Punch down the risen dough and divide it into 12 equal pieces. Shape each piece into a bun and place them on a lined baking sheet, leaving space between each.

5. Second Rise: Cover the buns with a cloth and let them rise again for about 30 minutes.

6. Preheat the Oven: Preheat your oven to 375°F (190°C).

7. Prepare the Cross Mixture: Mix 1/2 cup flour with enough water to make a thick paste. Transfer to a piping bag or a plastic bag with a small hole cut in one corner.

8. Pipe the Crosses: Pipe a line along each row of buns, then repeat in the opposite direction to create crosses.

9. Bake: Bake the buns for 20-25 minutes, or until they are golden brown.

10. Make the Glaze: While the buns are baking, heat the apricot jam with 1 tablespoon of water in a saucepan or microwave, then strain to remove any chunks.

11. Glaze the Buns: Brush the warm glaze over the hot buns as soon as they come out of the oven.

12. Cool and Serve: Let the buns cool on a wire rack before serving.

Enjoy your homemade Hot Cross Buns as part of your Easter brunch! They're best served warm, with a bit of butter if you like.

# Quiche Lorraine Recipe

Prep Time: 20 minutes
Cook Time: 35-40 minutes
Total Time: 55-60 minutes

Servings:
6-8

Ingredients:

For the Pie Crust:

- 1 1/4 cups all-purpose flour
- 1/2 teaspoon salt
- 1/2 cup unsalted butter, chilled and diced
- 3-4 tablespoons ice water

For the Filling:

- 8 slices bacon, chopped
- 1 medium onion, finely chopped
- 1 1/2 cups shredded Swiss or Gruyère cheese
- 4 large eggs
- 1 1/2 cups heavy cream
- 1/4 teaspoon salt
- 1/4 teaspoon ground black pepper
- 1/4 teaspoon ground nutmeg

Instructions:

1. Prepare the Pie Crust: In a large bowl, mix the flour and salt. Cut in the butter using a pastry cutter or your fingers until the mixture resembles coarse crumbs. Gradually add ice water, stirring until the dough comes together. Wrap in plastic wrap and refrigerate for at least 30 minutes.

2. Preheat the Oven: Preheat your oven to 375°F (190°C).

3. Roll Out the Dough: On a floured surface, roll out the dough to fit a 9-inch pie dish. Place the dough in the dish and trim any excess. Prick the bottom with a fork.

4. Blind Bake the Crust: Line the crust with parchment paper and fill with pie weights or dried beans. Bake for 10 minutes. Remove the weights and parchment and bake for another 5 minutes. Remove from the oven and reduce the temperature to 350°F (175°C).

5. Cook the Bacon and Onion: In a skillet, cook the chopped bacon until crisp. Remove the bacon and sauté the onion in the bacon fat until soft and translucent.

6. Combine Filling Ingredients: In a bowl, whisk together the eggs, heavy cream, salt, pepper, and nutmeg. Stir in the cheese, cooked bacon, and onion.

7. Assemble the Quiche: Pour the filling into the pre-baked pie crust.

8. Bake the Quiche: Bake for 30-35 minutes, or until the custard is set and the top is lightly golden.

9. Cool and Serve: Let the quiche cool for a few minutes before slicing. Serve warm or at room temperature.

Quiche Lorraine is a wonderful choice for Easter brunch, offering a rich and satisfying flavor that pairs well with a variety of side dishes. Enjoy!

# Easter Bread
# (also known as Pascha, Paska, or Pane di Pasqua)

Prep Time: 20 minutes
Cook Time: 35-40 minutes
Total Time: 55-60 minutes

Servings:
6-8

Ingredients:

- 4 to 4 1/2 cups all-purpose flour
- 1/2 cup sugar
- 1 packet (2 1/4 teaspoons) active dry yeast
- 1 teaspoon salt
- 2/3 cup warm milk (110°F to 115°F)
- 1/4 cup unsalted butter, softened
- 2 large eggs
- 1/2 teaspoon vanilla extract
- 1/4 teaspoon lemon zest
- 1/4 teaspoon orange zest
- 1/2 cup golden raisins (optional)
- 1 beaten egg (for egg wash)
- Nonpareils or sprinkles (optional, for decoration)

Instructions:

1. Prepare the Dough:

- In a large bowl, combine 1 1/2 cups flour, sugar, yeast, and salt.
- In a separate bowl, mix together the warm milk and butter. Add this to the flour mixture.
- Add the two eggs, vanilla extract, lemon zest, and orange zest. Beat until smooth.
- Stir in enough remaining flour to form a soft dough (the dough should be slightly sticky).

2. Knead the Dough:

- Turn the dough onto a floured surface and knead until smooth and elastic, about 6-8 minutes.
- Knead in the golden raisins, if using.

3. First Rise:

- Place the dough in a greased bowl, turning once to grease the top.
- Cover and let rise in a warm place until doubled, about 1 hour.

4. Shape the Bread:

- Punch down the dough and divide it into three equal parts.
- Roll each part into a 16-inch rope. Braid the ropes, and pinch the ends to seal.
- Form the braid into a ring and place it on a greased baking sheet.

5. Second Rise:

- Cover the dough ring and let it rise again until doubled, about 30-45 minutes.

6. Bake:

- Preheat the oven to 350°F (175°C).
- Brush the dough with beaten egg and sprinkle with nonpareils or sprinkles if desired.
- Bake for 25-30 minutes or until golden brown.
- Remove from the oven and let cool on a wire rack.

Serve this Easter Bread as part of your Easter breakfast or brunch. It's not only delicious but also makes a beautiful centerpiece for your table. Enjoy it plain, with butter, or with a spread of your choice!

# *Avocado Toast with Poached Eggs Recipe*

Prep Time: 15 minutes
Cook Time: 10 minutes
Total Time: 25 minutes

Servings:
4

Ingredients:

- 4 slices artisanal bread (such as sourdough or whole grain)
- 2 ripe avocados
- Juice of 1/2 lemon
- Salt and pepper, to taste
- 4 large eggs
- White vinegar (for poaching eggs)
- Optional: red pepper flakes or microgreens for garnish

Instructions:

1. Prepare the Avocado Spread: Cut the avocados in half, remove the pit, and scoop the flesh into a bowl. Add the lemon juice, salt, and pepper. Mash the ingredients together with a fork until you reach your desired consistency. Set aside.

2. Poach the Eggs: Fill a large saucepan with about 3 inches of water and add a splash of vinegar. Bring the water to a gentle simmer. Crack each egg into a small bowl and gently slide it into the simmering water. Poach the eggs for about 3-4 minutes until the whites are set but the yolks are still runny. Remove the eggs with a slotted spoon and set them on a warm plate.

3. Toast the Bread: While the eggs are poaching, toast the bread slices to your desired level of crispiness.

4. Assemble the Avocado Toast: Spread a generous layer of the mashed avocado mixture on each slice of toasted bread.

5. Top with Poached Eggs: Place a poached egg on top of each avocado toast.

6. Season and Garnish: Sprinkle a bit of salt and pepper over each egg. If you like, add a pinch of red pepper flakes for heat or a few microgreens for a fresh, colorful garnish.

7. Serve: Serve the avocado toasts immediately while the eggs are warm and the toast is crispy.

Avocado Toast with Poached Eggs is a light yet satisfying dish that's perfect for a springtime brunch like Easter. The combination of flavors and textures is sure to delight your guests!

# *Spinach and Goat Cheese Frittata Recipe*

Prep Time: 15 minutes
Cook Time: 25-30 minutes
Total Time: 40-45 minutes

Servings:
6-8

Ingredients:

- 8 large eggs
- 1/2 cup whole milk or heavy cream
- Salt and pepper, to taste
- 2 tablespoons olive oil
- 1 small onion, finely chopped
- 2 cloves garlic, minced
- 4 cups fresh spinach, roughly chopped
- 4 ounces goat cheese, crumbled
- 1 tablespoon fresh herbs (such as chives, parsley, or dill), chopped
- Additional herbs or goat cheese for garnish (optional)

Instructions:

1. Preheat the Oven: Preheat your oven to 375°F (190°C).

2. Prepare the Egg Mixture: In a large bowl, whisk together the eggs, milk (or cream), salt, and pepper. Set aside.

3. Cook the Vegetables: In an ovenproof skillet (about 10-12 inches in diameter), heat the olive oil over medium heat. Add the chopped onion and cook until translucent, about 3-4 minutes. Add the minced garlic and cook for another minute.

4. Add the Spinach: Add the chopped spinach to the skillet and cook until it wilts, about 2-3 minutes.

5. Combine with Egg Mixture: Spread the spinach and onion mixture evenly in the skillet. Pour the egg mixture over the vegetables. Sprinkle the crumbled goat cheese and chopped herbs evenly over the top.

6. Cook on Stovetop: Let the frittata cook on the stovetop for about 4-5 minutes until the edges start to set.

7. Bake the Frittata: Transfer the skillet to the preheated oven. Bake for 20-25 minutes, or until the frittata is set and slightly golden on top.

8. Garnish and Serve: Let the frittata cool for a few minutes. Garnish with additional herbs or goat cheese if desired. Slice and serve.

This Spinach and Goat Cheese Frittata is not only delicious but also visually appealing, making it a perfect dish for a special brunch like Easter. The creamy goat cheese pairs beautifully with the fresh spinach, creating a delightful flavor profile.

# Smoked Salmon and Cucumber Carpaccio Recipe

Prep Time: 15 minutes
Total Time: 15 minutes

Servings:
4

Ingredients:

For the Carpaccio:

- 8 oz smoked salmon, thinly sliced
- 1 large cucumber
- Fresh dill, for garnish
- Lemon wedges, for serving

For the Dill Cream Sauce:

- 1/2 cup sour cream or crème fraîche
- 2 tablespoons fresh dill, finely chopped
- 1 tablespoon lemon juice
- 1 teaspoon lemon zest
- 1 small garlic clove, minced
- Salt and pepper, to taste

Instructions:

1. Prepare the Dill Cream Sauce: In a small bowl, combine sour cream (or crème fraîche), chopped dill, lemon juice, lemon zest, and minced garlic. Season with salt and pepper to taste. Mix well until all ingredients are incorporated. Refrigerate the sauce until ready to serve.

2. Slice the Cucumber: Using a mandoline slicer or a very sharp knife, slice the cucumber into very thin rounds. If using a mandoline, be careful with your fingers.

3. Assemble the Carpaccio: Arrange the thinly sliced smoked salmon and cucumber slices on a serving platter. You can alternate between salmon and cucumber or create a separate section for each.

4. Garnish: Garnish the carpaccio with fresh dill sprigs. If desired, add a few lemon wedges to the platter.

5. Serve: Serve the smoked salmon and cucumber carpaccio immediately, accompanied by the dill cream sauce for drizzling or dipping.

6. Optional Serving Suggestion: For an added touch, you can drizzle a little bit of extra virgin olive oil over the carpaccio and sprinkle with a pinch of freshly ground black pepper before serving.

This Smoked Salmon and Cucumber Carpaccio with Dill Cream Sauce is a delightful and visually appealing dish, perfect for impressing your guests at a brunch or as an appetizer for a dinner party. Enjoy the fresh and harmonious blend of flavors!

# *Matcha Pancakes Recipe*

Prep Time: 10 minutes
Cook Time: 15 minutes
Total Time: 25 minutes

Servings:
4 (makes about 8-10 pancakes)

Ingredients:

- 1 1/2 cups all-purpose flour
- 2 tablespoons sugar
- 1 tablespoon matcha powder
- 2 teaspoons baking powder
- 1/2 teaspoon salt
- 1 1/4 cups milk
- 2 large eggs
- 2 tablespoons unsalted butter, melted, plus more for cooking
- 1 teaspoon vanilla extract
- Honey or maple syrup, for serving
- Fresh fruit or whipped cream for topping (optional)

Instructions:

1. Mix Dry Ingredients: In a large bowl, whisk together the flour, sugar, matcha powder, baking powder, and salt.

2. Combine Wet Ingredients: In another bowl, whisk together the milk, eggs, melted butter, and vanilla extract.

3. Make the Batter: Pour the wet ingredients into the dry ingredients. Stir until just combined; it's okay if the batter is a bit lumpy.

4. Heat the Pan: Heat a non-stick skillet or griddle over medium heat. Lightly brush with melted butter.

5. Cook the Pancakes: Pour about 1/4 cup of batter per pancake onto the skillet. Cook until bubbles form on the surface and the edges look set, about 2-3 minutes. Flip and cook for an additional 1-2 minutes on the other side, or until golden brown and cooked through.

6. Serve: Serve the matcha pancakes warm with honey or maple syrup and, if desired, top with fresh fruit or a dollop of whipped cream.

7. Optional Variations: For an extra matcha kick, you can mix a small amount of matcha powder into your syrup or whipped cream.

These Matcha Pancakes are a beautiful and tasty way to start your day. The matcha provides a subtle earthy flavor that pairs wonderfully with the sweetness of syrup and the richness of the pancake. Enjoy your green teainfused breakfast!

# *Acai Breakfast Bowl Recipe*

Prep Time: 10 minutes
Total Time: 10 minutes

Servings:
2

Ingredients:

For the Carpaccio:

- 2 packs (100g each) frozen acai berry puree, unsweetened
- 1/2 cup apple juice or any juice of your choice (alternatively, use almond milk for a creamier texture)
- 1 banana, sliced
- 1/2 cup mixed berries (like strawberries, blueberries, and raspberries)
- 1/2 cup granola
- 1 tablespoon honey or agave syrup (more to taste)
- 1 tablespoon coconut flakes
- Additional toppings (optional): sliced almonds, chia seeds, peanut butter, or sliced kiwi

Instructions:

1. Blend the Acai Puree: Break the frozen acai puree into chunks and place them in a blender. Add apple juice or almond milk to help the blending process. Blend until smooth and thick, similar to a thick smoothie or soft-serve ice cream.

2. Prepare the Base: Divide the blended acai mixture between two bowls.

3. Add Toppings: Top each bowl with sliced banana, mixed berries, and granola. Drizzle with honey or agave syrup. Sprinkle coconut flakes over the top.

4. Customize Your Bowl: Feel free to add additional toppings of your choice, such as sliced almonds, chia seeds, a dollop of peanut butter, or fresh kiwi slices.

5. Serve Immediately: Acai bowls are best enjoyed fresh. Serve immediately for a refreshing and energizing breakfast.

This Acai Breakfast Bowl is not only a feast for the eyes but also packed with antioxidants, vitamins, and fiber. It's a perfect light and healthy option that keeps you full and energized throughout the morning. Enjoy this superfood-packed treat!

# Easter Dinner
# Main Dishes

# Roast Leg of Lamb Recipe

Prep Time: 20 minutes
Cook Time: 1 hour 30 minutes
Total Time: About 1 hour 50 minutes (plus resting time)

Servings:
6-8

Ingredients:

- 1 leg of lamb (bone-in, about 5-7 pounds)
- 4 cloves garlic, minced
- 2 tablespoons fresh rosemary, chopped
- 1/4 cup olive oil
- Juice of 1 lemon
- 2 teaspoons Dijon mustard
- Salt and freshly ground black pepper, to taste
- 2 onions, quartered
- 2 cups chicken or lamb stock
- Fresh herbs (such as rosemary and thyme) for garnish

Instructions:

1. Preheat the Oven: Preheat your oven to 425°F (220°C).

2. Prepare the Lamb: If there is a thick layer of fat on the lamb, trim it off, leaving a thin layer for flavor. Make small incisions all over the lamb with a sharp knife.

3. Marinate: In a bowl, combine the minced garlic, chopped rosemary, olive oil, lemon juice, Dijon mustard, salt, and pepper. Rub this mixture all over the lamb, ensuring to get into the incisions.

4. Roast with Onions: Place the quartered onions in a roasting pan and set the lamb on top of them. Roast in the preheated oven for 20 minutes.

5. Reduce the Temperature: After 20 minutes, reduce the oven temperature to 350°F (175°C). Continue roasting the lamb, adding stock to the pan to keep the meat and onions moist and to prevent burning.

6. Check for Doneness: Roast for about 1 hour and 10 minutes more, or until a meat thermometer inserted into the thickest part of the lamb reads 145°F (63°C) for medium-rare, 160°F (70°C) for medium, or 170°F (77°C) for well done. Baste occasionally with the pan juices.

7. Rest the Lamb: Once cooked to your liking, remove the lamb from the oven. Cover it loosely with aluminum foil and let it rest for about 15-20 minutes before carving. This allows the juices to redistribute throughout the meat.

8. Serve: Carve the lamb and serve with the pan juices. Garnish with fresh herbs.

Enjoy your Roast Leg of Lamb as the centerpiece of your Easter meal. It pairs wonderfully with side dishes such as roasted vegetables, mashed potatoes, or a fresh salad.

# *Traditional Honey Glazed Ham Recipe*

Prep Time: 15 minutes
Cook Time: About 2 hours
(varies depending on the size of the ham)
Total Time: About 2 hours 15 minutes

Servings:
8-10

Ingredients:

- 1 fully cooked bone-in ham (about 8-10 pounds)
- Whole cloves (optional, for studding the ham)
- 1 cup honey
- 1/4 cup brown sugar
- 2 tablespoons Dijon mustard
- 1/4 cup apple cider vinegar
- 1 teaspoon ground cinnamon
- 1/2 teaspoon ground nutmeg
- 1/4 teaspoon ground cloves (if not using whole cloves)

Instructions:

1. Preheat the Oven: Preheat your oven to 325°F (163°C).

2. Prepare the Ham: Remove the ham from the packaging and place it on a rack in a large roasting pan. If your ham has a thick layer of skin, you may choose to trim it off, leaving a thin layer of fat. Score the surface of the ham in a diamond pattern, and if using, stud the intersections with whole cloves.

3. Make the Glaze: In a saucepan over medium heat, combine the honey, brown sugar, Dijon mustard, apple cider vinegar, cinnamon, nutmeg, and ground cloves (if not using whole cloves). Stir and cook until the brown sugar has dissolved and the mixture is well combined.

4. Glaze the Ham: Brush about one-third of the honey glaze over the ham.

5. Bake: Cover the ham loosely with aluminum foil to prevent it from drying out. Bake in the preheated oven for about 1.5 to 2 hours, or until the internal temperature reaches 140°F (60°C). Baste the ham with the remaining glaze every 30 minutes.

6. Broil for a Crisp Finish: During the last 15-20 minutes of cooking, remove the foil and set the oven to broil. Watch the ham carefully as the glaze caramelizes.

7. Rest and Serve: Remove the ham from the oven and let it rest for 10-15 minutes before carving. This allows the juices to redistribute throughout the meat.

8. Carve and Enjoy: Carve the ham into slices and serve.

This Honey Glazed Ham is sweet, moist, and full of flavor, making it the perfect main dish for your Easter celebration. Serve it alongside your favorite Easter sides, such as roasted vegetables, mashed potatoes, or a spring salad. Enjoy!

# *Pork Loin or Pork Roast Recipe*

Prep Time: 20 minutes

Cook Time: 1 hour to 1 hour 30 minutes
(depending on the size of the roast)

Total Time: 1 hour 40 minutes to 1 hour 50 minutes

Servings:
6-8

Ingredients:

- 1 whole pork loin or pork roast (about 3-5 pounds)
- 2 tablespoons olive oil
- 4 garlic cloves, minced
- 2 tablespoons fresh rosemary, finely chopped
- 2 tablespoons fresh thyme, finely chopped
- 1 tablespoon Dijon mustard (or more to ensure it covers the whole roast)
- Salt and freshly ground black pepper, to taste
- 1/2 cup white wine or chicken broth (for the roasting pan)
- Additional fresh herbs for garnish

Instructions:

1. Preheat the Oven: Preheat your oven to 375°F (190°C).

2. Prepare the Pork: If there is a thick layer of fat on the pork, you can trim it slightly, but leave a thin layer for flavor and moisture. Pat the pork dry with paper towels.

3. Make the Herb Rub: In a small bowl, mix together the olive oil, minced garlic, rosemary, thyme, Dijon mustard, salt, and pepper to form a paste.

4. Season the Pork: Rub the herb mixture all over the pork loin or roast, making sure to coat it evenly.

5. Roast the Pork: Place the pork in a roasting pan. Pour the white wine or chicken broth into the bottom of the pan (this will help keep the pork moist and add flavor to the pan juices). Roast in the preheated oven for about 20 minutes per pound, or until the internal temperature of the pork reaches 145°F (63°C).

6. Rest the Pork: Once the pork is cooked, remove it from the oven and let it rest for 10-15 minutes before slicing. This allows the juices to redistribute throughout the meat.

7. Serve: Slice the pork and arrange it on a serving platter. Garnish with additional fresh herbs.

8. Optional: Make a Pan Sauce: If desired, you can make a simple pan sauce with the drippings. Place the roasting pan over medium heat, add a bit more wine or broth, and scrape up any browned bits from the bottom of the pan. Simmer until slightly reduced, then strain and serve with the pork.

This Pork Loin or Pork Roast, with its aromatic herbs and succulent texture, makes for a delightful and impressive main course for your Easter dinner. Pair it with your favorite sides such as roasted vegetables, a fresh salad, or scalloped potatoes for a complete and satisfying meal.

# *Classic Roast Beef Recipe*

Prep Time: 20 minutes
Cook Time: Depends on the size of the roast
(approximately 1.5 to 2.5 hours)
Total Time: 2 to 3 hours (including rest time)

Servings:
6-8

Ingredients:

- 1 rib roast or beef tenderloin (about 4-6 pounds)
- 2 tablespoons olive oil
- 4-5 garlic cloves, minced
- 2 teaspoons coarse salt
- 1 teaspoon freshly ground black pepper
- 1 teaspoon dried thyme (or rosemary)
- 1/2 teaspoon paprika

For the Gravy:

- Pan drippings from the roast
- 2 tablespoons all-purpose flour
- 2 cups beef broth
- Salt and pepper, to taste

For the Horseradish Sauce:

- 1/2 cup sour cream
- 2 tablespoons prepared horseradish
- 1 teaspoon Dijon mustard
- 1 teaspoon white vinegar
- Salt and pepper, to taste

Instructions:

1. Prepare the Roast: Let the roast sit at room temperature for about 1 hour before cooking. Preheat your oven to 450°F (232°C). Rub the roast all over with olive oil. In a small bowl, mix together the minced garlic, salt, pepper, thyme (or rosemary), and paprika. Rub this seasoning mix evenly over the roast.

2. Roast the Beef: Place the roast on a rack in a roasting pan. Roast at 450°F (232°C) for 15 minutes, then reduce the oven temperature to 325°F (163°C). Continue roasting for approximately 15 minutes per pound for medium-rare. Use a meat thermometer to ensure the desired doneness; 125°F (52°C) for medium-rare is ideal.

3. Rest the Beef: Once cooked, remove the roast from the oven. Tent loosely with foil and let it rest for 20-30 minutes.

4. Make the Gravy: Skim off any excess fat from the pan drippings. Over medium heat, sprinkle flour into the pan and stir for about 1-2 minutes. Gradually whisk in the beef broth, cooking until the gravy thickens. Season with salt and pepper.

5. Prepare the Horseradish Sauce: Combine sour cream, horseradish, Dijon mustard, and white vinegar in a bowl. Season with salt and pepper to taste. Refrigerate until ready to serve.

6. Serve: Slice the roast beef and serve with the gravy and horseradish sauce on the side.

This classic roast beef recipe, seasoned with garlic and herbs, will make a delicious and memorable centerpiece for your Easter dinner. Enjoy it with traditional sides for a complete and satisfying meal.

# Roast Chicken Recipe

Prep Time: 20 minutes
Cook Time: 1 hour 30 minutes
Total Time: About 1 hour 50 minutes

Servings:
4-6

Ingredients:

- 1 whole chicken (about 4-5 pounds)
- 4 tablespoons unsalted butter, at room temperature
- 1 lemon, halved
- 4 garlic cloves, minced
- 2 tablespoons fresh rosemary, chopped
- 2 tablespoons fresh thyme, chopped
- 1 tablespoon fresh sage, chopped
- Salt and freshly ground black pepper, to taste
- 1 onion, quartered
- 2 carrots, cut into 2-inch pieces
- 2 celery stalks, cut into 2-inch pieces

Instructions:

1. Preheat the Oven: Preheat your oven to 425°F (220°C).

2. Prepare the Chicken: Remove the giblets and any excess fat from the chicken. Rinse the chicken inside and out with cold water, then pat dry with paper towels.

3. Season the Chicken: In a small bowl, mix the butter, minced garlic, rosemary, thyme, sage, salt, and pepper. Rub the mixture both under and over the skin of the chicken. Squeeze the lemon halves inside the chicken cavity and then place them inside along with any leftover herbs.

4. Arrange Vegetables and Chicken: In a roasting pan, spread the onion, carrots, and celery to create a bed for the chicken. Place the chicken on top of the vegetables.

5. Roast the Chicken: Roast the chicken in the preheated oven for about 1 hour and 30 minutes, or until the juices run clear when you cut between a leg and thigh. The internal temperature should reach 165°F (74°C) when measured in the thickest part of the thigh.

6. Rest Before Carving: Remove the chicken from the oven and let it rest for 10-15 minutes before carving. This allows the juices to redistribute, making for a moister chicken.

7. Serve: Carve the chicken and serve it with the roasted vegetables from the pan.

Suggested Side Dishes:

- Roasted potatoes or mashed potatoes
- Steamed green beans or a green salad
- Fresh dinner rolls or a loaf of crusty bread

This Roast Chicken, fragrant with herbs and garlic, makes for a beautiful and flavorful centerpiece for your Easter dinner. It's sure to satisfy your guests with its juicy and tender meat. Enjoy your Easter feast!

# *Salmon Recipe (Baked, Grilled, or Poached)*

Prep Time: 10 minutes
Cook Time: 15-20 minutes (for baking or grilling),
10-15 minutes (for poaching)
Total Time: 25-30 minutes

Servings:
4

Ingredients:

- 4 salmon fillets (about 6 ounces each)
- Salt and freshly ground black pepper, to taste
- 2 tablespoons olive oil (for baking or grilling)
- 1 lemon, thinly sliced
- Fresh dill and other herbs (such as parsley or thyme), for garnish

For Poaching Liquid (if poaching):

- 4 cups water (or a mix of water and white wine)
- 1 lemon, sliced
- 1 onion, sliced
- A few sprigs of fresh dill
- Salt and pepper

Instructions:

For Baked Salmon:

1. Preheat your oven to 400°F (200°C).
2. Season the salmon fillets with salt and pepper. Drizzle with olive oil.
3. Place the salmon in a baking dish. Top each fillet with lemon slices and a sprinkle of dill.
4. Bake in the preheated oven for 15-20 minutes, or until the salmon flakes easily with a fork.

For Grilled Salmon:

1. Preheat your grill to medium-high heat.
2. Season the salmon with salt and pepper and brush with olive oil.
3. Place the salmon, skin-side down, on the grill. Grill for about 5-7 minutes.
4. Carefully flip the salmon and continue grilling for another 5-7 minutes, or until desired doneness.
5. . Garnish with lemon slices and fresh dill.

For Poached Salmon:

1. In a large skillet, combine the water (and wine, if using), lemon slices, onion, dill, salt, and pepper. Bring to a simmer.
2. Add the salmon fillets to the poaching liquid. Cover and simmer for 10-15 minutes, or until the salmon is cooked through.
3. Remove the salmon with a slotted spoon and garnish with fresh herbs and lemon slices.

To Serve:

Garnish the salmon with additional fresh dill, lemon slices, and other fresh herbs. It pairs wonderfully with a variety of sides, such as roasted vegetables, a fresh salad, or rice.

This simple yet elegant salmon dish, with its delicate flavors and healthy profile, is perfect for an Easter dinner or any special occasion. Enjoy the tender and flavorful salmon prepared your favorite way!

# Easter Dinner
## Sides

# *Scalloped Potatoes Recipe*

Prep Time: 20 minutes
Cook Time: 1 hour
Total Time: 1 hour 20 minutes

Servings:
6

Ingredients:

- 2 pounds Yukon Gold potatoes, peeled and thinly sliced
- 3 tablespoons unsalted butter
- 3 tablespoons all-purpose flour
- 2 cups whole milk
- 1 cup heavy cream
- 2 garlic cloves, minced
- 1 teaspoon salt
- 1/2 teaspoon freshly ground black pepper
- 1/4 teaspoon ground nutmeg
- 1 cup grated Gruyère cheese (or cheddar cheese)
- 1/2 cup grated Parmesan cheese
- Fresh thyme leaves, for garnish (optional)

Instructions:

For Baked Salmon:

1. Preheat the Oven and Prepare the Pan: Preheat your oven to 375°F (190°C). Grease a 9x13-inch baking dish with butter or non-stick cooking spray.

2. Slice the Potatoes: Peel and thinly slice the potatoes, about 1/8-inch thick. Place them in a large bowl of cold water to prevent browning.

3. Make the Sauce: In a saucepan, melt the butter over medium heat. Add the flour and whisk for about 1 minute. Gradually whisk in the milk and heavy cream, ensuring no lumps form. Add the minced garlic, salt, pepper, and nutmeg. Continue to cook, stirring constantly, until the sauce thickens enough to coat the back of a spoon.

4. Assemble the Dish: Drain the potatoes and layer them in the prepared baking dish. Pour the cream sauce over the potatoes, ensuring all slices are coated. Sprinkle with the grated Gruyère and Parmesan cheeses.

5. Bake: Cover the dish with aluminum foil and bake for 30 minutes. Remove the foil and bake for an additional 30 minutes, or until the top is golden brown and the potatoes are tender.

6. Garnish and Serve: Let the scalloped potatoes rest for a few minutes before serving. Garnish with fresh thyme leaves if desired.

Serve these Scalloped Potatoes as a luxurious and rich side dish that complements a variety of main courses, from roast meats to vegetarian entrees. Their creamy texture and cheesy flavor are sure to be a hit at any gathering.

# Glazed Carrots and Parsnips Recipe

Prep Time: 15 minutes
Cook Time: 25 minutes
Total Time: 40 minutes

Servings:
4-6

Ingredients:

- 1 pound carrots, peeled and sliced diagonally
- 1 pound parsnips, peeled and sliced diagonally
- 3 tablespoons unsalted butter
- 3 tablespoons honey or brown sugar
- 1/4 cup chicken or vegetable broth
- Salt and freshly ground black pepper, to taste
- 2 tablespoons fresh parsley, chopped (optional for garnish)

Instructions:

1. Prepare the Vegetables: Begin by peeling and diagonally slicing both the carrots and parsnips into even pieces, about 1/4-inch thick.

2. Blanch the Vegetables: Bring a large pot of salted water to a boil. Add the carrots and parsnips, and blanch for about 3-4 minutes, just until they start to become tender. Drain and set aside.

3. Make the Glaze: In a large skillet, melt the butter over medium heat. Stir in the honey (or brown sugar) and broth. Bring the mixture to a simmer.

4. Add Vegetables to Glaze: Add the blanched carrots and parsnips to the skillet. Season with salt and pepper. Cook, occasionally stirring gently, until the vegetables are tender and glazed, about 15-20 minutes. If the glaze reduces too much before the vegetables are done, you can add a little more broth.

5. Garnish and Serve: Once the vegetables are tender and nicely glazed, check for seasoning and adjust if necessary. Garnish with chopped fresh parsley.

6. Serve Warm: Serve the glazed carrots and parsnips warm as a side dish to your main course.

These Glazed Carrots and Parsnips offer a lovely combination of sweet and savory flavors, with a slightly caramelized finish that enhances the natural flavors of the vegetables. They make a perfect accompaniment to a variety of dishes, especially roasted meats. Enjoy!

# *Asparagus with Hollandaise Sauce Recipe*

Prep Time: 15 minutes
Cook Time: 10 minutes
Total Time: 25 minutes

Servings:
4

Ingredients:

For the Asparagus:

- 1 pound fresh asparagus, ends trimmed
- Salt, for boiling water
- 1 tablespoon olive oil (optional, for roasting or grilling)

For the Hollandaise Sauce:

- 3 egg yolks
- 1 tablespoon lemon juice
- 1/2 cup (1 stick) unsalted butter, melted
- Pinch of cayenne pepper
- Salt, to taste

Instructions:

Prepare the Asparagus:

1. Boil: Bring a large pot of salted water to a boil. Add the asparagus and cook for 3-4 minutes until just tender but still crisp. Drain and plunge into ice water to stop the cooking process and retain the bright green color. Drain again and set aside.

2. Alternatively, Roast or Grill: Preheat your oven to 425°F (220°C) for roasting or preheat your grill for grilling. Toss the asparagus with olive oil and season with salt. Roast or grill until tender, about 8-10 minutes.

Make the Hollandaise Sauce:

1. Whisk Egg Yolks and Lemon Juice: In a heatproof bowl, whisk together the egg yolks and lemon juice until the mixture is thickened and doubled in volume.

2. Double Boiler Method: Place the bowl over a pot of simmering water (double boiler), ensuring the water doesn't touch the bottom of the bowl. Continue to whisk rapidly. Be careful not to let the eggs get too hot or they will scramble.

3. Add Melted Butter: Slowly drizzle in the melted butter and continue to whisk until the sauce is thickened and doubled in volume. Remove from heat.

4. Season the Sauce: Add a pinch of cayenne pepper and salt to taste. If the sauce is too thick, you can whisk in a few teaspoons of warm water.

Assemble and Serve:

1. Arrange Asparagus: Arrange the cooked asparagus on a serving platter.

2. Top with Hollandaise: Spoon the Hollandaise sauce over the asparagus.

3. Serve Immediately: Serve the asparagus while the sauce is warm and creamy.

This Asparagus with Hollandaise Sauce is a delightful combination of flavors and textures, with the tender asparagus complemented by the smooth and tangy sauce. It's a sophisticated addition to any meal, especially during the spring season or for special occasions. Enjoy!

# *Minted Peas Recipe*

Prep Time: 5 minutes
Cook Time: 10 minutes
Total Time: 15 minutes

Servings:
4

Ingredients:

- 2 cups frozen peas
- 2 tablespoons unsalted butter
- 2 tablespoons fresh mint, finely chopped
- Salt and freshly ground black pepper, to taste
- 1 teaspoon sugar (optional, to enhance sweetness)
- 1 tablespoon water or chicken/vegetable broth

Instructions:

1. Cook the Peas: In a medium saucepan, add the peas and water or broth. Bring to a simmer over medium heat. Cover and cook for about 5-7 minutes, or until the peas are just tender. Be careful not to overcook, as you want the peas to retain their bright green color and some bite.

2. Add Flavorings: Once the peas are cooked, drain any excess liquid. Stir in the butter, allowing it to melt with the warmth of the peas. Add the chopped fresh mint, salt, and pepper. If you prefer a slightly sweeter taste, you can also add a teaspoon of sugar.

3. Combine and Serve: Stir everything together until the peas are evenly coated with the butter and mint mixture. Taste and adjust the seasoning if necessary.

4. Serve Warm: Serve the minted peas warm as a side dish.

Minted Peas are not only easy and quick to prepare but also offer a burst of freshness to complement richer main dishes. They're particularly good in spring and summer or as part of a holiday meal. Enjoy this simple yet tasty side dish!

# *Spinach and Strawberry Salad Recipe*

Prep Time: 15 minutes
Total Time: 15 minutes

Servings:
4

Ingredients:

For the Salad:

- 6 cups fresh baby spinach, washed and dried
- 2 cups strawberries, hulled and sliced
- 1/2 cup feta cheese, crumbled
- 1/4 cup sliced almonds or walnuts, toasted
- 1/4 red onion, thinly sliced (optional)

For the Dressing:

- 1/4 cup extra virgin olive oil
- 2 tablespoons balsamic vinegar
- 1 tablespoon honey
- 1 teaspoon Dijon mustard
- Salt and pepper, to taste

Instructions:

1. Prepare the Dressing: In a small bowl, whisk together the olive oil, balsamic vinegar, honey, and Dijon mustard. Season with salt and pepper to taste. Set aside.

2. Combine Salad Ingredients: In a large salad bowl, combine the baby spinach, sliced strawberries, feta cheese, and toasted almonds or walnuts. If using, add the thinly sliced red onion.

3. Dress the Salad: Drizzle the dressing over the salad and gently toss to combine, ensuring all the ingredients are evenly coated.

4. Serve Immediately: Serve the salad immediately after dressing to maintain the freshness and crispness of the spinach.

5. Optional Additions: For added protein, consider topping the salad with grilled chicken or salmon. For a vegan option, omit the feta cheese or replace it with a vegan alternative.

This Spinach and Strawberry Salad is not only visually appealing but also packed with a variety of flavors and textures. It's a perfect dish for a spring or summer meal, and its lightness makes it an excellent choice for a healthy yet satisfying dish.

# *Lemon Butter Green Beans Recipe*

Prep Time: 10 minutes
Cook Time: 10 minutes
Total Time: 20 minutes

Servings:
4

Ingredients:

- 1 pound fresh green beans, trimmed
- 2 tablespoons unsalted butter
- Zest of 1 lemon
- 2 tablespoons lemon juice
- Salt and freshly ground black pepper, to taste
- Optional: 1-2 cloves garlic, minced, or red pepper flakes for heat

Instructions:

1. Blanch the Green Beans: Bring a large pot of salted water to a boil. Add the green beans and cook for about 3-4 minutes until they are bright green and tender but still crisp. Immediately plunge the beans into a bowl of ice water to stop the cooking process. This step helps retain their vibrant color and crisp texture. Drain well.

2. Prepare Lemon Butter Sauce: In a large skillet, melt the butter over medium heat. If using garlic, add it to the butter and sauté for about 1 minute until fragrant. Add the lemon zest and lemon juice, and stir to combine. If desired, you can also add a pinch of red pepper flakes for a bit of heat.

3. Toss Green Beans in Sauce: Add the blanched green beans to the skillet. Toss well to coat the beans with the lemon butter sauce. Season with salt and freshly ground black pepper.

4. Cook Until Heated Through: Cook the beans in the sauce for an additional 2-3 minutes, just until they are heated through.

5. Serve: Transfer the green beans to a serving dish. Serve warm.

6. Optional Garnishes: Garnish with additional lemon zest or freshly chopped parsley for an extra touch of freshness.

Lemon Butter Green Beans are a bright and flavorful side dish that pairs wonderfully with a variety of proteins, such as chicken, fish, beef, or lamb. They bring a light and refreshing element to any meal, especially in the spring and summer months. Enjoy!

# *Herbed Wild Rice Pilaf Recipe*

Prep Time: 10 minutes
Cook Time: 45-50 minutes
Total Time: About 1 hour

Servings:
6

Ingredients:

- 1 cup wild rice blend
- 2 cups chicken or vegetable broth
- 1 bay leaf
- 2 tablespoons olive oil
- 1 small onion, finely chopped
- 1 stalk celery, finely chopped
- 1 carrot, finely chopped
- 2 cloves garlic, minced
- 1/2 cup long-grain white rice
- 1/4 cup fresh parsley, chopped
- 2 tablespoons fresh thyme leaves
- Salt and freshly ground black pepper, to taste
- Optional additions: toasted nuts (such as almonds or pecans), dried
- cranberries, or diced mushrooms

Instructions:

1. Cook the Wild Rice: In a medium saucepan, bring the wild rice blend, chicken or vegetable broth, and a bay leaf to a boil. Reduce the heat to low, cover, and simmer for about 35-40 minutes, or until the rice is tender and has absorbed the liquid. Remove the bay leaf.

2. Sauté the Vegetables: While the wild rice is cooking, heat olive oil in a skillet over medium heat. Add the onion, celery, and carrot. Sauté until the vegetables are softened, about 5 minutes. Add the garlic and cook for another minute.

3. Add White Rice: Stir in the long-grain white rice to the skillet with the vegetables. Cook for 2-3 minutes, stirring constantly, until the rice is lightly toasted.

4. Combine Rice and Vegetables: Add the cooked wild rice blend to the skillet with the vegetables and white rice. Stir to combine.

5. Add Herbs and Season: Mix in the fresh parsley and thyme. Season with salt and freshly ground black pepper to taste. Cook for an additional 5 minutes, stirring occasionally.

6. Optional Additions: If desired, stir in toasted nuts, dried cranberries, or diced mushrooms for added texture and flavor.

7. Serve: Serve the herbed wild rice pilaf warm as a side dish.

This Herbed Wild Rice Pilaf is not just delicious but also a feast for the eyes, with its mix of colorful vegetables and herbs. It's a versatile side that goes well with chicken, fish, beef, or vegetarian main courses, making it perfect for a variety of occasions and meals.

# Easter Desserts and Sweet Treats

# Carrot Cake Recipe with Cream Cheese Frosting

Prep Time: 30 minutes
Cook Time: 30-35 minutes
Total Time: 1 hour to 1 hour 10 minutes

Servings:
8-10

Ingredients:

For the Cake:

- 2 cups all-purpose flour
- 2 teaspoons baking powder
- 1 teaspoon baking soda
- 1 1/2 teaspoons ground cinnamon
- 1/2 teaspoon ground nutmeg
- 1/2 teaspoon ground ginger
- 1/2 teaspoon salt
- 4 large eggs, at room temperature
- 1 cup vegetable oil
- 2 cups granulated sugar
- 2 teaspoons vanilla extract
- 3 cups grated carrots
- 1 cup chopped walnuts or pecans (optional)
- 1/2 cup crushed pineapple (drained, optional)

For the Cream Cheese Frosting:

- 1/2 cup unsalted butter, softened
- 8 ounces cream cheese, softened
- 4 cups powdered sugar
- 2 teaspoons vanilla extract

For Decorating:

- Marzipan carrots (optional)
- Additional chopped nuts or grated carrots (optional)

Instructions:

Make the Cake:

1. Preheat the Oven and Prepare Pans: Preheat your oven to 350°F (175°C). Grease and flour two 9-inch round cake pans.
2. Combine Dry Ingredients: In a medium bowl, whisk together flour, baking powder, baking soda, cinnamon, nutmeg, ginger, and salt.

3. Mix Wet Ingredients: In a large bowl, beat the eggs, vegetable oil, granulated sugar, and vanilla extract until well combined.
4. Add Dry Ingredients: Gradually add the dry ingredients to the wet mixture, mixing just until combined.
5. Fold in Carrots and Nuts: Stir in the grated carrots and, if using, chopped nuts and pineapple.
6. Bake: Divide the batter evenly between the prepared pans. Bake for 30-35 minutes, or until a toothpick inserted into the center comes out clean.
7. Cool Cakes: Let the cakes cool in the pans for 10 minutes, then transfer to wire racks to cool completely.

Make the Cream Cheese Frosting:

1. Beat Butter and Cream Cheese: In a large bowl, beat the butter and cream cheese together until smooth and creamy.
2. Add Powdered Sugar and Vanilla: Gradually add powdered sugar and vanilla extract, beating until the frosting is smooth and spreadable.

Assemble and Decorate the Cake:

1. Assemble: If the cakes have domed tops, trim them with a serrated knife to level. Place one cake layer on your serving plate. Spread a layer of frosting on top. Top with the second cake layer.
2. Frost the Cake: Spread a thin layer of frosting over the top and sides of the cake (crumb coat). Chill for 15-20 minutes, then apply a final, thicker layer of frosting.
3. Decorate: Decorate with marzipan carrots and additional nuts or grated carrots, if desired.
4. Serve: Slice and serve the carrot cake at room temperature.

This Carrot Cake is wonderfully moist and flavorful, with a perfect balance of sweetness and spice. The cream cheese frosting adds a rich and creamy finish that makes this cake a beloved dessert for any special occasion, especially Easter. Enjoy your homemade treat!

# *Simnel Cake Recipe*

Prep Time: 45 minutes
Cook Time: 2 hours 30 minutes
Total Time: About 3 hours 15 minutes
(including cooling time)

Servings:
12-14

Ingredients:

For the Cake:

- 1 1/2 cups mixed dried fruit (such as raisins, currants, and sultanas)
- 1/2 cup candied citrus peel, chopped
- 1/4 cup brandy or orange juice
- 2 cups all-purpose flour
- 1/2 teaspoon ground cinnamon
- 1/4 teaspoon ground nutmeg
- 1/4 teaspoon ground ginger
- 1 cup unsalted butter, softened
- 1 cup brown sugar
- 4 large eggs
- Zest of 1 lemon
- Zest of 1 orange
- 2 tablespoons apricot jam

For the Marzipan:

- 3 cups almond meal or ground almonds
- 1 1/2 cups powdered sugar
- 2 eggs, beaten
- 1 teaspoon almond extract

Instructions:

1. Soak the Fruit: In a bowl, combine the mixed dried fruit and candied citrus peel with the brandy or orange juice. Let soak for at least 1 hour, or overnight.

2. Prepare the Marzipan: In a separate bowl, mix together the almond meal and powdered sugar. Add the beaten eggs and almond extract, and knead to form a smooth marzipan. Divide the marzipan into three equal parts. Roll out one part into a circle the size of your cake pan for the middle layer. With another part, form 11 equal-sized balls for decorating. Reserve the third part for the top layer.

3. Preheat the Oven: Preheat your oven to 300°F (150°C). Grease and line an 8-inch round cake pan with parchment paper.

4. Make the Cake Batter: In a bowl, sift together the flour, cinnamon, nutmeg, and ginger. In another large bowl, cream the butter and brown sugar until fluffy. Beat in the eggs, one at a time, then mix in the lemon and orange zest. Gradually add the flour mixture, then fold in the soaked fruit.

5. Assemble the Cake: Spoon half of the cake batter into the prepared pan. Place the rolled-out marzipan circle over the batter. Add the remaining cake batter on top and smooth the surface.

6. Bake: Bake the cake for about 2 to 2.5 hours, or until a skewer inserted into the center comes out clean. Allow the cake to cool in the pan before turning it out onto a wire rack.

7. Decorate with Marzipan: Warm the apricot jam and brush it over the top of the cooled cake. Roll out the third part of the marzipan to cover the top of the cake. Place the marzipan over the jam. Arrange the 11 marzipan balls around the edge.

8. 8. Brown the Marzipan: Place the cake under a preheated broiler for 1-2 minutes to brown the marzipan topping. Watch carefully to prevent burning.

9. 9. Serve: Once the marzipan is lightly browned and the cake is cooled, it's ready to be served.

This Simnel Cake, rich with fruit and the distinctive flavor of marzipan, is a wonderful way to celebrate Easter and continue a time-honored tradition. Enjoy the moist cake and sweet marzipan with your Easter festivities!

# *Italian Easter Pie (Pastiera Napoletana) Recipe*

Prep Time: 1 hour (plus chilling and soaking time)
Cook Time: 1 hour
Total Time: 2 hours (plus chilling and soaking time)

Servings:
8-10

Ingredients:

For the Pastry:

- 2 1/2 cups all-purpose flour
- 1/2 cup granulated sugar
- 1/2 cup unsalted butter, cold and cubed
- 1 large egg
- Zest of 1 lemon

For the Filling:

- 1 cup wheat berries, soaked overnight
- 1 cup whole milk
- 1 strip of lemon peel
- 1 pound ricotta cheese, strained
- 4 large eggs
- 1 cup granulated sugar
- 1/4 cup candied orange peel, chopped
- 1/4 cup orange blossom water
- 1 teaspoon vanilla extract
- Powdered sugar, for dusting

Instructions:

Prepare the Wheat Berries:

1. Soak the wheat berries overnight in plenty of water.
2. Drain and rinse the wheat berries. Place them in a pot with the milk and lemon peel. Cook over low heat until the milk is absorbed and the wheat berries are tender, about 30 minutes. Let it cool.

Make the Pastry:

1. In a bowl, combine flour and sugar. Add the butter and use your fingers to rub it into the flour until the mixture resembles coarse crumbs.
2. Stir in the egg and lemon zest to form a dough. If the dough is too dry, add a little cold water. Wrap in plastic and chill for 30 minutes.

Prepare the Filling:

1. In a large bowl, mix the strained ricotta with the eggs and sugar. Stir in the cooled wheat berries, candied orange peel, orange blossom water, and vanilla extract.

Assemble the Pie:

1. Preheat your oven to 350°F (175°C).
2. Divide the pastry dough into two portions, one slightly larger than the other. Roll out the larger portion and line a 9-inch tart or springform pan, letting the excess hang over the edge.
3. Pour the filling into the crust. Roll out the second piece of dough and place it over the filling. Trim the excess dough and crimp the edges to seal.
4. Cut a few slits in the top crust to allow steam to escape.

Bake the Pie:

1. Bake in the preheated oven for about 1 hour, or until the crust is golden and the filling is set.
2. Let the pie cool completely, then refrigerate.

Serve:

1. Before serving, dust the top of the pie with powdered sugar.
2. Serve the Pastiera Napoletana chilled or at room temperature.

This Italian Easter Pie, with its rich flavors and creamy texture, is a true celebration of the holiday's traditions. The aromatic orange blossom water and sweet wheat berries create a unique and delightful dessert experience. Enjoy this special treat with your Easter festivities!

# *Lemon Tart Recipe*

Prep Time: 30 minutes
Cook Time: 40-45 minutes
Total Time: About 1 hour 15 minutes
(plus chilling time)

Servings:
8-10

Ingredients:

For the Tart Crust:

- 1 1/4 cups all-purpose flour
- 1/2 cup unsalted butter, cold and cubed
- 1/4 cup powdered sugar
- 1/4 teaspoon salt
- 1 large egg yolk
- 2 tablespoons ice water

For the Lemon Filling:

- 1 cup granulated sugar
- 2 tablespoons lemon zest (from about 2 lemons)
- 4 large eggs
- 2/3 cup fresh lemon juice (about 3-4 lemons)
- 1/4 cup heavy cream
- Powdered sugar, for dusting (optional)

Instructions:

Make the Tart Crust:

1. Combine Dry Ingredients: In a food processor, pulse together the flour, powdered sugar, and salt.
2. Add Butter: Add the cold, cubed butter and pulse until the mixture resembles coarse crumbs.
3. Add Egg Yolk and Water: Add the egg yolk and ice water. Pulse until the dough just starts to come together.
4. Chill the Dough: Turn the dough onto a piece of plastic wrap. Form into a disk, wrap, and chill in the refrigerator for at least 30 minutes.
5. Preheat the Oven: Preheat your oven to 375°F (190°C).
6. Roll and Press the Dough: On a lightly floured surface, roll out the dough to fit a 9-inch tart pan with a removable bottom. Press the dough into the pan and trim the edges. Prick the bottom with a fork.
7. Bake the Crust: Line the crust with parchment paper and fill with pie weights or dried beans. Bake for about 20 minutes. Remove the weights and parchment and

bake for another 10 minutes, or until lightly golden.

Make the Lemon Filling:

1. Combine Sugar and Lemon Zest: In a bowl, rub together the granulated sugar and lemon zest until the sugar is moist and fragrant.
2. Add Eggs and Lemon Juice: Whisk in the eggs and lemon juice until well combined.
3. Add Cream: Stir in the heavy cream.
4. Strain: Strain the mixture through a fine-mesh sieve into a bowl to remove any lumps and the zest.

Assemble and Bake the Tart:

1. Fill the Tart: Reduce the oven temperature to 350°F (175°C). Pour the lemon filling into the pre-baked tart crust.
2. Bake: Bake for 15-20 minutes, or until the filling is set but still slightly wobbly in the center.
3. Cool and Chill: Allow the tart to cool completely, then refrigerate until chilled.
4. Serve: Before serving, dust the tart with powdered sugar if desired.

Enjoy your Lemon Tart as a light and refreshing dessert, perfect for spring gatherings or as a sweet finish to any meal. The bright lemon flavor is sure to be a hit with anyone who enjoys a bit of tartness in their sweets.

# *Easter Egg Cheesecake Recipe*

Prep Time: 30 minutes

Cook Time: 1 hour

Chill Time: 4 hours to overnight

Total Time: About 5 hours 30 minutes to overnight (including chill time)

Servings:

10-12

## Ingredients:

### For the Crust:

- 2 cups graham cracker crumbs
- 1/2 cup unsalted butter, melted
- 1/4 cup granulated sugar

### For the Cheesecake Filling:

- 4 (8-ounce) packages cream cheese, softened
- 1 1/4 cups granulated sugar
- 4 large eggs
- 2 teaspoons vanilla extract
- 1 cup sour cream

### For the Decoration:

- Mini Easter egg candies
- Chocolate shavings or chocolate Easter egg nest

### For Chocolate Easter Egg Nest (Optional):

- 1/2 cup milk or dark chocolate chips
- 1 cup chow mein noodles or shredded coconut

## Instructions:

### Prepare the Crust:

1. Preheat the Oven: Preheat your oven to 325°F (160°C).
2. Mix Ingredients: Combine graham cracker crumbs, melted butter, and sugar in a bowl.
3. Press into Pan: Press the mixture into the bottom of a 9-inch springform pan. Set aside.

### Make the Pastry:

1. Beat Cream Cheese: In a large bowl, beat the cream cheese and sugar together until smooth.
2. Add Eggs: Add eggs one at a time, beating well after each addition.

3. Add Vanilla and Sour Cream: Mix in vanilla extract and sour cream until the filling is well combined and creamy.
4. Pour Over Crust: Pour the filling over the prepared crust.

### Bake the Cheesecake:

1. Bake: Place the cheesecake in the oven and bake for about 1 hour, or until the edges are set but the center still slightly jiggles.
2. Cool: Turn off the oven, open the oven door slightly, and let the cheesecake cool inside for 1 hour to prevent cracking.
3. Chill: Remove from the oven, run a knife around the edge, and chill in the refrigerator for at least 4 hours, preferably overnight.

### Prepare the Chocolate Easter Egg Nest (Optional):

1. Melt Chocolate: Melt chocolate chips in a microwave-safe bowl in 30-second intervals, stirring until smooth.
2. Mix with Noodles or Coconut: Gently mix in the chow mein noodles or shredded coconut until well coated.
3. Shape Nest: On a piece of parchment paper, form the mixture into a nest shape. Chill until set.

### Decorate the Cheesecake:

1. Add Easter Egg Candies: Once chilled, decorate the top of the cheesecake with mini Easter egg candies.
2. Add Chocolate Nest: If using, place the chocolate Easter egg nest in the center and fill with more candies or chocolate shavings.

### Serve:

Slice and serve the Easter Egg Cheesecake as a delightful and festive dessert perfect for your Easter celebration.

This Easter Egg Cheesecake is not only delicious but also a beautiful centerpiece

for your Easter dessert table. The combination of creamy cheesecake and playful Easter-themed decorations makes it a holiday favorite.

# *Pavlova with Fresh Berries Recipe*

Prep Time: 30 minutes
Cook Time: 1 hour 30 minutes
Cooling Time: 1 hour
Total Time: 3 hours

Servings:
6-8

Ingredients:

For the Meringue:

- 4 large egg whites, at room temperature
- 1 cup granulated sugar
- 2 teaspoons cornstarch
- 1 teaspoon white vinegar
- 1 teaspoon vanilla extract

For the Topping:

- 1 cup heavy whipping cream
- 2 tablespoons powdered sugar
- 1 teaspoon vanilla extract
- 2-3 cups mixed fresh berries (such as strawberries, blueberries, raspberries,
- and blackberries)
- Mint leaves for garnish (optional)

Instructions:

Make the Meringue:

1. Preheat the Oven: Preheat your oven to 250°F (120°C). Line a baking sheet with parchment paper and draw a 9-inch circle on the paper as a guide.

2. Beat Egg Whites: In a clean, dry bowl, beat the egg whites until soft peaks form. Gradually add the granulated sugar, about a tablespoon at a time, continuing to beat until the meringue is glossy and stiff peaks form.

3. Add Cornstarch, Vinegar, and Vanilla: Gently fold in the cornstarch, white vinegar, and vanilla extract.

4. Shape the Meringue: Spoon the meringue onto the parchment paper, using the circle as a guide. Shape it into a round with a slight well in the center.

5. Bake: Bake the meringue for about 1 hour and 30 minutes, or until it's dry and crisp on the outside and white. Turn off the oven and let the meringue cool completely inside the oven with the door ajar.

Prepare the Topping:

1. Whip the Cream: In a bowl, whip the heavy cream with powdered sugar and vanilla extract until it forms soft peaks.

2. Assemble the Pavlova: Carefully transfer the cooled meringue to a serving plate. Spoon the whipped cream over the top of the meringue.

3. Add Berries: Arrange the fresh berries on top of the whipped cream.

4. Garnish: Garnish with mint leaves if desired.

Serve:

Serve the Pavlova immediately after assembling to ensure the meringue remains crisp.

This Pavlova with Fresh Berries is a show-stopping dessert that's sure to impress. Its combination of a crunchy and marshmallowy meringue, rich whipped cream, and juicy fresh berries creates a delightful symphony of textures and flavors. Enjoy this beautiful and refreshing dessert at your next spring or summer gathering!

# Chocolate Easter Eggs Recipe

Prep Time: 45 minutes

Chilling Time: 1 hour

Total Time: 1 hour 45 minutes

Servings:

varies

Ingredients:

For the Chocolate Eggs:

- 12 ounces of high-quality chocolate (dark, milk, or white), chopped
- Easter egg molds

For the Filling:

- Small candies (like jelly beans or mini chocolate eggs)
- Chopped nuts (like almonds, walnuts, or hazelnuts)
- Nut butter or chocolate spread
- Crushed cookies or biscuit pieces
- Mini marshmallows

Additional Tools:

- Pastry brush or small spoon
- Piping bag (optional, for liquid fillings)

Instructions:

Prepare the Chocolate:

1. Melt the Chocolate: Slowly melt the chocolate in a heatproof bowl set over a pot of simmering water (double boiler), stiring occasionally. Alternatively, you can melt it in the microwave in 20-second bursts, stirring between each burst.
2. Cool the Melted Chocolate: Once the chocolate is melted, let it cool slightly to thicken. This will make it easier to coat the molds.

Mold the Chocolate Eggs:

1. Brush the Molds: Using a pastry brush or a small spoon, coat the insides of the Easter egg molds with a thin layer of melted chocolate. Make sure to cover all areas.
2. 2. Chill to Set: Place the chocolate-coated molds in the refrigerator for about 15 minutes to set.
3. 3. Add a Second Coat: For a stronger shell, apply a second coat of chocolate,
4. especially around the edges, and chill again until set.

Fill the Chocolate Eggs:

1. Remove from Molds: Once the chocolate is completely set, carefully remove the half egg shapes from the molds.
2. Fill the Eggs: Place your chosen fillings (candies, nuts, nut butter, etc.) into one half of each chocolate egg. If using a liquid filling like nut butter, a piping bag can help.
3. Seal the Eggs: Warm the edges of the filled egg half by placing it on a warm plate for a few seconds. Quickly press it against an empty egg half to seal. You can also use a little melted chocolate as 'glue' to help seal the edges.
4. Chill Again: Chill the completed eggs in the refrigerator for another 15 minutes to ensure they are fully set.

Decorate (Optional):

- Drizzle with different types of melted chocolate for a decorative effect.
- Apply edible glitter or paint for a festive look.

Serve:

Once set, your Homemade Chocolate Easter Eggs are ready to be enjoyed. They make excellent gifts or can be used for Easter egg hunts.

Creating these chocolate eggs is a delightful way to celebrate the Easter holiday. The possibilities for fillings and decorations are nearly endless, allowing for plenty of creativity in the kitchen.

# *Chocolate Babka Recipe*

Prep Time: 3 hours (includes rising time)
Cook Time: 45-50 minutes
Total Time: About 4 hours

Servings:
2 loaves

Ingredients:

For the Dough:

- 1/2 cup whole milk, warmed to about 110°F (43°C)
- 2 teaspoons active dry yeast
- 1/2 cup granulated sugar
- 4 cups all-purpose flour
- 1 teaspoon salt
- 2 large eggs
- 1/2 cup unsalted butter, room temperature, cut into small pieces

For the Chocolate Filling:

- 1 cup semi-sweet chocolate chips or chopped chocolate
- 1/2 cup unsalted butter
- 1/2 cup powdered sugar
- 1/3 cup cocoa powder
- 1 teaspoon ground cinnamon

For the Syrup:

- 1/3 cup water
- 1/3 cup granulated sugar

Instructions:

Make the Dough:

1. Activate the Yeast: In a small bowl, combine the warm milk and yeast. Let sit for 5-10 minutes until foamy.
2. Mix Dry Ingredients: In the bowl of a stand mixer fitted with the dough hook, mix together the flour, sugar, and salt.
3. Add Wet Ingredients: Add the eggs and yeast mixture to the flour. Mix until the dough starts to come together.
4. Add Butter: With the mixer on low, add the butter a few pieces at a time, mixing well after each addition. Continue to knead until the dough is smooth and pulls away from the side of the bowl.
5. First Rise: Place the dough in a greased bowl, cover with plastic wrap, and let it rise in a warm place until doubled in size, about 1-1.5 hours.

Prepare the Chocolate Filling:

1. 1. Melt Chocolate and Butter: In a saucepan over low heat, melt the chocolate and butter together. Remove from heat.
2. 2. Add Sugar, Cocoa, and Cinnamon: Stir in the powdered sugar, cocoa powder, and cinnamon until the mixture is smooth.

Assemble the Babka:

1. Roll Out Dough: Once the dough has risen, divide it in half. On a lightly floured surface, roll out one half into a rectangle.

2. Spread Filling: Spread half of the chocolate filling over the dough, leaving a small border around the edges.

3. Shape the Babka: Roll the dough into a tight log, starting from the long edge. Slice the log in half lengthwise, then twist the two halves together, keeping the cut sides up. Place in a greased 9x5 inch loaf pan.

4. Second Rise: Repeat with the second piece of dough and remaining filling. Cover the loaves and let them rise for another hour.

Bake the Babka:

1. Preheat Oven: Preheat the oven to 350°F (175°C).

2. Bake: Bake the babkas for 45-50 minutes, or until a skewer inserted into the center comes out clean.

Make the Syrup:

1. Combine Sugar and Water: While the babkas are baking, make the syrup by combining the water and sugar in a saucepan. Bring to a boil and simmer until the sugar has dissolved.

2. Brush the Babkas: As soon as the babkas come out of the oven, brush them with the syrup.

Cool and Serve:

1. Cool: Let the babkas cool in the pans for 10 minutes, then transfer to a wire rack to cool completely.

Enjoy your homemade Chocolate Babka as a sweet treat any time of the day. The combination of the rich chocolate filling and the soft, brioche-like bread is simply irresistible!

# Fourth of July Favorites

*The 4th of July, a day when the nation's heart beats in harmony with the colors of the flag, when the skies light up with fireworks, and the air is filled with the echoes of freedom. It's a day of unity, pride, and celebration — a time to gather with friends and family, bask in the summer sun, and revel in the traditions that make Independence Day truly special.*

*In this chapter of our cookbook, "4th of July Celebrations," we invite you to embrace the spirit of America's birthday with a culinary journey that pays homage to this beloved holiday. Whether you're hosting a backyard barbecue, a picnic in the park, or simply enjoying a meal at home, we've got you covered with a collection of recipes that capture the essence of the 4th of July.*

Grilling and barbecue hold a special place in the culinary world, bringing together people, flavors, and traditions in a unique and delightful way. The joy of grilling is not just about the delicious food it produces but also about the experience itself – the warmth of the fire, the sizzle of the grill, and the anticipation of a shared meal. Whether it's a backyard gathering, a family reunion, or a casual weekend treat, grilling and barbecue have a way of turning simple meals into memorable occasions.

Barbecue, in particular, is steeped in history and varies greatly from one culture to another. Its roots can be traced back to indigenous cooking methods, where meat was slow-cooked over an open fire or in a pit. Over time, these techniques evolved and spread, taking on different forms around the world. In the United States, barbecue is almost a way of life in regions like the Carolinas, Texas, and Kansas City, each boasting its own distinct style and flavors. From the tangy vinegar-based sauces of the Carolinas to the rich, smoky flavors of Texas brisket, American barbecue is a testament to the diverse culinary landscape of the country.

But barbecue is not limited to the United States. In Argentina, the asado is a cherished tradition, where succulent cuts of meat are grilled on a parrilla. In Korea, barbecue is a communal affair with marinated meats grilled right at the table. And in Australia, the barbie is a beloved national pastime, reflecting the country's outdoor lifestyle and love for fresh, grilled seafood and meats.

At its core, grilling and barbecue are about more than just cooking; they're about community, tradition, and the celebration of simple pleasures. It's a culinary art that engages all the senses and brings people together, creating not just meals but memories that last a lifetime.

# Barbecue Essentials and Grilling Recipes

# Grilling Equipment:
## Essential Tools for Perfect Barbecues

Grilling is an art that requires the right tools to achieve the perfect balance of flavor and texture. Whether you're a seasoned grill master or a novice, understanding the essential grilling equipment is key to your success. Here's an overview of the must-have tools for any grilling enthusiast.

### Grills and Smokers

- Charcoal Grills: Ideal for purists, charcoal grills are known for imparting a smoky flavor to the food. They require charcoal briquettes or lump charcoal and offer high heat ideal for searing meat.

- Gas Grills: Convenient and easy to control, gas grills are popular for their quick start-up and consistent heat. They use propane or natural gas and are great for direct and indirect grilling.

- Electric Grills: Perfect for those with limited outdoor space, electric grills only need a power outlet. While they don't offer a traditional smoky flavor, they are convenient and easy to use.

- Smokers: For low and slow cooking, smokers are essential. They come in various types like offset, vertical, or kettle-style and can use wood, charcoal, or even electric power to impart a deep smoky flavor to meats.

### Utensils and Accessories

- Tongs: Long-handled tongs are a necessity for flipping and moving food safely on the grill.

- Spatula: A sturdy spatula is ideal for maneuvering burgers, fish, and other delicate items.

- Grill Brush: For maintaining a clean grill, a good grill brush is crucial. It's used for scraping off the residue and keeping the grill grates clean.

- Meat Thermometer: To ensure meat is cooked to the perfect temperature, a meat thermometer is a must-have. Digital instant-read thermometers provide quick and accurate readings.

- Grill Gloves: Heat-resistant gloves protect your hands from the high heat of the grill and hot utensils.

- Basting Brush: A basting brush is used to apply marinades and sauces to food while grilling.

- Skewers: For kebabs and grilled vegetables, metal or bamboo skewers are essential.

### Optional Add-ons

- Grill Baskets: Handy for grilling small items like chopped vegetables and seafood without them falling through the grates.

- Rotisserie Kit: Perfect for slow-roasting meats evenly on all sides.

- Smoking Box/Chips: For gas grills, a smoking box with wood chips can add a smoky flavor to your grilled foods.

- Grill Covers: To protect your grill from the elements, a durable grill cover is a good investment.

With the right equipment in hand, grilling can be an enjoyable and rewarding experience. Each tool and accessory plays its part in helping you achieve grilling perfection, from the flavorful sear of a steak to the smoky aroma of slow-cooked ribs. So, gear up, fire up the grill, and get ready to savor the delights of outdoor cooking!

# *Preparation Techniques for Grilling*

Getting your grill ready and ensuring safety are crucial steps in the grilling process. Proper preparation not only affects the flavor and quality of your grilled food but also ensures a safe and enjoyable grilling experience. Here's a guide on how to prepare and preheat your grill, along with some essential safety tips.

Preparing and Preheating the Grill

1. Clean the Grill Grates: Before firing up your grill, make sure the grates are clean. Use a grill brush to scrape off any residue from previous grilling sessions. For a deeper clean, heat the grill for 10-15 minutes to loosen the residue before scrubbing.

2. Preheat the Grill:

- For Charcoal Grills: Light the charcoal using a chimney starter or by piling the charcoal and lighting it. Let the charcoal burn until it's covered with a light layer of ash (usually takes about 15-20 minutes). Spread the coals evenly for direct heat or to one side for indirect heat.

- For Gas Grills: Turn on the burners to high and close the lid. Preheat for about 10-15 minutes. Once preheated, adjust the burners to the desired temperature.

3. Oil the Grates: To prevent sticking, lightly oil the grill grates. Use tongs to hold a paper towel soaked in cooking oil and rub it over the grates.

Safety Tips

1. Location: Set up your grill in an open, well-ventilated area. Keep it away from structures, trees, and overhangs. Ensure the grill is on a stable surface.

2. Check for Leaks (Gas Grills): Before using a gas grill, check for leaks by applying a soap and water solution to the hose and connections. Turn on the gas and look for bubbles, which indicate a leak.

3. Keep a Safe Distance: Maintain a safe distance from the grill, especially when igniting it. Wear fitting clothing and use long-handled tools to avoid burns.

4. Never Leave the Grill Unattended: Always keep an eye on the grill when it's in use. This is crucial to prevent flare-ups and fires.

5. Be Ready to Extinguish Flames: Have baking soda on hand to control a grease fire and a fire extinguisher nearby for other fires. Never use water to put out a grease fire.

6. Proper Lighting: If using a charcoal grill, never use gasoline or kerosene as a starter. Always use lighter fluid designed for charcoal grilling.

7. Handling Food: Use separate plates and utensils for raw and cooked meats to avoid cross-contamination.

8. Let the Grill Cool: After grilling, let the grill cool completely before covering or storing it.

9. Regular Maintenance: Regularly check and maintain your grill to ensure it's in good working order. This includes checking burner jets for clogs and inspecting gas hoses for cracks.

Proper preparation and adherence to safety guidelines are the foundation of a successful grilling experience. By following these steps, you can focus on the enjoyable aspects of grilling while keeping yourself and your guests safe.

# *Marinating and Seasoning: Enhancing the Flavor of Your Grill*

Marinating and seasoning are key steps in infusing flavor into meats, vegetables, and seafood before grilling. A good marinade not only adds taste but can also help tenderize meats. Here are some tips and basic marinade recipes to elevate your grilling game.

Tips on Marinating

1. Time Matters:

- Meat: Marinate meat for at least 1 hour, but for more flavor, let it sit for up to 12 hours or overnight in the refrigerator. Larger cuts can be marinated longer.

- Seafood: Seafood should be marinated for a shorter time, typically 15-30 minutes, to avoid becoming mushy.

- Vegetables: Vegetables usually need just about 30 minutes to 1 hour.

Safety Tips

1. Use Acidic Components: Ingredients like lemon juice, vinegar, or yogurt help to break down proteins, making the meat tender.

2. Include Oil: Oil helps to carry fat-soluble flavors into the meat and keep it moist.

3. Balancing Flavors: A good marinade has a balance of salty, sweet, and acidic flavors. Adjust these elements to your taste.

4. Marinating Container: Use a non-reactive container like glass or plastic for marinating. Metal containers can react with acidic ingredients and alter the flavor.

5. Refrigerate: Always marinate in the refrigerator to prevent bacterial growth.

6. Avoid Cross-Contamination: Never reuse a marinade that has been in contact with raw meat unless it's boiled first.

Basic Marinade Recipes

1. Classic Meat Marinade:

- 1/2 cup olive oil
- 1/4 cup soy sauce
- 2 tablespoons Worcestershire sauce
- 2 tablespoons lemon juice or red wine vinegar
- 2 cloves garlic, minced
- 1 tablespoon honey or brown sugar
- 1 teaspoon black pepper

2. Simple Seafood Marinade:

- 1/4 cup olive oil
- 2 tablespoons lemon or lime juice
- 2 cloves garlic, minced
- 1 teaspoon dried dill or fresh parsley
- Salt and pepper to taste

3. Vegetable Marinade:

- 1/3 cup olive oil
- 2 tablespoons balsamic vinegar or apple cider vinegar
- 1 tablespoon Dijon mustard
- 1 teaspoon honey or maple syrup
- 1 clove garlic, minced
- Salt and pepper to taste
- Herbs like basil, thyme, or oregano

Tips on Seasoning

1. Season Generously: Especially for thick cuts of meat, be generous with salt and seasoning to ensure flavor throughout.

2. Season at the Right Time: Salt meats just before grilling to avoid drawing out moisture. Dry rubs can be applied a few hours in advance.

3. Experiment with Flavors: Don't be afraid to experiment with different herbs and spices. Classics like rosemary, thyme, and paprika are great for meats, while dill and lemon zest suit seafood well.

4. Let It Rest: After seasoning and before grilling, let the meat rest at room temperature for about 20-30 minutes. This allows the seasoning to penetrate and the meat to cook more evenly.

Marinating and seasoning are all about personal preference and experimentation. Feel free to adjust the ingredients to suit your taste and have fun creating your own signature blends!

Understanding different grilling techniques is crucial for achieving the best results. Whether you're grilling a steak, slow-cooking a brisket, or making the perfect vegetable kebabs, how you grill makes all the difference. Here's a guide to some fundamental grilling techniques, including direct vs. indirect grilling, smoking basics, temperature control, and testing for doneness.

# *Grilling Techniques: Mastering the Grill*

Direct vs. Indirect Grilling

1. Direct Grilling:

- Definition: Cooking food directly over the heat source.

- Best For: Foods that cook quickly, like steaks, burgers, fish, and vegetables.

- Technique: Preheat the grill on high. Place the food on the grill grate directly over the heat. Ideal for searing and getting those classic grill marks.

2. Indirect Grilling:

- Definition: Cooking food next to, not directly over, the heat source. This is similar to oven roasting.

- Best For: Larger or tougher cuts of meat that require longer cooking times, like roasts, whole chickens, or ribs.

- Technique: Light only one side of the grill or the outer burners, leaving the middle burner off. Place the food over the unlit part of the grill. Close the lid to create an oven-like environment.

Smoking Basics

1. Low and Slow: Smoking is all about cooking at low temperatures over a longer period. It imparts a distinct smoky flavor.

2. Wood Chips or Chunks: Use wood chips for short smokes and chunks for longer smokes. Different woods impart different flavors.

3. Temperature Control: Maintain a consistent temperature inside the smoker, typically between 225°F and 275°F.

4. Water Pan: Use a water pan to add moisture, balance the temperature, and catch drippings.

Temperature Control

1. Use a Thermometer: A grill thermometer helps maintain the desired temperature. Gas grills often have built-in thermometers, but for charcoal grills, an oven thermometer can be placed near the food.

2. Adjusting Heat: On gas grills, simply adjust the burners. For charcoal grills, control heat by adjusting the air vents. Opening vents lets in more oxygen and increases heat, while closing them reduces heat.

Testing for Doneness

1. Use a Meat Thermometer: This is the most accurate way to check for doneness. Insert it into the thickest part of the meat, not touching any bone.

2. Visual Cues: Look for changes in color, juices running clear, and meat firmness.

3. Touch Test: For steaks, use the touch test. Rare feels soft and spongy, medium feels firm but yielding, and well-done feels very firm.

4. Resting Time: Allow meat to rest after grilling. This lets the juices redistribute, ensuring a juicy meal.

Mastering these grilling techniques takes practice, but once you do, you'll be able to handle any grilling situation and cook a variety of dishes to perfection. Remember, every grill is different, so getting to know your grill is a key part of the journey to becoming a grill master.

# *Classic BBQ Chicken with Homemade BBQ Sauce Recipe*

BBQ chicken is a staple of outdoor cooking, loved for its smoky flavor and tender, juicy meat. Paired with a homemade BBQ sauce, it's a dish that's sure to be a crowd-pleaser. Here's a simple yet delicious recipe for making classic BBQ chicken.

Ingredients:

For the Chicken:

- 4-6 pieces of chicken (mix of thighs, drumsticks, and breasts)
- Salt and freshly ground black pepper, to taste
- 2 tablespoons olive oil

Filling:

- 1 cup ketchup
- 1/2 cup apple cider vinegar
- 1/2 cup brown sugar
- 1/4 cup honey
- 2 tablespoons Worcestershire sauce
- 1 tablespoon lemon juice
- 1 teaspoon smoked paprika
- 1/2 teaspoon garlic powder
- 1/2 teaspoon onion powder
- 1/2 teaspoon ground black pepper
- 1/4 teaspoon cayenne pepper (adjust for heat preference)
- Salt to taste

Topping:

- Powdered sugar for dusting
- Additional chocolate hazelnut spread for drizzling
- Whipped cream (optional)

Instructions:

Prepare the BBQ Sauce:

1. Combine Ingredients: In a saucepan, combine all the BBQ sauce ingredients. Stir well to combine.
2. Simmer: Bring the mixture to a simmer over medium heat. Reduce the heat and let it simmer for 20-30 minutes, stirring occasionally, until the sauce thickens.
3. Cool and Reserve: Remove the sauce from the heat and let it cool. Reserve some sauce for serving.

Prepare the Chicken:

1. Season the Chicken: Pat the chicken pieces dry with paper towels. Season generously with salt and pepper.
2. Preheat the Grill: Preheat your grill to medium-high heat and lightly oil the grates.
3. Grill the Chicken: Brush the chicken with olive oil. Grill the chicken pieces, skin-side down first, over indirect heat for about 25-30 minutes, turning occasionally.
4. Add BBQ Sauce: Once the chicken is almost cooked through (internal temperature should be about 165°F for breasts and 175°F for thighs and drumsticks), start basting with the BBQ sauce. Continue to grill, turning frequently and basting with sauce, until the chicken is glazed and beautifully charred.
5. Rest the Chicken: Remove the chicken from the grill and let it rest for a few minutes.

Serve:

1. Serve Warm: Serve the BBQ chicken warm with the reserved BBQ sauce on the side.
2. Suggested Sides: Classic sides like coleslaw, corn on the cob, or baked beans complement BBQ chicken perfectly.

This BBQ chicken, slathered in a rich, flavorful homemade sauce, is a perfect main dish for any backyard barbecue or family gathering. The key to great BBQ chicken is to cook it slowly over indirect heat and then finish it over direct heat with plenty of sauce for that perfect caramelization. Enjoy your homemade BBQ feast!

# Grilled Steak Perfection: A Step-by-Step Guide to Grilling Various Cuts of Steak

Grilling the perfect steak is an art form. The type of cut, the seasoning, and the grilling technique all play crucial roles in the outcome. Here's a comprehensive guide to help you achieve steak perfection on the grill.

### Selecting Your Steak

1. Choose the Right Cut: Popular cuts for grilling include ribeye, sirloin, T-bone, porterhouse, and filet mignon. Ribeye is rich in flavor due to its marbling, while sirloin offers a leaner option. T-bone and porterhouse provide two different textures and flavors in one cut, and filet mignon is known for its tenderness.

### Preparing Your Steak

1. Bring to Room Temperature: Remove the steaks from the refrigerator about 30-40 minutes before grilling to allow them to come to room temperature. This helps in cooking the steak evenly.

2. Season Generously: Season the steaks with coarse salt and freshly ground black pepper. For added flavor, you can also use garlic powder, onion powder, or your favorite steak seasoning.

3. Oil Lightly: Brush each steak lightly with oil. This helps in creating a good sear and prevents sticking to the grill.

### Grilling Your Steak

1. Preheat Your Grill: Preheat your grill to high heat. You want to get a good sear on the steaks, which seals in the juices.

2. Sear the Steak: Place the steaks on the grill and sear them for about 2-4 minutes on each side, depending on the thickness of the steak and desired level of doneness.

3. Use a Thermometer: To ensure perfect doneness, use a meat thermometer. Here's a quick guide:

- Rare: 120-125°F (49-52°C)
- Medium-rare: 130-135°F (54-57°C)
- Medium: 140-145°F (60-63°C)
- Medium-well: 150-155°F (65-68°C)
- Well-done: 160-165°F (71-74°C)

4. Let it Rest: Once your steaks reach the desired internal temperature, remove them from the grill and let them rest on a plate for about 5 minutes. Resting allows the juices to redistribute throughout the steak.

### Serving Your Steak

- Serve the steak with your choice of sides like grilled vegetables, a fresh salad, or a baked potato.

- For an extra touch of flavor, consider topping your steak with a pat of butter or a drizzle of olive oil just before serving.

Remember, each cut of steak might require slight adjustments in cooking time due to thickness and marbling. With practice, you'll get a feel for grilling each type of steak to perfection. Enjoy the process and the delicious results!

158

# Pork Ribs with a Twist: Grilling with a Unique Spice Rub or Marinade

Pork ribs are a barbecue favorite, known for their rich flavor and tender meat. Adding a unique twist with a custom spice rub or marinade can elevate this classic dish to new heights. Here's a recipe that includes both a distinctive spice rub and a flavorful marinade to give your pork ribs an unforgettable flavor.

Ingredients:

For the Ribs:

- 2 racks of pork ribs (about 3-4 pounds each)

For the Spice Rub:

- 2 tablespoons brown sugar
- 1 tablespoon smoked paprika
- 1 tablespoon ground coffee (fine grind)
- 1 teaspoon garlic powder
- 1 teaspoon onion powder
- 1 teaspoon ground cumin
- 1 teaspoon chili powder
- 1 teaspoon coarse salt
- 1/2 teaspoon ground black pepper

For the Marinade:

- 1/2 cup apple cider vinegar
- 1/2 cup soy sauce
- 1/4 cup olive oil
- 1/4 cup honey
- 2 cloves garlic, minced
- 1 teaspoon ginger, grated
- Juice of 1 lime

Instructions:

Prepare the Ribs:

1. Remove the Membrane: Start by removing the membrane from the back of the ribs. Slide a knife under the membrane and lift to loosen. Grab it with a paper towel and pull it off.

Make the Spice Rub:

1. 1. Combine Ingredients: In a bowl, mix together all the ingredients for the spice rub.
2. 2. Apply the Rub: Generously apply the rub to both sides of the ribs, massaging it into the meat. Let the ribs sit with the rub for at least 30 minutes, or ideally, refrigerate them overnight for deeper flavor.

Make the Marinade:

1. 1. Combine Marinade Ingredients: In a bowl, whisk together all the marinade ingredients.
2. 2. Marinate the Ribs: Place the ribs in a large resealable bag. Pour in the marinade, ensuring the ribs are well coated. Marinate in the refrigerator for at least 2 hours, or overnight for best results.

Grill the Ribs:

1. Preheat the Grill: Preheat your grill to medium-low heat (about 275°F) for indirect grilling.
2. Grill Ribs: Remove the ribs from the marinade and discard the excess marinade. Place the ribs on the grill, away from the direct heat. Cover and grill for about 2-2.5 hours, or until the ribs are tender and the meat starts to pull away from the bone.
3. Optional Glaze: During the last 30 minutes of grilling, you can brush the ribs with your favorite BBQ sauce for a sticky glaze.

Grill the Ribs:

1. Rest and Cut: Let the ribs rest for 10 minutes after removing them from the grill. Then cut between the bones to separate them.
2. Enjoy: Serve the ribs hot, with extra BBQ sauce on the side if desired.

The combination of the rich spice rub and the tangy marinade will make these pork ribs a standout dish at any barbecue. The coffee in the rub adds a unique depth of flavor, while the marinade ensures the meat stays moist and tender. Enjoy this delicious twist on a classic!

# Burgers and Hot Dogs: Classic and Gourmet Recipes

Burgers and hot dogs are quintessential grill favorites, loved for their simplicity and versatility. Whether you prefer them classic or gourmet, these recipes will help you elevate these traditional barbecue staples.

*Classic Burger Recipe*

Ingredients:

- 2 pounds ground beef (80/20 blend for optimal juiciness)
- Salt and freshly ground black pepper, to taste
- 4-6 hamburger buns
- Optional toppings: lettuce, tomato slices, onions, pickles, cheese slices

Instructions:

1. Form Patties: Divide the ground beef into 4-6 portions, depending on desired size. Gently form each into a patty without overworking the meat.
2. Season: Season both sides of each patty with salt and pepper.
3. Grill: Preheat the grill to high. Grill the patties for about 3-4 minutes per side for medium-rare, or longer for well-done.
4. Add Cheese: If making cheeseburgers, add cheese slices during the last minute of grilling.
5. Assemble Burgers: Place each patty on a bun and add your favorite toppings.

*Gourmet Burger Recipe: Blue Cheese and Caramelized Onion Burger*

Ingredients:

- 2 pounds ground beef (80/20 blend)
- Salt and freshly ground black pepper, to taste
- 1 tablespoon olive oil
- 2 large onions, thinly sliced
- 1/2 cup blue cheese crumbles
- Arugula or mixed greens
- 4-6 gourmet hamburger buns

Instructions:

1. Caramelize Onions: In a skillet, heat the olive oil over medium heat. Add the sliced onions and cook slowly, stirring occasionally, until golden and caramelized, about 15-20 minutes. Set aside.
2. Form and Season Patties: Form the beef into 4-6 patties. Season with salt and pepper.
3. Grill Patties: Grill the patties as above.

4. Assemble Burgers: Place a patty on each bun. Top with a generous spoonful of caramelized onions, blue cheese crumbles, and arugula.

*Classic Hot Dog Recipe*

Ingredients:

- 8 high-quality hot dogs
- 8 hot dog buns
- Optional toppings: ketchup, mustard, relish, sauerkraut, onions

Instructions:

1. Prep Hot Dogs: Make small diagonal cuts on the hot dogs. This helps them cook evenly and prevent curling.
2. Grill: Grill the hot dogs over medium heat, turning occasionally, until heated through and slightly charred, about 5 minutes.
3. Serve: Place each hot dog in a bun and add your favorite toppings.

*Gourmet Hot Dog Recipe: Chicago-Style Hot Dog*

Ingredients:

- 8 beef hot dogs
- 8 poppy seed hot dog buns
- Yellow mustard
- Bright green relish
- Fresh chopped onions
- Tomato wedges
- Pickle spears
- Sport peppers
- Celery salt

Instructions:

1. Grill Hot Dogs: Grill the hot dogs as above.
2. Assemble: Place a hot dog in each bun. Add mustard, relish, onions, tomato wedges, and a pickle spear on each side of the hot dog. Add a couple of sport peppers and a dash of celery salt.

From the timeless appeal of classic burgers and dogs to the enhanced flavors of their gourmet counterparts, these recipes cater to a range of tastes and occasions. Experiment with toppings and condiments to create your own signature versions!

# Seafood Recipes

### Grilled Salmon

Grilled salmon is a delicious and healthy meal option that's simple to prepare. Here's a straightforward recipe to make flavorful grilled salmon:

Ingredients:

- Salmon fillets (4 pieces, about 6 ounces each)
- Olive oil (2 tablespoons)
- Lemon juice (from 1 lemon)
- Garlic (2 cloves, minced)
- Salt (to taste)
- Black pepper (to taste)
- Dill or parsley (for garnish, optional)

Instructions:

1. Preparation: Start by preheating your grill to medium-high heat. While the grill is heating up, rinse the salmon fillets and pat them dry with paper towels.

2. Marinade: In a small bowl, mix together olive oil, lemon juice, minced garlic, salt, and black pepper. This will be your marinade for the salmon. Brush the salmon fillets with this mixture, ensuring that they are evenly coated.

3. Grilling the Salmon: Place the salmon fillets on the grill, skin side down. Grill for about 4-6 minutes per side, depending on the thickness of the fillets. The salmon is done when it flakes easily with a fork. Be careful not to overcook the salmon, as it can dry out quickly.

4. Serving: Once the salmon is cooked, remove it from the grill and place it on a serving plate. You can garnish it with fresh dill or parsley and serve with a wedge of lemon.

5. Sides: Grilled salmon pairs well with a variety of sides, such as grilled vegetables, a fresh salad, or roasted potatoes.

Enjoy your simple yet flavorful grilled salmon!

### Grilled Shrimp Skewers

Barbecued Shrimp Skewers are a great choice for a spicy and savory appetizer, perfect for any gathering or a family dinner. Here's a simple recipe to make these delicious skewers:

Ingredients:

- Large shrimp (peeled and deveined, 1 pound)
- Olive oil (2 tablespoons)
- Garlic (3 cloves, minced)
- Lemon juice (from 1 lemon)
- Paprika (1 teaspoon)
- Cayenne pepper (1/2 teaspoon, adjust for spiciness)
- Salt (to taste)
- Black pepper (to taste)
- Wooden or metal skewers

Instructions:

1. Preparation: Start by soaking the wooden skewers in water for at least 30 minutes if you're using them. This prevents them from burning on the grill. Preheat your grill to medium-high heat.

2. Marinade: In a large bowl, combine olive oil, minced garlic, lemon juice, paprika, cayenne pepper, salt, and black pepper. Add the shrimp to the bowl and toss them until they are well coated with the marinade. Let the shrimp marinate for about 15-20 minutes.

3. Skewering the Shrimp: Thread the marinated shrimp onto the skewers. If you're using wooden skewers, make sure the shrimp are not packed too tightly to allow even cooking.

4. Grilling the Skewers: Place the shrimp skewers on the grill. Cook for about 2-3 minutes per side, or until the shrimp turn pink and opaque. Be careful not to overcook the shrimp, as they can become tough.

5. Serving: Once cooked, remove the shrimp skewers from the grill and place them on a serving platter. They can be served with lemon wedges and a dipping sauce of your choice, like a spicy mayo or a garlic aioli.

Enjoy your spicy barbecued shrimp skewers, perfect as a flavorful appetizer!

*Grilled Tuna Steaks with Avocado Salsa*

A delectable and healthy dish that's perfect for a sophisticated yet easy meal. This recipe can also be adapted for other firm types of fish, such as swordfish, mahi-mahi, or halibut, offering versatility depending on what's available or preferred.

Ingredients:

For the Grilled Tuna Steaks:

- Tuna steaks (4 pieces, about 6 ounces each)
- Olive oil (2 tablespoons)
- Lemon juice (from 1 lemon)
- Garlic (2 cloves, minced)
- Salt and pepper (to taste)

For the Avocado Salsa:

- Ripe avocados (2, diced)
- Red onion (1/4 cup, finely chopped)
- Cherry tomatoes (1/2 cup, halved)
- Fresh cilantro (1/4 cup, chopped)
- Lime juice (from 1 lime)
- Jalapeño (1, seeded and minced; optional for heat)
- Salt and pepper (to taste)

Instructions:

1. Preparing the Tuna Steaks:

- Preheat the grill to high heat.
- In a small bowl, whisk together olive oil, lemon juice, minced garlic, salt, and pepper. Brush this mixture on both sides of the tuna steaks.

2. Grilling the Tuna:

- Place the tuna steaks on the hot grill. Grill for about 2-3 minutes per side for medium-rare (adjust the time based on desired doneness and thickness of the steaks).
- Remove the tuna from the grill and let it rest for a few minutes.

3. Making the Avocado Salsa:

- In a medium bowl, combine diced avocados, red onion, cherry tomatoes, cilantro, lime juice, jalapeño (if using), and a pinch of salt and pepper.
- Gently toss to mix the ingredients without mashing the avocado.

4. Serving:

- Serve the grilled tuna steaks topped with a generous scoop of the avocado salsa.
- This dish pairs well with a side of grilled vegetables or a light salad.

Note:

- If using an alternative firm fish like swordfish, mahi-mahi, or halibut, follow the same grilling instructions, adjusting the cooking time as needed based on the thickness and type of fish.

Enjoy your Grilled Tuna Steaks with Avocado Salsa, a fresh and flavorful dish that's sure to impress!

# Patriotic Desserts and Snacks

In this delightful chapter, we explore the colorful and creative world of Patriotic Desserts, a collection of recipes that are not only a treat to the taste buds but also a feast for the eyes. These desserts are perfect for celebrating the spirit of national pride and unity, making them ideal for a variety of patriotic holidays including Memorial Day, Veterans Day, and the 4th of July.

Each recipe in this chapter is crafted with the theme of patriotism in mind, featuring the vibrant red, white, and blue colors of the flag. From the visually stunning American Flag Cake to the refreshing Firecracker Popsicles, these desserts are designed to add a festive touch to your holiday gatherings. Whether you're hosting a large party or enjoying a quiet celebration at home, these treats are sure to bring a sense of joy and festivity to the occasion.

So, preheat your ovens and get your baking tools ready! Whether you're a seasoned baker or trying your hand at festive treats for the first time, this chapter offers a range of recipes that are both delicious and symbolically rich, perfect for any patriotic celebration. Let's embark on a culinary journey that pays homage to our nation's colors and the spirit of our holidays.

# Red, White, and Blue Fruit Salad

A delightful and easy-to-make dessert that's perfect for any patriotic occasion or simply as a refreshing treat. The combination of strawberries, blueberries, and bananas (or marshmallows) creates a vibrant and tasty mix. Here's how to prepare it:

Ingredients:

- Strawberries (2 cups, hulled and halved)
- Blueberries (1 cup)
- Bananas (2, sliced) or Mini Marshmallows (1 cup)
- Lemon juice (from 1 lemon, if using bananas)
- Fresh mint leaves (for garnish, optional)
- Honey or maple syrup (optional, for sweetness)

Instructions:

1.  Prepare the Fruit:

    - Wash the strawberries and blueberries thoroughly. Hull and halve the strawberries. If you're using bananas, peel and slice them. If you opt for marshmallows, ensure they're ready to use.

2.  Preventing Banana Browning (if using bananas):

    - To keep the bananas from browning, toss the sliced bananas in lemon juice. This adds a nice citrusy flavor and maintains the fresh look of the bananas.

3.  Assemble the Salad:

    - In a large mixing bowl, combine the strawberries, blueberries, and either the banana slices or marshmallows. Gently toss the ingredients to mix them evenly.

4.  Add Sweetness (optional):

    - If you prefer your fruit salad a bit sweeter, drizzle a small amount of honey or maple syrup over the salad and toss it again gently.

5.  Garnish and Serve:

    - Garnish with fresh mint leaves for an extra touch of freshness and flavor.
    - Serve the fruit salad immediately if using bananas to ensure they don't brown. If you're using marshmallows, the salad can be refrigerated for a short time before serving.

Enjoy your Red, White, and Blue Fruit Salad, a simple, healthy, and visually appealing dessert that's sure to be a hit at any gathering!

# The American Flag Cake

A festive and eye-catching dessert, ideal for patriotic celebrations or as a themed treat. It involves decorating a rectangular sheet cake with white frosting and arranging blueberries and raspberries or sliced strawberries to mimic the American flag. Here's a step-by-step recipe to create this beautiful cake:

Ingredients:

For the Cake:

- All-purpose flour (2 cups)
- Granulated sugar (1 ½ cups)
- Baking powder (1 tablespoon)
- Salt (½ teaspoon)
- Unsalted butter (½ cup, softened)
- Eggs (4, large)
- Milk (1 cup)
- Vanilla extract (2 teaspoons)

For the Frosting and Decoration:

- Cream cheese (8 ounces, softened)
- Unsalted butter (½ cup, softened)
- Powdered sugar (4 cups)
- Vanilla extract (1 teaspoon)
- Blueberries (1 cup)
- Raspberries or sliced strawberries (2 cups)

Instructions:

1. Bake the Cake:

- Preheat your oven to 350°F (175°C). Grease and flour a 9x13 inch rectangular baking pan.
- In a large bowl, mix flour, sugar, baking powder, and salt. Add softened butter, eggs, milk, and vanilla extract. Beat until the mixture is smooth and well combined.
- Pour the batter into the prepared baking pan. Bake for 30-35 minutes, or until a toothpick inserted into the center of the cake comes out clean.
- Allow the cake to cool completely before frosting.

2. Prepare the Frosting:

- In a large bowl, beat together the softened cream cheese and butter until smooth. Gradually add powdered sugar and vanilla extract, continuing to beat until the frosting is smooth and creamy.

3. Frost the Cake:

- Spread the white frosting evenly over the cooled cake, creating a smooth surface.

4. Decorate the Cake:

- For the stars: Arrange the blueberries in the top left corner of the cake to create a blue square. The blueberries represent the stars in the flag.
- For the stripes: Place rows of raspberries or sliced strawberries across the cake to represent the red stripes. Leave space between the rows to let the white frosting show through, mimicking the white stripes of the flag.

5. Serving:

- Refrigerate the cake until you're ready to serve. This dessert is best enjoyed the same day it's made to maintain the freshness of the fruit and the appearance of the flag.

Enjoy your American Flag Cake, a delicious and visually stunning centerpiece for your patriotic celebration!

# The Patriotic Trifle

A visually striking and delicious dessert that beautifully layers red, white, and blue components, making it perfect for patriotic celebrations or themed parties. Using a clear glass trifle bowl allows the colorful layers to be displayed, enhancing its appeal. Here's how to create this delightful dessert:

Ingredients:

Red Layer:

- Strawberries or Raspberries (4 cups, fresh and sliced for strawberries)

White Layer:

- Whipped Cream (4 cups) or Vanilla Pudding (if using pudding, prepare according to package instructions, enough for 4 cups)

Blue Layer:

- Blueberries (4 cups, fresh)

Additional:

- Sponge Cake or Angel Food Cake (1, cut into cubes)
- Optional: A splash of liqueur or fruit juice for moistening the cake layers

Instructions:

1. Prepare the Ingredients:

- If using strawberries, wash and slice them. Wash the blueberries and set aside. Prepare the whipped cream or vanilla pudding. Cut the sponge cake or angel food cake into bite-sized cubes.

2. Layer the Trifle:

- First Layer (Red): Start by placing a layer of red fruit (strawberries or raspberries) at the bottom of the trifle bowl.
- Second Layer (White): Add a layer of white component over the red fruit. This can be either whipped cream or vanilla pudding, depending on your preference.
- Third Layer (Cake): Place a layer of cake cubes over the white layer. Optionally, you can moisten the cake with a little liqueur or fruit juice for added flavor.
- Fourth Layer (Blue): Add a layer of blueberries over the cake.

3. Repeat the Layers:

- Continue layering in the same order (red, white, cake, blue) until the trifle bowl is filled. Aim to end with a layer of whipped cream or pudding on top for a neat presentation.

4. Garnish:

- For a patriotic touch, you can create a flag design on top using blueberries and raspberries/strawberries or simply garnish with a mix of the fruits.

5. Chill and Serve:

- Refrigerate the trifle for at least an hour before serving. This allows the layers to set and the flavors to meld together.

Enjoy your Patriotic Trifle, a delightful and eye-catching dessert that's sure to be a hit at any festive gathering!

# *Star-Spangled Berry Tart*

Celebrate in style with this Star-Spangled Berry Tart. A simple yet elegant dessert, featuring a buttery crust, creamy cream cheese frosting, and fresh berries arranged in a beautiful star pattern. Perfect for patriotic celebrations!

## Ingredients

### For the Crust:

- 1 1/4 cups all-purpose flour
- 1/2 cup unsalted butter, chilled and diced
- 1/4 cup granulated sugar
- 1/4 teaspoon salt
- 1 egg yolk
- 2-3 tablespoons cold water

### For the Cream Cheese Frosting:

- 8 ounces cream cheese, softened
- 1/2 cup powdered sugar
- 1 teaspoon vanilla extract
- 1/2 cup heavy cream

### For the Topping:

- 1 cup fresh strawberries, sliced
- 1 cup fresh blueberries

## Instructions

### Making the Crust:

1. Prep the Dough: In a food processor, combine flour, sugar, and salt. Add butter and pulse until mixture resembles coarse crumbs. Add egg yolk and 1 tablespoon water, pulsing until dough clumps together. Add more water if necessary.

2. Chill the Dough: Turn out the dough onto a work surface, form into a disc, wrap in plastic, and chill for at least 30 minutes.

3. Preheat Oven: Preheat your oven to 375°F (190°C).

4. Roll and Fit the Dough: Roll out the dough on a lightly floured surface and fit it into a 9-inch tart pan with a removable bottom. Trim the edges and prick the bottom with a fork.

5. Bake the Crust: Bake for 12-15 minutes or until golden. Let it cool completely.

### Preparing the Cream Cheese Frosting:

1. Cream the Cheese: Beat the cream cheese, powdered sugar, and vanilla extract together until smooth.

2. Whip the Cream: In another bowl, whip the heavy cream until stiff peaks form.

3. Combine: Gently fold the whipped cream into the cream cheese mixture until well combined.

### Assembling the Tart:

1. Fill the Tart: Spread the cream cheese frosting evenly over the cooled tart crust.

2. Arrange the Berries: Place the strawberries and blueberries on the frosting, arranging them in a star pattern or as desired.

### Serving:

- Chill the tart for at least 1 hour before serving. This allows the frosting to set and makes it easier to slice.

- Serve as a festive end to your patriotic celebration, and enjoy the blend of creamy, fruity, and buttery flavors!

This Star-Spangled Berry Tart is not only a visually stunning addition to your table but also a deliciously balanced dessert that's sure to impress.

# Firecracker Popsicles

A fun and refreshing treat, perfect for summer celebrations or patriotic events. These layered popsicles feature vibrant red, white, and blue colors, achieved using strawberry, coconut milk, and blueberry purees. Here's how to make them:

Ingredients:

Red Layer:

- Strawberries (2 cups, fresh or frozen)
- Sugar or honey (to taste, optional)

White Layer:

- Coconut milk (1 can, full-fat for creamier texture)
- Sugar or honey (to taste, optional)

Blue Layer:

- Blueberries (2 cups, fresh or frozen)
- Sugar or honey (to taste, optional)

Additional:

- Popsicle molds and sticks

Instructions:

1. Prepare the Fruit Purees:

- Red Layer: Puree the strawberries in a blender. Add sugar or honey if you desire more sweetness. Strain the mixture to remove seeds for a smoother texture.

- Blue Layer: Similarly, puree the blueberries and add sweetener if needed. Strain if desired.

2. Assemble the Popsicles:

- First Layer (Red): Pour the strawberry puree into the popsicle molds, filling each one about a third of the way. Freeze for about 30-45 minutes or until set but not completely frozen.

- Second Layer (White): Once the red layer is set, pour the coconut milk over it to create the second layer. Insert popsicle sticks at this stage. Freeze again for another 30-45 minutes.

- Third Layer (Blue): After the white layer is set, complete the popsicles with the blueberry puree as the final layer.

3. Freeze Completely:

- • Freeze the popsicles until they are completely solid, preferably overnight, to ensure they are fully set.

4. Serve:

- To remove the popsicles from the molds, run warm water over the outside of the molds for a few seconds, then gently pull the sticks.

Enjoy your Firecracker Popsicles, a delightful and patriotic treat that's as visually appealing as it is delicious!

# Patriotic Rice Krispie Treats

A colorful twist to the traditional recipe, making them perfect for festive occasions. By incorporating red and blue food coloring into separate batches and creatively shaping or layering them, you can create a fun and patriotic dessert. Here's how to do it:

Ingredients:

- Butter (6 tablespoons, divided into 2 tablespoons per batch)
- Mini marshmallows (6 cups, divided into 2 cups per batch)
- Rice Krispie cereal (9 cups, divided into 3 cups per batch)
- Red food coloring
- Blue food coloring
- Non-stick cooking spray or additional butter for greasing
- Optional: White icing or sprinkles for decoration

Instructions:

1. Prepare Batches Separately:

- You will make three batches of Rice Krispie treats – one red, one blue, and one plain. Start with either the red or blue batch.

2. Making the Colored Batches:

- In a large pot, melt 2 tablespoons of butter over low heat. Add 2 cups of marshmallows and stir until completely melted.
- Add a few drops of red or blue food coloring to the melted marshmallows and mix until you achieve the desired color.
- Remove the pot from heat and stir in 3 cups of Rice Krispie cereal until they are well coated with the colored marshmallow mixture.
- Press the mixture into a greased or buttered pan (you can use a 9x13 inch pan or a similar size). Use a spatula or wax paper to press it down evenly without sticking. Set aside to cool.

3. Repeat for Each Color:

- Clean the pot, and repeat the process for the other colored batch and the plain batch.

4. Assemble the Treats:

- Layering Option: If you are layering, gently press each colored layer on top of the other in the pan (e.g., blue, then plain, then red).
- Star Shapes Option: Alternatively, if you want to cut them into star shapes, spread each batch in separate pans.

5. Cutting and Decorating:

- Once all the layers are set (if layered) or each batch is cooled (if separate), cut the treats into squares or use a star-shaped cookie cutter for a festive look.
- Optionally, you can decorate with white icing or sprinkles for an added patriotic flair.

6. Serving:

- Serve the Patriotic Rice Krispie Treats as a colorful addition to your celebration. They're best enjoyed the same day but can be stored in an airtight container for a short period.

Enjoy creating and indulging in these fun and festive Patriotic Rice Krispie Treats!

# Flag Fruit Pizza

A delightful and visually appealing dessert that combines the sweetness of a large cookie crust with the freshness of fruit, arranged to resemble the American flag. It's perfect for patriotic celebrations or as a creative dessert option for any gathering. Here's how to make it:

Ingredients:

For the Cookie Crust:

- All-purpose flour (2 cups)
- Baking powder (1 teaspoon)
- Salt (1/2 teaspoon)
- Unsalted butter (3/4 cup, softened)
- Granulated sugar (1 cup)
- Egg (1 large)
- Vanilla extract (1 teaspoon)

For the Cream Cheese Frosting:

- Cream cheese (8 ounces, softened)
- Unsalted butter (1/4 cup, softened)
- Powdered sugar (2 cups)
- Vanilla extract (1 teaspoon)

For the Fruit Decoration:

- Strawberries or raspberries (for the red stripes)
- Blueberries (for the star section)
- Bananas or white chocolate chips (optional, for the white stripes)

Instructions:

1. Bake the Cookie Crust:

- Preheat your oven to 350°F (175°C). Line a pizza pan or a large baking sheet with parchment paper.
- In a bowl, whisk together flour, baking powder, and salt.
- In another bowl, cream together softened butter and sugar until light and fluffy. Beat in the egg and vanilla extract.
- Gradually mix in the dry ingredients until well combined.
- Press the cookie dough evenly onto the prepared pan, forming a large circle.
- Bake for 10-15 minutes or until lightly golden. Allow it to cool completely.

2. Prepare the Cream Cheese Frosting:

- Beat together the softened cream cheese and butter until smooth. Add powdered sugar and vanilla extract, and continue beating until the frosting is creamy and spreadable.

3. Assemble the Fruit Pizza:

- Spread the cream cheese frosting evenly over the cooled cookie crust.
- Arrange the fruit on the frosting to mimic the American flag: use blueberries to create a square in the top left corner for the stars, and create alternating stripes with strawberries or raspberries and bananas or white chocolate chips.

4. Chill and Serve:

- Refrigerate the fruit pizza for about an hour to set the frosting and make it easier to slice.
- Slice the pizza into squares or wedges and serve.

Enjoy your Flag Fruit Pizza, a sweet and patriotic treat that's as fun to make as it is to eat!

# Berry and Yogurt Parfaits

A quick, healthy, and delicious snack that combines the natural sweetness of berries with creamy vanilla yogurt. They are visually appealing, especially when layered in clear cups, making them perfect for a nutritious breakfast, snack, or light dessert. Here's a simple recipe to make them:

Ingredients:

- Blueberries (1 cup)
- Vanilla yogurt (2 cups; Greek yogurt for a thicker texture)
- Strawberries (1 cup, hulled and sliced)
- Optional: Granola or nuts for added crunch
- Optional: Honey or maple syrup for extra sweetness

Instructions:

1. Prepare the Ingredients:

- Wash the blueberries and strawberries. Hull and slice the strawberries. If using granola or nuts, have them ready.

2. Assemble the Parfaits:

- Begin by placing a layer of blueberries at the bottom of each clear cup.
- Add a layer of vanilla yogurt over the blueberries. You can sweeten the yogurt with honey or maple syrup if desired.
- Next, add a layer of sliced strawberries on top of the yogurt.

3. Repeat the Layers:

- Continue layering the blueberries, yogurt, and strawberries until the cups are filled to your desired level. The quantity of ingredients can be adjusted based on the size of your cups and your preference for more fruit or yogurt.

4. Add the Final Touches (optional):

- For a bit of crunch and additional flavor, top each parfait with a sprinkle of granola or nuts.

5. Serving:

- The Berry and Yogurt Parfaits can be served immediately or refrigerated for a short time before serving. If you plan to refrigerate them for longer, add granola just before serving to maintain its crunch.

Enjoy your Berry and Yogurt Parfaits, a delightful and healthy treat that's as aesthetically pleasing as it is tasty!

# Patriotic Cupcakes

A delightful and festive treat, perfect for any patriotic celebration like Memorial Day, Veterans Day, or the 4th of July. These vanilla cupcakes are adorned with red, white, and blue frosting, and can be topped with mini American flags or star sprinkles for an added festive touch. Here's how to make them:

Ingredients:

For the Cupcakes:

- All-purpose flour (2 cups)
- Granulated sugar (1 ½ cups)
- Baking powder (2 teaspoons)
- Salt (½ teaspoon)
- Unsalted butter (½ cup, softened)
- Eggs (3, large)
- Milk (1 cup)
- Vanilla extract (2 teaspoons)

For the Frosting:

- Unsalted butter (1 cup, softened)
- Powdered sugar (4 cups)
- Vanilla extract (1 teaspoon)
- Milk or cream (2-3 tablespoons)
- Red and blue food coloring

For Decoration:

- Mini American flags or star sprinkles

Instructions:

1. Bake the Cupcakes:

- Preheat your oven to 350°F (175°C) and line a muffin tin with cupcake liners.
- In a bowl, mix together flour, sugar, baking powder, and salt.
- In another bowl, beat the softened butter, eggs, milk, and vanilla extract until smooth.
- Gradually mix the dry ingredients into the wet ingredients until well combined.
- Fill the cupcake liners about two-thirds full with the batter.
- Bake for 18-20 minutes, or until a toothpick inserted into the center of a cupcake comes out clean.
- Let the cupcakes cool completely before frosting.

2. Prepare the Frosting:

- Beat the softened butter until creamy. Gradually add powdered sugar, vanilla extract, and milk or cream, beating until smooth and fluffy.
- Divide the frosting into three portions. Leave one portion white, and use food coloring to dye one portion red and the other blue.

3. Frost the Cupcakes:

- Use a piping bag with a star tip to create a patriotic design. You can pipe each color separately or combine them in one bag for a swirled effect.
- Alternatively, you can use a knife or spatula to apply the frosting in layers or dollops of red, white, and blue.

4. Decorate:

- Top each cupcake with a mini American flag or star sprinkles for a festive finish.

5. Serve and Enjoy:

- The Patriotic Cupcakes are now ready to be served and enjoyed as a sweet part of your patriotic celebration!

These cupcakes are not only delicious but also a beautiful way to show your patriotic spirit. Enjoy baking and sharing these treats!

# Patriotic Cocktails

# Watermelon Margaritas

A refreshing and delightful twist on the classic margarita, perfect for summer gatherings or as a vibrant cocktail to enjoy any time. The combination of fresh watermelon, tequila, lime juice, and triple sec creates a sweet and tangy flavor that's both invigorating and delicious. Here's how to make it:

Ingredients:

- Fresh watermelon cubes (4 cups, seeds removed)
- Tequila (1 cup)
- Lime juice (1/2 cup, freshly squeezed)
- Triple sec (1/4 cup)
- Ice cubes
- Salt (for rimming the glasses)
- Lime wedges (for garnish)

Instructions:

1. Prepare the Watermelon:
   - Remove any seeds from the watermelon cubes. You can use a seedless watermelon for convenience.

2. Blend the Ingredients:
   - In a blender, combine the watermelon cubes, tequila, lime juice, and triple sec. Blend until smooth.

3. Chill the Mixture (optional):
   - For a colder drink, you can refrigerate the watermelon-tequila mixture for about 1 hour before serving.

4. Prepare the Glasses:
   - Run a lime wedge around the rim of each glass. Dip the rims into salt to coat them lightly.
   - Fill the glasses with ice cubes.

5. Serve:
   - Pour the blended watermelon margarita over the ice in the prepared glasses.
   - Garnish each glass with a lime wedge.

6. Enjoy:
   - Your Watermelon Margaritas are ready to be enjoyed! They're perfect for sipping on a warm day or serving at a summer party.

This recipe can easily be adjusted to make a larger batch for a group, or you can add more or less tequila and triple sec to suit your taste. Enjoy this refreshing twist on a classic cocktail!

# Blueberry Mojito

A delightful and refreshing cocktail that adds a fruity twist to the classic Mojito. The combination of fresh blueberries, mint, and lime creates a vibrant and flavorful drink, perfect for summer evenings or as a special treat. Here's how to make a Blueberry Mojito:

Ingredients:

- Fresh blueberries (1/2 cup)
- Fresh mint leaves (10-12 leaves, plus extra for garnish)
- Sugar (2 teaspoons)
- White rum (2 ounces)
- Lime juice (1 ounce, freshly squeezed)
- Club soda
- Ice cubes
- Lime wedges (for garnish)

Instructions:

1. Muddle the Ingredients:

- In a sturdy glass, add the fresh blueberries, mint leaves, and sugar.
- Use a muddler or the back of a spoon to gently crush and muddle the blueberries and mint with the sugar. This releases the flavors and juices.

2. Add Rum and Lime Juice:

- Pour the white rum and freshly squeezed lime juice into the glass.

3. Add Ice:

- Fill the glass with ice cubes.

4. Top with Club Soda:

- Gently pour club soda into the glass to top it off.

5. Mix the Drink:

- Use a spoon or a stirrer to lightly mix the ingredients together, bringing some of the muddled blueberries and mint to the top.

6. Garnish and Serve:

- Garnish the drink with a few extra mint leaves and a lime wedge.
- Serve immediately.

7. Enjoy:

- Your Blueberry Mojito is ready to enjoy! The mix of sweet blueberries, refreshing mint, and tangy lime makes it an irresistible summer cocktail.

This recipe can be easily adjusted to make more servings for guests. For a non-alcoholic version, simply omit the rum and add more club soda. Enjoy your vibrant and refreshing Blueberry Mojito!

# Peach Sangria

A wonderfully refreshing and fruity beverage, perfect for warm weather gatherings or as a delightful drink to enjoy on any relaxing day. The combination of white wine, juicy peaches, a hint of brandy, and a medley of berries creates a beautifully balanced and tasty concoction. Here's how to make it:

Ingredients:

- White wine (1 bottle, such as Pinot Grigio or Sauvignon Blanc)
- Fresh peaches (2-3, sliced)
- Brandy (1/4 cup)
- Sugar (2-3 tablespoons, adjust to taste)
- Mixed berries (1 cup, such as strawberries, raspberries, blueberries)
- Sparkling water
- Ice cubes
- Optional: Fresh mint leaves or a cinnamon stick for added flavor

Instructions:

1. Prepare the Fruit:

- Wash and slice the peaches. If you're using strawberries, hull and halve them. Leave other berries whole.

2. Combine Ingredients:

- In a large pitcher, combine the sliced peaches, mixed berries, and sugar.
- Pour the brandy over the fruit and gently stir to help dissolve the sugar.
- Add the entire bottle of white wine to the pitcher.

3. Chill the Sangria:

- Cover the pitcher and refrigerate for at least 2-3 hours, ideally overnight. This allows the flavors to meld together and the fruit to infuse the wine.

4. Serve:

- Just before serving, add ice cubes to the pitcher to keep the sangria cold.
- Pour the sangria into glasses, making sure to get some of the fruit in each glass.
- Top each glass with a splash of sparkling water for a refreshing fizz.

5. Garnish (optional):

- Garnish each glass with a sprig of fresh mint or a cinnamon stick for an extra layer of flavor.

6. Enjoy:

- Your Peach Sangria is ready to be enjoyed! It's a perfect drink for sipping on a sunny day or serving at a social gathering.

This Peach Sangria recipe is versatile and can be modified to suit your taste. For a sweeter sangria, add more sugar, or for a stronger drink, increase the amount of brandy. Enjoy crafting and savoring this delightful and fruity beverage!

# The Strawberry Basil Lemonade Cocktail

A refreshing and aromatic drink, combining the sweetness of strawberries, the herbal notes of basil, and the tartness of lemonade, all enhanced by the smoothness of vodka. This cocktail is perfect for a summer day, a brunch, or any occasion where you want to serve a unique and flavorful beverage. Here's how to make it:

Ingredients:

- Fresh strawberries (6-8, hulled and halved)
- Fresh basil leaves (6-8 leaves, plus extra for garnish)
- Vodka (2 ounces)
- Lemonade (4 ounces, homemade or store-bought)
- Ice cubes
- Lemon slice (for garnish)

Instructions:

1. Muddle the Strawberries and Basil:

- In a cocktail shaker or a sturdy glass, add the halved strawberries and basil leaves.
- Use a muddler or the back of a spoon to gently crush the strawberries and basil, releasing their juices and flavors.

2. Add Vodka and Lemonade:

- Pour the vodka and lemonade into the shaker or glass with the muddled strawberry and basil mixture.

3. Shake or Stir the Cocktail:

- If using a shaker, add ice, close the shaker, and shake well until the mixture is chilled. If you're mixing in a glass, stir well to combine all the ingredients.

4. Prepare the Serving Glass:

- Fill a serving glass with ice cubes.

5. Serve:

- Strain the cocktail mixture into the prepared glass over the ice. If you prefer a more rustic look, you can pour the mixture without straining to include bits of strawberry and basil.

6. Garnish and Enjoy:

- Garnish the cocktail with a fresh basil leaf and a slice of lemon on the rim of the glass.
- Serve immediately and enjoy the delightful combination of flavors in your Strawberry Basil Lemonade Cocktail.

This cocktail is not only delicious but also visually appealing with its vibrant colors and fresh ingredients. It's sure to be a hit at any gathering or a relaxing treat for yourself!

# Cucumber Gin and Tonic

A crisp and refreshing twist on the classic gin and tonic, perfect for a hot summer day or a relaxing evening. The addition of thinly sliced cucumber and a splash of lime juice brings a fresh, clean taste to this timeless cocktail. Here's how to make it:

Ingredients:

- Gin (2 ounces)
- Tonic water
- Cucumber (1, thinly sliced)
- Lime juice (splash)
- Ice cubes
- Lime wedge or cucumber slice (for garnish)

Instructions:

1. Prepare the Cucumber:

- Wash the cucumber and thinly slice it. You'll need a few slices for each drink.

2. Mix the Drink:

- In a highball glass or a gin and tonic glass, add a few slices of cucumber.
- Fill the glass with ice cubes.
- Pour the gin over the ice.
- Add a splash of fresh lime juice.

3. Add Tonic Water:

- Gently pour tonic water into the glass to the top, or to your desired level depending on how strong you like your drink.

4. Garnish:

- Stir the drink gently to mix the flavors.
- Garnish with a lime wedge or an extra slice of cucumber on the rim of the glass.

5. Serve and Enjoy:

- Your Cucumber Gin and Tonic is ready to serve. Enjoy the subtle, refreshing flavors that make this cocktail a delightful variation of the classic.

This cocktail is not only easy to make but also offers a sophisticated flavor profile. The coolness of the cucumber complements the botanicals in the gin, while the lime adds just the right amount of tartness. It's a perfect choice for those who appreciate a less sweet cocktail.

# The Piña Colada

A classic tropical cocktail known for its rich, sweet, and refreshing flavors. This drink, which combines the tastes of coconut, pineapple, and rum, is a favorite for beach vacations or for bringing a bit of the tropics into your home. Here's a classic recipe for making a Piña Colada:

Ingredients:

- Light rum (2 ounces)
- Cream of coconut (1 and 1/2 ounces)
- Pineapple juice (2 ounces)
- Fresh pineapple chunks (optional, for a more textured drink)
- Ice cubes
- Pineapple slice and maraschino cherry (for garnish)

Instructions:

1. Prepare the Ingredients:

- If you're using fresh pineapple chunks, cut a few pieces into smaller chunks. Reserve a slice of pineapple and a maraschino cherry for garnish.

2. Blend the Drink:

- In a blender, combine the light rum, cream of coconut, pineapple juice, and fresh pineapple chunks (if using).
- Add a generous amount of ice. The amount of ice can vary depending on how thick you want your Piña Colada to be.

3. Blend Until Smooth:

- Blend the mixture until it's smooth. If the consistency is too thick, you can add a bit more pineapple juice or a splash of water to thin it out. If it's too thin, add more ice and blend again.

4. Serve:

- Pour the blended Piña Colada into a chilled glass.

5. Garnish and Enjoy:

- Garnish the rim of the glass with a slice of pineapple and place a maraschino cherry on top.
- Serve immediately and enjoy your tropical cocktail.

The Piña Colada is the epitome of a tropical drink, with its creamy texture and blend of sweet coconut and tangy pineapple flavors. Whether you're lounging by the pool, hosting a summer party, or just in the mood for something delightful and refreshing, this cocktail is sure to transport you to a tropical paradise.

# Red, White, and Blue Sangria

A festive and visually stunning drink, perfect for patriotic celebrations like the 4th of July, Memorial Day, or any summer gathering. This sangria combines the flavors of red and blue fruits with the crispness of white wine, creating a refreshing and delicious beverage. Here's how to make it:

Ingredients:

- White wine (1 bottle, such as Pinot Grigio, Sauvignon Blanc, or Chardonnay)
- Brandy (1/2 cup)
- Honey or sugar (2-3 tablespoons, adjust to taste)
- Fresh strawberries (1 cup, hulled and halved)
- Fresh blueberries (1 cup)
- Fresh raspberries (1/2 cup)
- Apple (1, sliced into star shapes for the "white" component)
- Lemon-lime soda or sparkling water (for topping up)
- Ice cubes

Instructions:

1. Prepare the Fruit:

- Wash all the berries thoroughly. Hull and halve the strawberries. Slice the apple into thin slices, and use a small cookie cutter or a knife to cut them into star shapes for a festive touch.

2. Combine Wine and Brandy:

- In a large pitcher, pour the bottle of white wine.
- Add the brandy to the wine. If you prefer a less strong sangria, you can reduce the amount of brandy.

3. Add Sweetener:

- Stir in honey or sugar to sweeten the mixture. Adjust the amount according to your taste preference.

4. Add the Fruit:

- Add the prepared strawberries, blueberries, raspberries, and apple stars to the pitcher.

5. Chill the Sangria:

- Cover the pitcher and place it in the refrigerator. Let it chill for at least 2-3 hours, preferably overnight. This allows the flavors to meld together and the fruit to infuse the wine.

6. Serve:

- Just before serving, add ice cubes to the pitcher to keep the sangria cold.
- Pour the sangria into glasses, making sure to get some of the fruit in each glass.
- Top each glass with a splash of lemon-lime soda or sparkling water for a refreshing fizz.

7. Garnish and Enjoy:

- Garnish each glass with a skewer of extra red, white, and blue fruits if desired.
- Serve and enjoy your festive Red, White, and Blue Sangria!

This colorful and patriotic sangria is not only delicious but also a beautiful centerpiece for your celebration. The combination of fruits and wine creates a refreshing and enjoyable drink that's perfect for sipping on a warm day.

# Patriotic Layered Cocktail

A visually striking drink, showcasing the colors of the American flag in layers of red, white, and blue. This cocktail is perfect for patriotic celebrations like the Fourth of July or Memorial Day. The key to achieving distinct layers in the cocktail is the careful pouring of liquids based on their sugar content and density. Here's how to make a Patriotic Layered Cocktail:

Ingredients:

- Grenadine syrup (for the red layer)
- Blue Curaçao (for the blue layer)
- Vodka or light rum (for the white layer)
- Lemon-lime soda or club soda (to lighten the alcohol for layering)
- Ice cubes

Instructions:

1. Prepare the Ingredients:

- Chill all the ingredients beforehand as using cold liquids helps maintain the layers.

2. Start with the Red Layer:

- Fill a tall glass about one-third of the way with ice cubes.
- Slowly pour grenadine over the ice until it fills about one-third of the glass. The grenadine should sink to the bottom as it's denser than theother ingredients.

3. Create the White Layer:

- In a separate container, mix vodka or light rum with an equal part of lemon-lime soda or club soda. This mixture should be less dense than the grenadine but denser than the blue Curaçao.
- Carefully layer this mixture over the grenadine by pouring it slowly over the back of a spoon or by using a pourer to gently disperse the liquid. Fill the glass another third of the way.

4. Add the Blue Layer:

- Finally, slowly pour the blue Curaçao over the back of a spoon or a pourer to create the top layer. Being less dense, it should float above the vodka or rum mixture.

5. Garnish and Serve:

- Garnish with a cherry or a small American flag on a skewer if desired.
- Serve the cocktail with a stirrer on the side. Guests can stir the cocktail to mix the layers before drinking.

Enjoy your Patriotic Layered Cocktail! This drink is not only a festive addition to any patriotic celebration but also a fun way to show off your bartending skills with its striking layered appearance.

# The Firecracker Martini

A vibrant and exciting cocktail, perfect for festive occasions, especially those that call for a bit of flair and sparkle. This drink combines the sharpness of vodka with the sweetness of fruit flavors, and a hint of spiciness to create a memorable experience. Here's how to make a Firecracker Martini:

Ingredients:

- Vodka (2 ounces)
- Blue Curaçao (1 ounce)
- Grenadine (1 ounce)
- Lemon juice (1/2 ounce, freshly squeezed)
- Simple syrup (1/2 ounce, optional for extra sweetness)
- Ice cubes
- Jalapeño (1 slice, seeds removed - optional for a spicy kick)
- Red, white, and blue sugar crystals (for rimming the glass)
- Lemon twist or a small firework/sparkler (for garnish)

Instructions:

1. Prepare the Glass:

- Rim a martini glass with lemon juice, then dip it in a plate of red, white, and blue sugar crystals to create a festive rim.

2. Combine Ingredients:

- In a cocktail shaker, combine the vodka, blue Curaçao, grenadine, lemon juice, and simple syrup. If you want a spicy twist, add a slice of jalapeño.

3. Shake the Cocktail:

- Fill the shaker with ice and shake well until the mixture is chilled.

4. Strain and Serve:

- Strain the cocktail into the prepared martini glass.

5. Garnish:

- Garnish with a lemon twist for a citrus aroma or add a small firework/sparkler on the rim for a true "firecracker" effect (ensure safety and remove before drinking).

6. Enjoy:

- Serve the Firecracker Martini immediately and enjoy the burst of flavors with a festive presentation.

Remember, the key to a great Firecracker Martini is balancing the sweet and tart flavors with a hint of heat if you choose to add jalapeño. This cocktail is sure to be a showstopper at any party or special occasion!

# The Stars and Stripes Frozen Daiquiri

A festive and visually stunning cocktail, perfect for patriotic celebrations. This drink layers red, white, and blue frozen daiquiris, each flavored differently to not only look great but also taste delicious. Here's how to make a Stars and Stripes Frozen Daiquiri:

Ingredients:

Red Layer (Strawberry Daiquiri):

- Fresh or frozen strawberries (1 cup)
- White rum (1 ounce)
- Lime juice (1/2 ounce)
- Simple syrup (1/2 ounce)
- Ice cubes

White Layer (Classic Daiquiri):

- White rum (1 ounce)
- Lime juice (1 ounce)
- Simple syrup (1/2 ounce)
- Ice cubes

Blue Layer (Blueberry Daiquiri):

- Fresh or frozen blueberries (1 cup)
- Blue Curaçao (1 ounce)
- White rum (1 ounce)
- Lime juice (1/2 ounce)
- Simple syrup (1/2 ounce)
- Ice cubes

Instructions:

1.  Prepare Each Layer Separately:

- For each layer, blend the ingredients in a blender until smooth. Start with the red layer, followed by the white, and then the blue layer. Rinse the blender between each layer to keep the colors distinct.

2.  Red Layer:

- Blend strawberries, white rum, lime juice, simple syrup, and ice until smooth. Pour into a separate container and set aside in the freezer to keep it chilled.

3.  White Layer:

- Blend white rum, lime juice, simple syrup, and ice until smooth. Pour into a separate container and place it in the freezer.

4.  Blue Layer:

- Blend blueberries, blue Curaçao, white rum, lime juice, simple syrup, and ice until smooth. Transfer to a separate container and keep in the freezer.

5.  Assemble the Drink:

- Take a clear glass and carefully layer the daiquiris. Start with the red strawberry layer, followed by the white classic daiquiri, and then top with the blue blueberry layer. Work quickly to prevent the layers from melting.

6.  Garnish and Serve:

- Garnish with a strawberry or a skewer of blueberries, if desired.
- Serve immediately with a straw.

Enjoy your Stars and Stripes Frozen Daiquiri! This visually impressive drink not only celebrates the patriotic theme but also offers a delightful mix of flavors, making it a perfect choice for festive summer gatherings.

# Hauntingly Delicious
# Halloween Delights

*Welcome to the spine-tingling chapter of our cookbook, "Hauntingly Delicious Halloween Delights." Halloween is a bewitching time of year when the ordinary transforms into the extraordinary, and everyday ingredients become enchanting creations. In this chapter, we'll guide you through crafting an eerie yet delectable Halloween feast, featuring appetizers that will give your guests goosebumps, main courses that will haunt their taste buds, and desserts that will cast a sweet spell.*

# Spooky Treats
# and Appetizers

# Mummy Mini Pizzas

A fun and easy-to-make treat, perfect for Halloween parties or as a spooky snack for kids and adults alike. Using English muffins as the base, these pizzas can be quickly assembled and customized. The mozzarella strips create the look of mummy bandages, and olives serve as the eyes, making them not only tasty but also playful. Here's how to make Mummy Mini Pizzas:

Ingredients:

- English muffins (6, split in half)
- Marinara sauce (1 cup)
- Mozzarella cheese (8 ounces, sliced into thin strips)
- Black olives (sliced, for the eyes)
- Optional: Other toppings like pepperoni, bell peppers, or mushrooms, cut into small pieces

Instructions:

1. Preheat the Oven:

- Preheat your oven to 350°F (175°C).

2. Prepare the English Muffins:

- Split the English muffins in half and place them on a baking sheet, cut side up.

3. Add Marinara Sauce:

- Spread a thin layer of marinara sauce on each English muffin half.

4. Create the Mummy Bandages:

- Lay strips of mozzarella cheese over the marinara sauce to resemble mummy bandages. Leave some space for the eyes. It's okay if the cheese overlaps a bit, as it will melt.

5. Add the Eyes:

- Place two olive slices on each mini pizza for the eyes. You can nestle the olives into the cheese so they stay in place.

6. Bake:

- Bake in the preheated oven for about 10-15 minutes, or until the cheese is melted and slightly golden.

7. Serve:

- Remove the mini pizzas from the oven and let them cool for a couple of minutes.
- Serve warm and enjoy your spooky Mummy Mini Pizzas!

These mini pizzas are not only adorable but also customizable. You can add additional toppings under the cheese for more flavor, such as pepperoni, diced bell peppers, or mushrooms. They're sure to be a hit at any Halloween gathering!

# Spider Deviled Eggs

A creative and fun twist on classic deviled eggs, perfect for Halloween parties or spooky-themed events. The addition of black olive slices transforms these appetizers into little "spiders" sitting atop the eggs. Here's how to make Spider Deviled Eggs:

Ingredients:

- Eggs (12, hard-boiled and peeled)
- Mayonnaise (1/2 cup)
- Mustard (1 tablespoon, Dijon or yellow)
- Salt and pepper (to taste)
- Paprika (for garnish, optional)
- Black olives (large, pitted, about 6-12 depending on size)

Instructions:

1. Prepare the Hard-Boiled Eggs:

- Place eggs in a saucepan and cover with water. Bring to a boil, then turn off the heat, cover, and let sit for about 12 minutes. Transfer eggs to cold water to cool.
- Once cooled, peel the eggs and cut them in half lengthwise.

2. Make the Deviled Egg Filling:

- Gently remove the yolks and place them in a mixing bowl.
- Mash the yolks with a fork and add mayonnaise, mustard, salt, and pepper. Mix until smooth and creamy.
- Taste and adjust the seasoning as needed.

3. Fill the Egg Whites:

- Spoon or pipe the yolk mixture back into the egg white halves.

4. Create the Spider Decoration:

- Cut the black olives in half lengthwise. Use one half for the spider's body, placing it in the center of the yolk mixture.
- Slice the other half of the olive into thin strips for the spider's legs. You'll need eight strips for each spider.
- Carefully place four strips on each side of the olive half to form the legs of the spider.

5. Garnish and Serve:

- Sprinkle a bit of paprika over the eggs for extra color and flavor, if desired.
- Arrange the Spider Deviled Eggs on a platter and serve.

Enjoy your spooky and delicious Spider Deviled Eggs! They're sure to be a hit with guests, adding a fun and eerie touch to your Halloween spread.

# Witch's Finger Pretzel Rods

A spooky and fun Halloween treat, perfect for parties or as a creative snack for the season. These eerie fingers are made by dipping pretzel rods in green-colored white chocolate and using almond slices to mimic fingernails. Adding wrinkle lines with a toothpick gives them a more realistic and creepy effect. Here's how to make Witch's Finger Pretzel Rods:

Ingredients:

- Pretzel rods (about 20)
- White chocolate (16 ounces)
- Green food coloring
- Almond slices (about 20, for the fingernails)
- Toothpick (for adding wrinkle lines)

Instructions:

1. Melt the White Chocolate:

- Break the white chocolate into pieces and place it in a microwave-safe bowl.
- Microwave in 30-second intervals, stirring in between, until the chocolate is completely melted and smooth.

2. Color the Chocolate:

- Once the white chocolate is melted, add green food coloring. Stir well until you achieve the desired shade of green.

3. Prepare the Pretzel Rods:

- Line a baking sheet with parchment paper or a silicone baking mat.
- Hold a pretzel rod by one end and dip it into the green chocolate, covering about three-quarters of the rod to resemble a finger. Gently shake off any excess chocolate.

4. Add the Fingernails:

- While the chocolate is still wet, carefully place an almond slice at the tip of the coated pretzel rod to resemble a fingernail.

5. Add Wrinkle Lines:

- Use a toothpick to gently draw wrinkle lines near the almond slice and in the middle of the pretzel rod to mimic the creases of a finger.

6. Set the Chocolate:

- Place the chocolate-coated pretzel rod on the prepared baking sheet. Repeat with the remaining pretzel rods.
- Allow the chocolate to harden completely. You can speed up this process by placing the baking sheet in the refrigerator for about 15-20 minutes.

7. Serve:

- Once the chocolate is set and the pretzel rods are firm, they are ready to be served. Arrange them on a platter for a spooky presentation.

Enjoy your Witch's Finger Pretzel Rods! These treats are not only eerie and perfect for Halloween but also delicious and fun to make. They're sure to be a hit at any Halloween gathering!

# Monster Mouths

A fun, easy-to-make, and healthy Halloween treat that's perfect for parties or as a creative snack for kids. Made with apple slices, peanut butter, and mini marshmallows, these treats resemble spooky monster mouths and are sure to be a hit. Here's how to make Monster Mouths:

Ingredients:

- Apples (2-3, any variety)
- Peanut butter (smooth or crunchy)
- Mini marshmallows

Instructions:

1. Prepare the Apples:

- Wash the apples and pat them dry.
- Cut each apple into quarters and remove the core.
- Slice each quarter into thin wedges, about 1/4 inch thick. You'll need two slices for each monster mouth.

2. Assemble the Monster Mouths:

- Take an apple slice and spread a layer of peanut butter on one side.
- Stick mini marshmallows onto the peanut butter along the edge of the apple slice to resemble teeth.
- Take another apple slice and spread peanut butter on one side. Place this slice on top of the marshmallows, peanut butter side down, to create a sandwich. The marshmallows should be visible, resembling teeth in a mouth.

3. Repeat:

- Repeat the process with the remaining apple slices and mini marshmallows until you have used all the apple wedges.

4. Serve:

- Serve the Monster Mouths immediately after assembling.

5. Optional Variations:

- For a nut-free version, use sunflower seed butter, cream cheese, or a chocolate-hazelnut spread instead of peanut butter.
- To make the monster mouths more colorful, you can use red apple slices for a 'bloody' effect.

Monster Mouths are not only adorable and spooky but also a healthier alternative to traditional Halloween sweets. They're easy enough for kids to help make and are perfect for Halloween parties or as a fun snack during the Halloween season. Enjoy making and munching on these playful treats!

# Ghostly Cheese Balls

A spooktacular and tasty treat for Halloween parties or any spooky-themed event. These adorable ghost-shaped cheese balls are easy to make and can be decorated with peppercorns or black olives to create the eyes, giving them a charming ghostly appearance. Here's a simple recipe to make Ghostly Cheese Balls:

Ingredients:

- Cream cheese (8 ounces, softened)
- Sharp cheddar cheese (1 cup, grated)
- Garlic powder (1/2 teaspoon)
- Onion powder (1/2 teaspoon)
- Salt and pepper (to taste)
- Whole peppercorns or small pieces of black olives (for the eyes)
- Optional: Chives or parsley (finely chopped, for extra flavor)

Instructions:

1. Prepare the Cheese Mixture:

- In a mixing bowl, combine the softened cream cheese with the grated cheddar cheese. Mix well until the ingredients are fully incorporated.

- • Add garlic powder, onion powder, salt, and pepper to the cheese mixture. Mix again until all the seasonings are evenly distributed. If you're using chives or parsley, add them in this step.

2. Shape the Cheese Balls:

- Once the cheese mixture is ready, use your hands to shape small portions of it into ghost-like figures. Aim for an elongated shape with a rounded head and a flowing bottom, like a ghost.

3. Add the Eyes:

- Place two peppercorns or small pieces of black olive on each cheese ball to make the eyes. Position them to mimic the look of a ghost's face.

4. Chill the Cheese Balls:

- Place the shaped cheese balls on a plate or a tray lined with parchment paper. Refrigerate them for at least 30 minutes to an hour to firm up. This makes them easier to handle and serve.

5. Serve:

- Once chilled and firm, serve your Ghostly Cheese Balls. They can be placed on a platter as is or served with crackers, breadsticks, or vegetable sticks.

Enjoy your Ghostly Cheese Balls, a perfect combination of spooky and delicious! These charming treats are sure to be a hit at any Halloween gathering and are as fun to make as they are to eat.

# Pumpkin Veggie Platter

A creative and healthy way to celebrate the fall season, especially around Halloween and Thanksgiving. This platter is arranged to look like a pumpkin, using colorful vegetables like carrots, bell peppers, cucumbers, and broccoli. It's not only visually appealing but also a great way to encourage healthy snacking. Here's how to make a Pumpkin Veggie Platter:

Ingredients:

- Carrots (2-3 cups, baby carrots or thinly sliced)
- Bell peppers (1-2, preferably orange for the pumpkin color, sliced)
- Cucumbers (2, sliced)
- Broccoli (a few florets for the stem)
- Your choice of dip (hummus, ranch, yogurt-based dips, etc.)
- A small bowl for the dip

Instructions:

1. Prepare the Vegetables:

- Wash all the vegetables thoroughly.
- Slice the bell peppers and cucumbers into strips.
- If you're not using baby carrots, peel and slice the carrots into thin sticks.

2. Arrange the Pumpkin Base:

- On a large round platter, start arranging the carrots and bell pepper slices in a circular pattern, alternating them to create a pumpkin-like appearance. The outer circle should be larger, gradually getting smaller as you move towards the center.

3. Fill the Center with Dip:

- Place a small bowl of your chosen dip in the center of the arranged vegetables. This will be the "center" of the pumpkin.

4. Add the Cucumber Layer:

- Arrange the cucumber slices around the dip bowl, further enhancing the pumpkin shape.

5. Create the Pumpkin Stem:

- At the top of the pumpkin, place a few broccoli florets to mimic the stem of the pumpkin.

6. Serve:

- Once your veggie pumpkin is assembled, it's ready to be served.

This Pumpkin Veggie Platter is not only a festive addition to any fall gathering but also a delightful way to enjoy a variety of vegetables. You can customize the platter with your favorite veggies and dips, making it versatile and suitable for different tastes and dietary preferences. Enjoy creating and sharing this fun and healthy platter!

# Zombie Meatloaf

A gruesomely delightful dish perfect for Halloween parties or any spooky-themed event. This recipe transforms a classic meatloaf into a creepy zombie face, using onion slices for eyes and teeth and ketchup for blood, to create a frighteningly fun presentation. Here's how to make Zombie Meatloaf:

Ingredients:

For the Meatloaf:

- Ground beef (2 pounds)
- Bread crumbs (1 cup)
- Milk (1/2 cup)
- Eggs (2, beaten)
- Onion (1, finely chopped)
- Garlic (2 cloves, minced)
- Salt (1 teaspoon)
- Pepper (1/2 teaspoon)
- Worcestershire sauce (1 tablespoon)
- Mixed herbs (1 teaspoon, optional, such as thyme or oregano)

For the Zombie Features:

- Large onion (1, sliced into rings for eyes and teeth)
- Ketchup (for blood effect)
- Optional: Green food coloring (to give the meatloaf a more ghoulish color)

Instructions:

1. Preheat Oven:

- Preheat your oven to 375°F (190°C).

2. Mix the Meatloaf Ingredients:

- In a large bowl, combine the ground beef, bread crumbs, milk, beaten eggs, finely chopped onion, minced garlic, salt, pepper, Worcestershire sauce, and mixed herbs (if using).
- If you want a more zombie-like color for your meatloaf, mix in a few drops of green food coloring.

3. Shape the Meatloaf:

- On a baking sheet lined with parchment paper, shape the meatloaf mixture into a rough face shape - think of a flattened oval for the face with areas built up for the brow and cheekbones.

4. Create the Zombie Face:

- Use onion rings to form the eyes, placing them in the appropriate spot on the meatloaf face.
- Shape additional onion pieces into jagged teeth and place them around the mouth area.
- You can also shape the nose using either meat or onions.

5. Bake the Meatloaf:

- Place the baking sheet in the oven and bake for about 45-60 minutes, or until the meatloaf is cooked through (internal temperature of 160°F or 70°C).

6. Add the Ketchup:

- After removing the meatloaf from the oven, let it rest for a few minutes.
- Drizzle ketchup around the meatloaf for a 'bloody' effect, focusing on the mouth and eyes.

7. Serve:

- Once your Zombie Meatloaf is garnished, it's ready to be served.

Enjoy this eerie yet delicious centerpiece for your Halloween feast! This Zombie Meatloaf is sure to be the talk of any Halloween party, offering both a creepy visual and a tasty meal. Feel free to get creative with the shaping and decorating to make your zombie as scary as you like!

# Bat Wings

A fun and spooky twist on classic chicken wings, perfect for Halloween parties or themed events. By marinating the wings in a dark sauce, such as black bean sauce or soy sauce with black food coloring, they take on a creepy, bat-like appearance. Here's how to make Bat Wings:

Ingredients:

- Chicken wings (2 pounds)
- Black bean sauce or soy sauce (1 cup)
- Black food coloring (a few drops, optional)
- Garlic (3 cloves, minced)
- Ginger (1 tablespoon, grated)
- Honey (2 tablespoons)
- Rice vinegar (1 tablespoon)
- Sesame oil (1 teaspoon)
- Optional spices: chili flakes, five-spice powder
- Salt and pepper (to taste)
- Optional: Sesame seeds or chopped green onions for garnish

Instructions:

1.  Prepare the Marinade:

- In a large bowl, combine black bean sauce or soy sauce with black food coloring (if using) until you achieve a very dark color.
- Add minced garlic, grated ginger, honey, rice vinegar, and sesame oil to the sauce. Mix well. Include chili flakes or five-spice powder if you want some extra flavor.
- Season the mixture with salt and pepper to taste.

2.  Marinate the Chicken Wings:

- Add the chicken wings to the marinade, ensuring they are well coated.
- Cover the bowl and refrigerate for at least 2 hours, or overnight for a deeper flavor and color.

3.  Cook the Wings:

- Preheat your oven to 400°F (200°C) if baking. For frying, fill a pan with enough oil to cover the wings and heat it to 375°F (190°C).
- Remove the wings from the marinade and shake off any excess.
- If baking, place the wings on a baking sheet lined with parchment paper or a wire rack and bake for 40-45 minutes until crispy. Turn them halfway through cooking.
- If frying, fry the wings in batches until they are crispy and fully cooked, about 10-15 minutes.

4.  Garnish and Serve:

- Once cooked, place the Bat Wings on a serving platter. Sprinkle sesame seeds or chopped green onions on top for garnish if desired.

5.  Enjoy:
6.  Serve your Bat Wings hot. They are perfect as a spooky appetizer or main dish for your Halloween festivities.

These Bat Wings, with their dark and mysterious look, are sure to be a conversation starter and a hit at any Halloween celebration. Enjoy creating and serving this eerie yet delicious treat!

# Creepy Crawly Jello

A simple yet delightfully spooky dessert, perfect for Hallowe-en parties or any occasion that calls for a bit of eerie fun. This dessert features clear gelatin filled with gummy worms or other gummy insects, creating a creepy, crawly effect. Here's how to make Creepy Crawly Jello:

Ingredients:

- Unflavored gelatin (4 packets, about 1 ounce total)
- Water (4 cups, divided)
- Sugar (1/2 cup, optional for sweetness)
- Gummy worms or other gummy insects
- Individual serving cups or a large bowl for serving

Instructions:

1. Prepare the Gelatin:

- In a small bowl, sprinkle the gelatin over 1 cup of cold water. Allow it to sit for about 5 minutes to "bloom."
- Heat the remaining 3 cups of water in a saucepan. If you're adding sugar for sweetness, dissolve it in the hot water.
- Once the water is hot (but not boiling), add the bloomed gelatin and stir until completely dissolved.

2. Cool the Gelatin Mixture:

- Remove the gelatin mixture from the heat and let it cool to room temperature. It should still be liquid.

3. Assemble the Jello:

- Place a few gummy worms or insects in the bottom of each serving cup or at the bottom of a large bowl.
- Carefully pour the cooled gelatin mixture over the gummy creatures.
- Add more gummy worms or insects, suspending them in the gelatin. Some can be partially sticking out of the gelatin for a more dramatic effect.

4. Chill the Jello:

- Refrigerate the jello for at least 4 hours, or until it's completely set.

5. Serve:

- Once set, the Creepy Crawly Jello is ready to be served. If you used individual cups, they're ready as is. If you made a large bowl, you can scoop servings onto plates or into smaller cups.

Enjoy your Creepy Crawly Jello, a playful and spooky treat that's perfect for adding a touch of fun to any Halloween-the-med event. The gummy creatures suspended in the clear ge-latin create an eerie effect that's sure to delight guests of all ages!

197

# Creative Halloween-Themed Main Courses

# Jack-o'-Lantern Stuffed Peppers

A festive and delicious meal, perfect for Halloween or any fall-themed dinner. These stuffed peppers are carved to resemble Jack-o'-lanterns and filled with a savory mixture of ground beef, rice, tomato sauce, and cheese. Here's how to make them:

Ingredients:

- Bell peppers (4-6, any color, but orange looks most like pumpkins)
- Ground beef (1 pound)
- Cooked rice (1 cup)
- Tomato sauce (1 cup)
- Onion (1, diced)
- Garlic (2 cloves, minced)
- Shredded cheese (1 cup, cheddar or a blend)
- Salt and pepper (to taste)
- Olive oil (for cooking)
- Optional: spices such as cumin, paprika, or Italian seasoning

Instructions:

1.  Preheat the Oven:

- Preheat your oven to 350°F (175°C).

2.  Prepare the Peppers:

- Slice off the tops of the bell peppers and set them aside. Remove the seeds and membranes.
- Carefully carve faces into the sides of the peppers to resemble Jack-o'- lanterns, using a small knife.

3.  Cook the Filling:

- Heat olive oil in a skillet over medium heat. Add the diced onion and minced garlic, sautéing until softened.
- Add the ground beef, breaking it up with a spoon, and cook until browned. Drain any excess fat.
- Stir in the cooked rice, tomato sauce, and any optional spices. Season with salt and pepper.
- Cook the mixture for a few more minutes until everything is heated through.

4.  Stuff the Peppers:

- Fill each carved pepper with the beef and rice mixture. Top with shredded cheese.

5.  Bake the Peppers:

- Place the stuffed peppers in a baking dish. Put the pepper tops back on or leave them off if you prefer.
- Bake in the preheated oven for about 25-30 minutes, or until the peppers are tender and the cheese is melted and bubbly.

6.  Serve:

- Remove the peppers from the oven and let them cool for a few minutes.
- Serve the Jack-o'-Lantern Stuffed Peppers warm.

Enjoy your Jack-o'-Lantern Stuffed Peppers, a fun and tasty meal that brings the spirit of Halloween to your dinner table. These stuffed peppers are not only visually appealing but also packed with flavor, making them a hit with both kids and adults!

# Spooky Spaghetti and Eyeballs

A fun and slightly eerie dish, perfect for Halloween dinner or any spooky-themed event. This recipe pairs classic spaghetti with marinara sauce and transforms ordinary meatballs into creepy "eyeballs" using olive slices. Here's how to make it:

Ingredients:

For the Meatball Eyeballs:

- Ground beef (1 pound)
- Bread crumbs (1/2 cup)
- Egg (1, beaten)
- Garlic (1 clove, minced)
- Onion (1/2, finely chopped)
- Salt and pepper (to taste)
- Black olives (sliced, one slice per meatball)
- Olive oil (for frying)

For the Spaghetti:

- Spaghetti (1 pound)
- Marinara sauce (24 ounces, homemade or store-bought)
- Optional: grated Parmesan cheese, basil leaves for garnish

Instructions:

1. Prepare the Meatballs:

- In a bowl, combine ground beef, bread crumbs, beaten egg, minced garlic, chopped onion, salt, and pepper. Mix until well combined.
- Form the mixture into small meatballs, about the size of a golf ball.
- Press a slice of black olive into the center of each meatball to resemble the iris of an eyeball.

2. Cook the Meatballs:

- Heat olive oil in a skillet over medium heat.
- Cook the meatballs, turning occasionally, until they are browned on all sides and cooked through, about 10-15 minutes.

3. Cook the Spaghetti:

- Meanwhile, bring a large pot of salted water to a boil.
- Cook the spaghetti according to the package instructions until al dente.
- Drain the spaghetti and return it to the pot.

4. Prepare the Marinara Sauce:

- In a separate saucepan, heat the marinara sauce over medium heat until it's simmering.

5. Assemble the Dish:

- Toss the cooked spaghetti with the marinara sauce.
- Serve the spaghetti on plates or in a large serving dish.
- Place the meatball eyeballs on top of the spaghetti.

6. Garnish and Serve:

- Garnish with grated Parmesan cheese and fresh basil leaves if desired.
- Serve your Spooky Spaghetti and Eyeballs hot and enjoy the creepy yet delicious meal!

This dish is sure to be a hit, especially with kids, as it brings a playful and spooky twist to a family favorite. The olive "eyeballs" add a fun element to the savory meatballs, making the dish both visually interesting and tasty.

# Witches' Brew Soup

A fun and healthy Halloween dish that combines the goodness of broccoli and spinach to create a vibrant green soup, perfect for setting a spooky mood. Serving this delicious soup in small soup pots, or "cauldrons," with a breadstick "broomstick" on the side, adds to the witchy theme. Here's how to make it:

Ingredients:

For the Soup:

- Broccoli (2 cups, chopped)
- Spinach (2 cups, fresh or frozen)
- Onion (1, diced)
- Garlic (2 cloves, minced)
- Vegetable or chicken broth (4 cups)
- Olive oil (2 tablespoons)
- Salt and pepper (to taste)
- Cream or milk (optional, for creaminess)
- Optional: a pinch of nutmeg or cayenne pepper for extra flavor

For the Breadstick Broomsticks:

- Store-bought breadstick dough or homemade dough
- Optional: butter and garlic powder for seasoning

Instructions:

1. Cook the Vegetables:

- In a large pot, heat olive oil over medium heat.
- Add diced onion and minced garlic, cooking until the onion is translucent.
- Add chopped broccoli and cook for a few more minutes.
- Pour in the broth and bring the mixture to a boil. Reduce heat and simmer until the broccoli is tender.

2. Add Spinach:

- Stir in the spinach and cook until it's wilted and bright green. If using frozen spinach, thaw and squeeze out excess water before adding.

3. Puree the Soup:

- Use an immersion blender to puree the soup directly in the pot until smooth. Alternatively, transfer to a blender in batches and blend until smooth. Be careful with hot liquids in a blender.
- Season the soup with salt, pepper, and optional nutmeg or cayenne pepper.
- For a creamier soup, stir in some cream or milk to your desired consistency.

4. Prepare the Breadstick Broomsticks:

- Preheat the oven according to the breadstick dough instructions.
- Roll out the dough and cut it into thin strips. Wrap the strips around the
- top of each breadstick to resemble the bristles of a broomstick.
- Optional: Brush with melted butter and sprinkle with garlic powder for extra flavor.
- Bake according to the dough package instructions or until golden brown.

5. Serve:

- Ladle the soup into small soup pots or bowls to resemble cauldrons.
- Serve each "cauldron" of Witches' Brew Soup with a breadstick broomstick on the side.

Enjoy your Witches' Brew Soup, a delightfully green and nutritious dish that's as fun to make as it is to eat. The breadstick broomsticks add a whimsical touch, perfect for a Halloween feast!

# Mummy Meatloaf

A whimsical and delicious dish perfect for Halloween festivities. This recipe transforms the classic meatloaf into a mummy by wrapping it in strips of pastry dough to resemble bandages and using olives or peas for the eyes. Here's how to make it:

Ingredients:

For the Meatloaf:

- Ground beef (2 pounds)
- Bread crumbs (1 cup)
- Onion (1, finely chopped)
- Garlic (2 cloves, minced)
- Egg (1, beaten)
- Ketchup (1/2 cup)
- Worcestershire sauce (1 tablespoon)
- Salt and pepper (to taste)
- Mixed herbs (1 teaspoon, such as thyme or oregano)

For the Mummy Wrapping:

- Puff pastry or refrigerated croissant dough (1 package)
- Black olives or peas (for the eyes)

Instructions:

1. Preheat the Oven:

- Preheat your oven to 350°F (175°C).

2. Make the Meatloaf Mixture:

- In a large bowl, combine the ground beef, bread crumbs, finely chopped onion, minced garlic, beaten egg, ketchup, Worcestershire sauce, salt, pepper, and mixed herbs. Mix until well combined.

3. Shape the Meatloaf:

- On a baking sheet lined with parchment paper, shape the meatloaf mixture into a rough oval or mummy shape.

4. Prepare the Pastry:

- Roll out the puff pastry or croissant dough and cut it into strips.
- Wrap the strips around the meatloaf, leaving some space for the mummy's eyes. Overlap the strips slightly to resemble bandages.

5. Bake the Meatloaf:

- Bake in the preheated oven for about 45 minutes. If the pastry is browning too quickly, cover it with foil.

6. Add the Eyes:

- About 10 minutes before the meatloaf is done, remove it from the oven and add two black olives or peas where the eyes should be.
- Return to the oven and finish baking.

7. Serve:

- Once the meatloaf is cooked through and the pastry is golden brown, remove it from the oven and let it rest for a few minutes before slicing.
- Serve the Mummy Meatloaf warm, and enjoy your spooky creation!

This Mummy Meatloaf is not only a fun centerpiece for your Halloween table but also a hearty and delicious meal that guests are sure to love. The pastry adds a delightful crispness to the meatloaf, making it a perfect dish for a festive occasion.

# *Zombie Brain Meatballs*

A gruesomely delightful dish that's perfect for Halloween parties or any spooky-themed event. These meatballs are designed to resemble brains, with shallow channels carved into them to mimic brain grooves. Served with a "bloody" marinara sauce, they're both creepy and delicious. Here's how to make them:

Ingredients:

For the Meatballs:

- Ground beef or a mix of beef and pork (2 pounds)
- Bread crumbs (1 cup)
- Egg (1, beaten)
- Garlic (2 cloves, minced)
- Onion (1, finely chopped)
- Milk (1/2 cup)
- Salt and pepper (to taste)
- Worcestershire sauce (1 tablespoon)

For the Marinara Sauce:

- Canned crushed tomatoes (28 ounces)
- Garlic (2 cloves, minced)
- Olive oil (2 tablespoons)
- Onion (1, diced)
- Dried basil and oregano (1 teaspoon each)
- Salt and pepper (to taste)
- Red food coloring (optional, for added "bloody" effect)

Instructions:

1. Prepare the Meatball Mixture:

- In a large bowl, combine ground meat, bread crumbs, beaten egg, minced garlic, chopped onion, milk, salt, pepper, and Worcestershire sauce. Mix until well combined.

2. Shape the Meatballs:

- Form the mixture into large, round meatballs.
- Using a small knife or a spatula, gently carve shallow channels on the top of each meatball to resemble the grooves of a brain.

3. Cook the Meatballs:

- Preheat your oven to 375°F (190°C).
- Place the meatballs on a baking sheet lined with parchment paper.
- Bake for 25-30 minutes or until the meatballs are cooked through.

4. Prepare the Marinara Sauce:

- In a saucepan, heat olive oil over medium heat. Add diced onion and minced garlic, cooking until softened.
- Pour in the crushed tomatoes and add dried basil, oregano, salt, and pepper. Simmer for 15-20 minutes.
- For a more "bloody" appearance, stir in a few drops of red food coloring.

5. Serve:

- Serve the meatballs hot, drizzled with the marinara sauce or with the sauce on the side for dipping.
- Garnish with fresh herbs if desired.

Enjoy your Zombie Brain Meatballs, a creepy yet delicious addition to your Halloween feast! These meatballs are not only visually striking but also packed with savory flavors that are sure to please your guests.

# *Bat Bites*

A fun and spooky treat that's perfect for Halloween parties or any eerie-themed gathering. This recipe involves making cut-out bat shapes from a large quesadilla and serving them with dips like guacamole or salsa for a ghoulish effect. Here's how to make them:

Ingredients:

- Large flour tortilla (1)
- Shredded cheese (1 cup, any variety)
- Cooked chicken, shredded (1/2 cup, optional)
- Olive oil or cooking spray
- Dips of your choice (guacamole, salsa, sour cream, etc.)

Equipment:

- Bat-shaped cookie cutter or a printed bat template to cut out the shapes

Instructions:

1. Prepare the Quesadilla:

- Lay the large flour tortilla flat on a clean surface.
- Sprinkle the shredded cheese evenly over one-half of the tortilla.
- If desired, add the cooked shredded chicken on top of the cheese.

2. Fold and Cook:

- Fold the other half of the tortilla over the cheese and chicken, creating a half-moon shape.
- Heat a skillet or griddle over medium heat and lightly grease it with olive oil or cooking spray.
- Place the folded quesadilla on the skillet and cook until the cheese is melted and the tortilla is golden brown on both sides, about 2-3 minutes per side.

3. Cut Out Bat Shapes:

- Allow the quesadilla to cool slightly.
- Use a bat-shaped cookie cutter or a printed bat template to cut out bat shapes from the quesadilla. Press the cutter firmly to create the shapes.

4. Serve with Dips:

- Arrange the bat-shaped quesadilla bites on a serving platter.
- Place small bowls of guacamole, salsa, sour cream, or other dips alongside the bat bites for a spooky effect.

5. Enjoy:

- Serve your Bat Bites to your delighted guests, and watch them disappear into the night!

These Bat Bites are not only a creative and festive addition to your Halloween spread, but they also taste fantastic with the savory quesadilla filling and your choice of dips. They're sure to be a hit at your next Halloween gathering.

# Ghastly Goulash

A spooky twist on the classic goulash, perfect for Halloween or any eerie-themed dinner. This recipe adds a creepy touch to the dish by incorporating black food coloring into the pasta or using squid ink pasta for an eerie appearance. Here's how to make it:

Ingredients:

- Ground beef or pork (1 pound)
- Onion (1, finely chopped)
- Bell pepper (1, diced)
- Garlic (3 cloves, minced)
- Tomatoes (2, diced)
- Tomato paste (2 tablespoons)
- Paprika (2 tablespoons)
- Beef broth (1 cup)
- Salt and pepper (to taste)
- Black food coloring or squid ink pasta (8 ounces)
- Olive oil (2 tablespoons)
- Sour cream (optional, for garnish)
- Chopped fresh parsley (optional, for garnish)

Instructions:

1. Prepare the Goulash:

- In a large skillet or pot, heat olive oil over medium heat.
- Add the finely chopped onion and diced bell pepper. Sauté until they become soft and translucent.
- Add the minced garlic and continue to sauté for another minute until fragrant.

2. Cook the Meat:

- Add the ground beef or pork to the skillet and cook until browned, breaking it into small pieces as it cooks.

3. Add Tomatoes and Seasonings:

- Stir in the diced tomatoes, tomato paste, and paprika. Cook for a few minutes to combine the flavors.
- Pour in the beef broth and season with salt and pepper to taste.

4. Simmer:

- Reduce the heat to low and let the goulash simmer for about 20-30 minutes, allowing the flavors to meld and the sauce to thicken. Stir occasionally.

5. Prepare the Black Pasta:

- While the goulash is simmering, cook the black pasta or squid ink pasta according to the package instructions. Drain and set aside.

6. Serve:

- To serve, place a portion of the eerie black pasta on each plate.
- Ladle the ghastly goulash over the pasta.
- Garnish with a dollop of sour cream and chopped fresh parsley, if desired.

Enjoy your Ghastly Goulash, a chillingly delicious dish that's both eerie and satisfying. The jet-black pasta or squid ink pasta adds a spooky visual element to this classic comfort food. It's sure to be a hit at your Halloween dinner or any creepy-themed gathering.

# Cauldron Curry

A fun and spooky treat that's perfect for Halloween parties A delightful and seasonally-inspired dish that's perfect for autumn gatherings, especially around Halloween. This recipe serves a hearty pumpkin curry in mini cauldrons, creating a whimsical and flavorful experience. Here's how to make it:

Ingredients:

- Pumpkin or squash chunks (2 cups, peeled and cubed)
- Onion (1, finely chopped)
- Garlic (2 cloves, minced)
- Curry paste (2 tablespoons, red or green)
- Coconut milk (1 can, 13.5 ounces)
- Vegetable broth (1 cup)
- Fresh ginger (1 tablespoon, grated)
- Red bell pepper (1, diced)
- Carrots (2, peeled and sliced)
- Snow peas (1 cup, trimmed)
- Fresh cilantro (1/4 cup, chopped, for garnish)
- Lime wedges (for garnish)
- Salt and pepper (to taste)
- Cooking oil (2 tablespoons)

Instructions:

1. Sauté the Aromatics:

- In a large pot or cauldron (or a regular pot if cauldrons aren't available), heat the cooking oil over medium heat.
- Add the finely chopped onion and minced garlic. Sauté until the onion becomes translucent and aromatic.

2. Add the Curry Paste:

- Stir in the curry paste and grated fresh ginger. Cook for a minute or two to release their flavors.

3. Cook the Pumpkin:

- Add the cubed pumpkin or squash chunks to the pot. Cook for about 5 minutes, allowing them to soften slightly and absorb the flavors.

4. Pour in the Liquids:

- Pour in the coconut milk and vegetable broth. Stir well to combine.

5. Add Vegetables:

- Add the diced red bell pepper, sliced carrots, and trimmed snow peas to the pot.

6. Simmer:

- Reduce the heat to low and let the curry simmer for about 15-20 minutes, or until the vegetables are tender and the flavors have melded together. Stir occasionally.

7. Season:

- Season the Cauldron Curry with salt and pepper to taste.

8. Serve in Mini Cauldrons:

- Carefully ladle the pumpkin curry into mini cauldrons or small soup pots for a spooky presentation.

9. Garnish:

- Garnish each cauldron with a sprinkle of fresh chopped cilantro and serve with lime wedges on the side.

Enjoy your Cauldron Curry, a delightful and cozy autumn dish served with a touch of Halloween whimsy. The mini cauldrons add a festive and spooky element to this flavorful pumpkin curry. It's sure to warm both your heart and your taste buds.

# *Bloody Beet Risotto*

A visually striking and delicious dish that's perfect for Halloween or any spooky-themed dinner. This recipe creates a vibrant deep red beetroot risotto, garnished with goat cheese to resemble blood and bones. Here's how to make it:

Ingredients:

- Arborio rice (1 cup)
- Beetroot (2 medium-sized, peeled and grated)
- Onion (1, finely chopped)
- Garlic (2 cloves, minced)
- Vegetable broth (4 cups, kept warm)
- Dry white wine (1/2 cup)
- Butter (2 tablespoons)
- Olive oil (2 tablespoons)
- Goat cheese (1/2 cup, crumbled)
- Parmesan cheese (1/2 cup, grated)
- Salt and pepper (to taste)
- Fresh parsley (1/4 cup, chopped, for garnish)

Instructions:

1. Prepare the Beetroot:
   - Grate the peeled beetroot and set it aside.

2. Sauté the Aromatics:
   - In a large skillet or saucepan, heat the olive oil over medium heat.
   - Add the finely chopped onion and minced garlic. Sauté until the onion becomes translucent and fragrant.

3. Toast the Rice:
   - Add the Arborio rice to the skillet and cook for about 2-3 minutes, stirring frequently, until the rice becomes slightly translucent at the edges.

4. Deglaze with Wine:
   - Pour in the dry white wine and stir until it's mostly absorbed by the rice.

5. Add the Beetroot:
   - Stir in the grated beetroot, allowing it to infuse its vibrant color into the risotto.

6. Begin Adding Broth:
   - Start adding the warm vegetable broth one ladleful at a time, stirring constantly.
   - Allow each ladle of broth to be mostly absorbed before adding the next. Continue this process until the rice is creamy and cooked to your desired level of tenderness (usually about 18-20 minutes).

7. Finish with Butter and Cheese:
   - Stir in the butter and grated Parmesan cheese, ensuring they are fully incorporated and adding creaminess to the risotto.
   - Season with salt and pepper to taste.

8. Serve:
   - Ladle the Bloody Beet Risotto into individual serving bowls or onto a platter.

9. Garnish:
   - Crumble the goat cheese over the top of the risotto to resemble "bones" and create a visually striking contrast.
   - Sprinkle chopped fresh parsley on top for added color and freshness.

Enjoy your Bloody Beet Risotto, a visually captivating and flavorful dish that's sure to impress your guests at Halloween or any spooky dinner gathering.

# Haunted Pizza

A creative and fun Halloween-themed dish that allows you to let your imagination run wild with spooky toppings. You can design spiders, ghosts, or skeletons on your pizza using various ingredients. Here's a basic recipe to get you started:

Ingredients:

- Pizza dough (store-bought or homemade)
- Pizza sauce
- Shredded mozzarella cheese
- Toppings for decorating:
- Black olives (for spiders)
- Sliced black olives or green bell peppers (for spider legs)
- Sliced mozzarella cheese (for ghosts)
- Sliced bell peppers (for skeleton shapes)
- Mini pepperoni slices (for additional decorations)
- Red or green bell pepper strips (for "bloody" effects, optional)
- Any other Halloween-themed toppings you prefer

Instructions:

1. Preheat Your Oven:

- Preheat your oven to the temperature recommended for your pizza dough (usually around 450°F or as directed on the dough package).

2. Prepare the Pizza Dough:

- Roll out the pizza dough on a lightly floured surface to your desired thickness. You can shape it into a round or rectangular pizza.

3. Spread Pizza Sauce:

- Spread a layer of pizza sauce evenly over the rolled-out dough.

4. Add Cheese:

- Sprinkle a generous amount of shredded mozzarella cheese over the sauce to create the base for your haunted toppings.

5. Create Your Halloween Designs:

- Use the toppings to create spooky shapes on your pizza. Here are some ideas:
- For spiders: Place whole black olives in the center for the body and add sliced olives or green bell pepper strips as legs.
- For ghosts: Cut mozzarella cheese slices into ghostly shapes and arrange them on the pizza.
- For skeletons: Create a skeleton shape using sliced bell peppers or other toppings.

6. Add Extra Decorations:

- If you'd like, use mini pepperoni slices or additional toppings to add more Halloween-themed decorations to your pizza. You can also use red or green bell pepper strips to create "bloody" effects.

7. Bake:

- Carefully transfer your decorated pizza onto a pizza stone or baking sheet lined with parchment paper.
- Bake in the preheated oven according to the dough's instructions or until the crust is golden brown, and the cheese is bubbly and slightly browned (usually 12-15 minutes).

8. Serve and Enjoy:

- Once your Haunted Pizza is out of the oven, let it cool for a minute or two, then slice it and serve it to your excited Halloween guests.

Feel free to get creative with your Haunted Pizza and let your imagination run wild with spooky designs. It's a fun and interactive way to celebrate Halloween with a delicious twist on pizza night!

# Sinfully Sweet
# Desserts and Candies

# The Wicked Witch's Chocolate Cauldron Cake

A show-stopping dessert that's perfect for Halloween or any witch-themed gathering. This decadent chocolate cake is shaped like a cauldron, filled with gooey chocolate ganache, and topped with green icing to resemble a bubbling potion. Here's how to make it:

Ingredients:

For the Chocolate Cake:
- All-purpose flour (2 cups)
- Cocoa powder (1 cup)
- Baking powder (2 teaspoons)
- Baking soda (1 1/2 teaspoons)
- Salt (1/2 teaspoon)
- Unsalted butter (1 cup, softened)
- Granulated sugar (2 cups)
- Eggs (4, room temperature)
- Vanilla extract (2 teaspoons)
- Buttermilk (1 1/2 cups, room temperature)
- Hot water (1 1/2 cups)

For the Chocolate Ganache:
- Semi-sweet chocolate chips (1 1/2 cups)
- Heavy cream (1 cup)

For the Green Icing:
- Powdered sugar (2 cups)
- Unsalted butter (1/2 cup, softened)
- Green food coloring
- Milk (2-4 tablespoons, as needed)
- Edible glitter or sprinkles (optional, for extra sparkle)

Additional Decorations:
- Witch's cauldron-shaped cake mold or bundt pan
- Witch's cauldron-shaped cake topper (optional)

Instructions:

For the Chocolate Cake:

1. Preheat Your Oven:
- Preheat your oven to 350°F (175°C) and grease and flour your witch's cauldron-shaped cake mold or bundt pan.

2. Mix Dry Ingredients:
- In a large mixing bowl, whisk together the all-purpose flour, cocoa powder, baking powder, baking soda, and salt. Set aside.

3. Cream Butter and Sugar:
- In another large bowl, cream together the softened butter and granulated sugar until light and fluffy.

4. Add Eggs and Vanilla:
- • Beat in the eggs one at a time, ensuring each egg is fully incorporated. Stir in the vanilla extract.

5. Alternate Wet and Dry Ingredients:
- Gradually add the dry ingredients to the butter mixture, alternating with buttermilk. Begin and end with the dry ingredients. Mix until just combined.

6. Add Hot Water:
- Carefully add the hot water to the batter and mix until the batter is smooth. The batter will be thin, but that's okay.

7. Bake:
- Pour the batter into your greased and floured cake mold or bundt pan.
- Bake in the preheated oven for 40-45 minutes or until a toothpick inserted into the center comes out clean.
- Allow the cake to cool in the pan for about 10 minutes before transferring it to a wire rack to cool completely.

For the Chocolate Ganache:

1. Prepare Chocolate Ganache:
- In a heatproof bowl, heat the heavy cream until it just begins to simmer (you can do this in the microwave or on the stovetop).
- Pour the hot cream over the semi-sweet chocolate chips.
- Let it sit for a minute to melt the chocolate, then stir until smooth and glossy.

2. Fill the Cauldron Cake:
- Once the cake is completely cooled, use a serrated knife to level the top if needed.
- Carefully hollow out the center of the cake to create a cauldron shape. Save the cake scraps for later.

3. Fill with Ganache:
- Pour the chocolate ganache into the hollowed-out cauldron, allowing it to overflow slightly for a bubbling effect.
- Replace the cake scraps over the ganache to "seal" the cauldron.

For the Green Icing:

1. Prepare Icing:
- In a mixing bowl, beat together the softened butter and powdered sugar until creamy.
- Add green food coloring until you achieve your desired "witch's potion" green color.
- If the icing is too thick, add milk a tablespoon at a time until it reaches a spreadable consistency.

2. Decorate the Cake:
- Spread the green icing over the top of the cauldron cake, allowing it to drip down the sides for a spooky effect.
- If desired, sprinkle edible glitter or sprinkles over the icing for extra sparkle.

3. Optional Cake Topper:
- Place a witch's cauldron-shaped cake topper on the cake for added decoration (if available).

Your Wicked Witch's Chocolate Cauldron Cake is ready to serve! This bewitching dessert is sure to impress your guests with its spooky appearance and rich, chocolatey flavor. Enjoy the magic!

# *Vampire Blood Velvet Cupcakes*

A delightfully spooky treat for Halloween or any vampire--themed event. These red velvet cupcakes have a surprise raspberry filling, are topped with cream cheese frosting, and feature a drizzle of raspberry sauce to mimic dripping blood. Here's how to make them:

Ingredients:

For the Red Velvet Cupcakes:

- All-purpose flour (1 1/2 cups)
- Cocoa powder (2 tablespoons)
- Baking powder (1 teaspoon)
- Baking soda (1/2 teaspoon)
- Salt (1/4 teaspoon)
- Unsalted butter (1/2 cup, softened)
- Granulated sugar (1 cup)
- Eggs (2, room temperature)
- Red food coloring (1 ounce bottle)
- Vanilla extract (1 teaspoon)
- Buttermilk (1 cup, room temperature)
- White vinegar (1 teaspoon)
- Baking soda (1 teaspoon)

For the Raspberry Filling:

- Fresh raspberries (1 cup)
- Sugar (1/4 cup)
- Water (1/4 cup)
- Cornstarch (1 tablespoon, dissolved in 2 tablespoons of water)

For the Cream Cheese Frosting:

- Cream cheese (8 ounces, softened)
- Unsalted butter (1/2 cup, softened)
- Powdered sugar (4 cups)
- Vanilla extract (1 teaspoon)

For the Raspberry Sauce (Blood Drizzle):

- Fresh raspberries (1 cup)
- Sugar (1/4 cup)
- Water (1/4 cup)

Instructions:

For the Red Velvet Cupcakes:

1. Preheat Your Oven:
- Preheat your oven to 350°F (175°C).
- Line a cupcake tin with cupcake liners.
2. Mix Dry Ingredients:
- In a mixing bowl, sift together the flour, cocoa powder, baking powder, baking soda, and salt. Set aside.
3. Cream Butter and Sugar:
- In a separate bowl, cream together the softened butter and granulated sugar until light and fluffy.
4. Add Eggs and Red Food Coloring:
- Beat in the eggs, one at a time.
- Stir in the red food coloring and vanilla extract until well combined.

5. Alternate Wet and Dry Ingredients:
- Gradually add the dry ingredients to the butter mixture, alternating with buttermilk, beginning and ending with the dry ingredients.
- In a small bowl, mix the white vinegar and baking soda until it fizzes, then quickly fold it into the batter.
6. Fill Cupcake Liners:
- Fill each cupcake liner about 2/3 full with the red velvet batter.
7. Bake:
- Bake in the preheated oven for 18-20 minutes or until a toothpick inserted into the center of a cupcake comes out clean.
- Allow the cupcakes to cool in the pan for a few minutes, then transfer them to a wire rack to cool completely.

For the Raspberry Filling:

1. Prepare Raspberry Sauce:
- In a saucepan, combine the fresh raspberries, sugar, and water.
- Cook over medium heat, stirring and mashing the raspberries until they break down and the mixture thickens (about 5-7 minutes).
- Add the cornstarch mixture to further thicken the sauce.
- Remove from heat and let it cool.

For the Cream Cheese Frosting:

1. Make Cream Cheese Frosting:
- In a mixing bowl, beat together the softened cream cheese, softened butter, powdered sugar, and vanilla extract until smooth and creamy.

Assemble the Cupcakes:

1. Fill with Raspberry Filling:
- Once the cupcakes are completely cool, use a cupcake corer or a knife to create a hole in the center of each cupcake.
- Fill each hole with raspberry filling.
2. Frost with Cream Cheese Frosting:
- Pipe or spread cream cheese frosting on top of each cupcake.

For the Raspberry Sauce (Blood Drizzle):

1. Prepare Raspberry Sauce:
- In a saucepan, combine the fresh raspberries, sugar, and water.
- Cook over medium heat, stirring and mashing the raspberries until they break down and the mixture thickens (about 5-7 minutes).
- Strain the sauce to remove seeds.
2. Drizzle Over Cupcakes:
- Drizzle the raspberry sauce over the frosted cupcakes to mimic dripping blood.

Your Vampire Blood Velvet Cupcakes are now ready to sink your teeth into! These deliciously eerie cupcakes are sure to be a hit at your Halloween gathering. Enjoy!

# *Mummy Rice Krispies Treats*

A fun and adorable Halloween treat that combines the classic Rice Krispies Treats with a spooky twist. These treats are wrapped in white chocolate and decorated with edible candy eyes to resemble cute mummies. Here's how to make them:

Ingredients:

- Rice Krispies cereal (6 cups)
- Mini marshmallows (10 ounces)
- Unsalted butter (3 tablespoons)
- White chocolate chips (12 ounces)
- Edible candy eyes
- Cooking spray or butter (for greasing)
- Black icing gel or melted chocolate (for decorating)

Instructions:

1. Prepare a 9x13-inch Baking Pan:

- Grease a 9x13-inch baking pan with cooking spray or butter, or line it with parchment paper, leaving an overhang on the sides for easy removal.

2. Make Rice Krispies Treats:

- In a large saucepan, melt the unsalted butter over low heat.

- Add the mini marshmallows to the melted butter and stir continuously until they are completely melted and the mixture is smooth.

- Remove the saucepan from the heat and quickly stir in the Rice Krispies cereal. Mix until the cereal is evenly coated with the marshmallow mixture.

3. Press into the Pan:

- Transfer the Rice Krispies mixture into the prepared baking pan.

- Use a buttered spatula or your hands (be careful, it's hot) to press the mixture firmly and evenly into the pan.

4. Cool and Cut:

- Allow the Rice Krispies mixture to cool and set in the pan for about 30 minutes.

5. Cut into Rectangles:

- Once the Rice Krispies treats have cooled, use a sharp knife to cut them into rectangular bars. You can make them as wide or narrow as you prefer.

6. Prepare the White Chocolate Coating:

- In a microwave-safe bowl or using a double boiler, melt the white chocolate chips until smooth and creamy. Be sure to follow the melting instructions on the chocolate chip package.

7. Dip in White Chocolate:

- Dip each Rice Krispies treat into the melted white chocolate, allowing any excess chocolate to drip off.

- Place the dipped treats on a parchment paper-lined tray.

8. Add Edible Candy Eyes:

- While the white chocolate coating is still wet, press edible candy eyes onto each treat. You can have fun arranging them to give the mummies different expressions.

9. Allow to Set:

- Allow the white chocolate to set and harden, which will take about 30 minutes at room temperature or less if you place them in the refrigerator.

10. Decorate with Icing Gel or Chocolate:

- Once the white chocolate has set, use black icing gel or melted chocolate to add mummy-like bandages across the treats. You can make them as messy or neat as you like for a fun look.

Your Mummy Rice Krispies Treats are now ready to enjoy! These cute and tasty treats are perfect for Halloween parties, and they're sure to bring a smile to everyone's face. Enjoy your spooky snack!

# Candy Corn Panna Cotta

A delightful dessert that captures the iconic candy corn colors of orange, yellow, and white in creamy panna cotta layers. Served in clear glasses, it creates a striking visual effect. Here's how to make it:

Ingredients:

For the Orange Layer:

- Heavy cream (1 cup)
- Granulated sugar (1/4 cup)
- Orange extract or orange zest (1 teaspoon)
- Orange gelatin powder (1 packet, about 3 ounces)
- Cold water (1/4 cup)
- Orange food coloring (a few drops, optional)

For the Yellow Layer:

- Heavy cream (1 cup)
- Granulated sugar (1/4 cup)
- Lemon extract or lemon zest (1 teaspoon)
- Lemon gelatin powder (1 packet, about 3 ounces)
- Cold water (1/4 cup)
- Yellow food coloring (a few drops, optional)

For the White Layer:

- Heavy cream (1 cup)
- Granulated sugar (1/4 cup)
- Vanilla extract (1 teaspoon)
- Unflavored gelatin powder (1 packet, about 2 1/4 teaspoons)
- Cold water (1/4 cup)

Instructions:

For the Orange Layer:

1. In a saucepan, combine the heavy cream and granulated sugar. Heat over medium-low heat, stirring until the sugar is completely dissolved. Do not let it boil.
2. Remove the saucepan from heat and stir in the orange extract or orange zest. Let it cool slightly.
3. In a separate small bowl, sprinkle the orange gelatin powder over the cold water. Allow it to bloom for a few minutes.
4. Add the bloomed gelatin mixture to the warm cream mixture and stir until the gelatin is fully dissolved. If desired, add a few drops of orange food coloring to achieve the desired color.
5. Carefully pour the orange panna cotta mixture into clear glasses, filling them about one-third full. Place the glasses in the refrigerator to set for about 30 minutes.

For the Yellow Layer:

1. Follow the same steps as the Orange Layer, substituting lemon extract or lemon zest for the flavor and yellow food coloring if desired.
2. Carefully pour the yellow panna cotta mixture on top of the set orange layer, filling the glasses another one-third full. Return the glasses to the refrigerator to set for about 30 minutes.

For the White Layer:

1. In a saucepan, combine the heavy cream and granulated sugar. Heat over medium-low heat, stirring until the sugar is completely dissolved. Do not let it boil.
2. Remove the saucepan from heat and stir in the vanilla extract. Let it cool slightly.
3. In a separate small bowl, sprinkle the unflavored gelatin powder over the cold water. Allow it to bloom for a few minutes.
4. Add the bloomed gelatin mixture to the warm cream mixture and stir until the gelatin is fully dissolved.
5. Carefully pour the white panna cotta mixture on top of the set yellow layer, filling the glasses to the top.
6. Place the glasses in the refrigerator and let the Candy Corn Panna Cotta layers set for at least 2 hours or until completely firm.
7. Once set, you can optionally garnish the panna cotta with whipped cream or candy corn pieces.

Your Candy Corn Panna Cotta is now ready to be served. The layers of creamy goodness in the iconic candy corn colors make it a perfect Halloween or fall dessert. Enjoy the visual delight and delicious taste!

# Poisoned Candy Apples

A spooky and sinister twist on the classic candy apple, perfect for a Snow White-inspired Halloween treat. These glossy black candy apples are coated in a shiny black candy shell. Here's how to make them:

Ingredients:

- • Apples (6-8, preferably Granny Smith or any variety you prefer)
- • Sugar (2 cups)
- • Water (1/2 cup)
- • Light corn syrup (1/2 cup)
- • Black food coloring (gel or paste)
- • Candy apple sticks or wooden popsicle sticks
- • Cooking spray (for greasing)

Instructions:

Prepare the Apples:

1. Wash and thoroughly dry the apples. Remove any wax coating by dipping them briefly in boiling water and then wiping them dry with a clean kitchen towel or paper towels. This will help the candy coating adhere better.

2. Insert candy apple sticks or wooden popsicle sticks into the top of each apple, making sure they are secure. Set aside.

Make the Candy Coating:

1. In a heavy-bottomed saucepan, combine sugar, water, and light corn syrup. Stir gently over medium heat until the sugar dissolves completely.

2. Once the sugar has dissolved, stop stirring and attach a candy thermometer to the side of the saucepan. Increase the heat to medium-high and bring the mixture to a boil. Continue boiling without stirring until it reaches the "hard crack" stage, which is around 300°F (149°C). This should take about 20-25 minutes.

3. Remove the saucepan from heat as soon as it reaches the desired temperature. Be cautious as the syrup is extremely hot.

Add Black Food Coloring:

1. Wearing gloves to protect your hands, add black food coloring to the hot sugar syrup and stir until the color is evenly distributed and reaches your desired shade of black.

Dip the Apples:

1. Working quickly, carefully dip each apple into the black candy coating, tilting and rotating the apple to ensure even coverage. Allow any excess syrup to drip back into the saucepan.

2. Place the coated apples onto a parchment paper-lined baking sheet or a silicone mat. Be cautious as the coating will be very hot.

Let the Coating Set:

1. Allow the Poisoned Candy Apples to cool and the candy coating to harden completely. This can take about 20-30 minutes.

Serve:

1. Once the candy coating has set and hardened, your Poisoned Candy Apples are ready to serve.

These sinister-looking candy apples are a wickedly fun Halloween treat, and they make a great addition to any spooky-themed party or event. Just be sure to warn your guests that they might be under a wicked spell! Enjoy!

# Spiderweb Cheesecake

A delightful and spooky dessert perfect for Halloween. It features a creamy cheesecake with a spiderweb design made from chocolate ganache on top, complete with a chocolate spider in the center. Here's how to make it:

Ingredients:

For the Cheesecake:

- Cream cheese (4 packages, 8 ounces each), softened
- Granulated sugar (1 cup)
- Sour cream (1 cup)
- Vanilla extract (1 teaspoon)
- Eggs (4)
- Graham cracker crumbs (1 1/2 cups)
- Unsalted butter (1/2 cup, melted)

For the Chocolate Ganache:

- Heavy cream (1/2 cup)
- Semi-sweet chocolate chips (1 cup)
- White chocolate chips (1/4 cup)

For the Chocolate Spider:

- Semi-sweet chocolate chips (1/4 cup)
- Candy eyes or small edible decorations (for spider eyes)
- Red gel food coloring (optional, for decorating)

Instructions:

For the Cheesecake:

1. Preheat your oven to 325°F (160°C). Grease a 9-inch springform pan with butter or cooking spray.
2. In a mixing bowl, combine the graham cracker crumbs and melted unsalted butter. Press the mixture firmly into the bottom of the prepared springform pan to create the crust.
3. In a large mixing bowl, beat the softened cream cheese until it's smooth and creamy.
4. Gradually add the granulated sugar and continue to beat until well combined.
5. Mix in the sour cream and vanilla extract until the mixture is smooth.
6. Add the eggs one at a time, mixing well after each addition.
7. Pour the cheesecake batter over the graham cracker crust in the springform pan.
8. Tap the pan on the counter a few times to remove any air bubbles.
9. Bake the cheesecake in the preheated oven for about 45-50 minutes or until the edges are set, and the center is slightly jiggly.
10. Turn off the oven, crack the oven door open, and let the cheesecake cool inside for about 1 hour.
11. Remove the cheesecake from the oven, run a knife around the edge to loosen it from the pan, and then refrigerate it for at least 4 hours or until completely chilled.

For the Chocolate Ganache:

1. In a microwave-safe bowl, heat the heavy cream until it's hot but not boiling, about 30 seconds in the microwave.
2. Add the semi-sweet chocolate chips to the hot cream and let it sit for a minute to soften. Then, stir until smooth and creamy.
3. Allow the ganache to cool slightly.

For the Chocolate Spider:

1. Melt the semi-sweet chocolate chips in a microwave-safe bowl until smooth. Be careful not to overheat it.
2. Place the melted chocolate into a piping bag or a small plastic sandwich bag with a tiny corner snipped off.
3. Pipe spider shapes onto a parchment paper-lined tray. You can make round bodies with eight legs.
4. While the chocolate is still wet, place small candy eyes or edible decorations on the spiders as eyes.
5. Allow the chocolate spiders to cool and harden.

Assembling the Spiderweb Cheesecake:

1. Once the cheesecake is completely chilled, carefully remove it from the springform pan.
2. Pour the slightly cooled chocolate ganache over the top of the cheesecake and use a spatula to create a spiderweb design.
3. Place one of the chocolate spiders in the center of the cheesecake.
4. Optionally, use red gel food coloring to create a spooky effect by adding a few red lines to the spiderweb.
5. Slice and serve your Spiderweb Cheesecake to delight your guests with this Halloween treat.

This Spiderweb Cheesecake is not only delicious but also a spooky showstopper that's sure to impress at your Halloween celebration. Enjoy your creamy, spiderweb-adorned dessert!

# Zombie Brain Gelatin

A delightfully gruesome yet tasty treat that's perfect for Halloween or themed parties. It features green-colored gelatin molded into brain shapes and served in a pool of raspberry syrup. Here's how to make it:

Ingredients:

For the Green Gelatin Brains:

- Lime-flavored gelatin mix (2 packages, 3 ounces each)
- Boiling water (2 cups)
- Cold water (2 cups)
- Red gel food coloring (optional)

For the Raspberry Syrup:

- Fresh or frozen raspberries (2 cups)
- Sugar (1/2 cup)
- Water (1/2 cup)
- Red gel food coloring (optional)

Brain Mold:

- Brain-shaped gelatin mold or silicone brain mold

Instructions:

For the Green Gelatin Brains:

1. In a large mixing bowl, empty the contents of the lime-flavored gelatin packages.
2. Pour 2 cups of boiling water over the gelatin mix and stir until completely dissolved.
3. Add 2 cups of cold water to the mixture and stir until well combined. If desired, add a few drops of red gel food coloring to achieve a realistic brain color. Stir until evenly colored.
4. Prepare your brain-shaped gelatin mold by lightly greasing it with cooking spray.
5. Carefully pour the green gelatin mixture into the brain mold.
6. Refrigerate the mold for at least 4 hours or until the gelatin is completely set.

For the Raspberry Syrup:

1. In a saucepan, combine the fresh or frozen raspberries, sugar, and water.
2. Heat the mixture over medium heat, stirring occasionally, until the raspberries break down and the syrup thickens, which should take about 10-15 minutes.
3. Use a fine-mesh strainer to strain the raspberry syrup into a bowl, removing any seeds.
4. If desired, add a few drops of red gel food coloring to intensify the color of the syrup. Stir until well combined.

Assembling Zombie Brain Gelatin:

1. Once the gelatin brains are set, carefully unmold them onto a serving platter.
2. Pour the raspberry syrup onto the platter around the gelatin brains, creating a gruesome "pool of blood" effect.
3. Serve your Zombie Brain Gelatin by slicing the brains and letting your guests enjoy the eerie and delicious treat.

These Zombie Brain Gelatin desserts are sure to be a hit at your Halloween or themed party, and they'll leave your guests marveling at your creative and spooky culinary skills! Enjoy the creepy but tasty brains!

# Caramel Apple Monsters

A fun and spooky treat that combines the sweetness of caramel-dipped apples with colorful candy eyes and monster faces made from candies and marshmallows. Here's how to make them:

Ingredients:

- Apples (6-8, preferably Granny Smith or any variety you prefer)
- Caramel candies (1 package, about 14 ounces)
- Candy eyes (large and small)
- Assorted colorful candies (such as M&M's, Skittles, or similar)
- Mini marshmallows
- Wooden popsicle sticks or candy apple sticks
- Cooking spray (for greasing)
- Wax paper or parchment paper

Optional Decoration:

- Colored icing or edible markers for drawing monster features

Instructions:

Prepare the Apples:

1. Wash and thoroughly dry the apples. Remove any wax coating by dipping them briefly in boiling water and then wiping them dry with a clean kitchen towel or paper towels. This will help the caramel adhere better.

2. Insert wooden popsicle sticks or candy apple sticks into the top of each apple, making sure they are secure. Set aside.

Melt the Caramel:

1. Unwrap the caramel candies and place them in a microwave-safe bowl.

2. Microwave the caramels in 30-second intervals, stirring in between, until they are completely melted and smooth. Be careful as the caramel can get very hot.

Dip the Apples:

1. Line a baking sheet or tray with wax paper or parchment paper and lightly grease it with cooking spray.

2. Hold an apple by the stick and dip it into the melted caramel, rotating and tilting to ensure an even coating.

3. Allow any excess caramel to drip back into the bowl, and then place the caramel-coated apple onto the prepared baking sheet.

Decorate the Monsters:

1. While the caramel is still warm, quickly attach candy eyes to create the monster's eyes. You can use large candy eyes for a whimsical look or a combination of large and small eyes for variety.

2. Use colorful candies, such as M&M's or Skittles, to create the monster's mouth, nose, and other facial features. Mini marshmallows can be used for teeth.

3. You can get creative with your monster designs, making each apple unique.

Let the Caramel Set:

1. Allow the caramel on the apples to cool and set for at least 30 minutes.

Optional Decoration:

1. If desired, use colored icing or edible markers to draw additional details on your caramel apple monsters, such as eyebrows, scars, or hair.

Serve:

1. Your Caramel Apple Monsters are now ready to serve. Enjoy these fun and spooky treats!

These Caramel Apple Monsters are a fantastic addition to Halloween parties or any festive occasion where you want to add a touch of whimsy and spookiness to your dessert table. Kids and adults alike will love creating and devouring these delightful monsters!

# Haunted House Gingerbread Cookies

Creating Haunted House Gingerbread Cookies is a delightful way to celebrate Halloween. These spooky gingerbread cookies are shaped like haunted houses and are adorned with intricate icing details and edible silver or black dust for a spooky finish. Here's how to make them:

Ingredients:

For the Gingerbread Cookies:

- All-purpose flour (3 cups)
- Ground ginger (1 tablespoon)
- Ground cinnamon (1 tablespoon)
- Baking soda (1 teaspoon)
- Salt (1/2 teaspoon)
- Unsalted butter (1 cup, softened)
- Brown sugar (1 cup, packed)
- Large egg
- Molasses (1/2 cup)
- Vanilla extract (1 teaspoon)

For the Royal Icing:

- Egg whites (2 large)
- Lemon juice (1 teaspoon)
- Powdered sugar (3 cups)
- Black or silver edible dust (for decoration)

Additional Supplies:

- Haunted house-shaped cookie cutter
- Piping bags with fine tips
- Edible black or silver gel food coloring (optional)

Instructions:

For the Gingerbread Cookies:

1. In a large mixing bowl, whisk together the flour, ground ginger, ground cinnamon, baking soda, and salt. Set aside.

2. In another mixing bowl, beat the softened unsalted butter and brown sugar together until creamy and smooth.

3. Add the large egg, molasses, and vanilla extract to the butter-sugar mixture. Mix until well combined.

4. Gradually add the dry ingredients to the wet ingredients, mixing until a smooth dough forms. If the dough is too sticky, you can add a little more flour.

5. Divide the dough into two portions, wrap each in plastic wrap, and refrigerate for at least 2 hours or until firm.

6. Preheat your oven to 350°F (175°C) and line baking sheets with parchment paper.

7. Roll out one portion of the chilled dough on a lightly floured surface to about 1/4-inch thickness.

8. Use the haunted house-shaped cookie cutter to cut out your haunted house shapes and place them on the prepared baking sheets.

9. Bake the cookies for 10-12 minutes or until they are lightly browned around the edges. Allow them to cool on the baking sheets for a few minutes before transferring them to a wire rack to cool completely.

10. Repeat the rolling and cutting process with the remaining dough.

For the Royal Icing:

1. In a clean mixing bowl, beat the egg whites and lemon juice until frothy.

2. Gradually add the powdered sugar, beating until the icing forms stiff peaks. If the icing is too thick, you can add a few drops of water to thin it out.

3. Optionally, add black or silver edible gel food coloring to achieve the desired color for your haunted house details.

4. Transfer the royal icing to piping bags with fine tips to create intricate designs on your gingerbread haunted houses.

Assembling the Haunted House Gingerbread Cookies:

1. Once the cookies are completely cooled, use the royal icing to decorate them with spooky details. You can create windows, doors, ghosts, bats, cobwebs, or any other hauntingly delightful decorations you like.

2. Sprinkle edible black or silver dust over the cookies to add a spooky finish.

3. Allow the royal icing to set before serving or packaging your Haunted House Gingerbread Cookies.

These spooky gingerbread cookies are not only delicious but also a fantastic creative outlet for your Halloween decorating skills. Whether you're making them for a Halloween party or as a fun family activity, they're sure to impress and delight everyone who sees and tastes them!

# Ghostly White Chocolate Truffles

Creating Ghostly White Chocolate Truffles is a delightful way to add a spooky touch to your Halloween dessert table. These creamy white chocolate truffles are shaped like ghosts and dusted with powdered sugar for a ghostly appearance. Here's how to make them:

Ingredients:

- White chocolate chips or white chocolate bars (8 ounces)
- Heavy cream (1/2 cup)
- Unsalted butter (2 tablespoons)
- Vanilla extract (1 teaspoon)
- Powdered sugar (for dusting)
- Edible candy eyes (small size)
- Black gel food coloring (optional, for ghostly eyes and mouths)

Instructions:

Prepare the White Chocolate Truffle Mixture:

1. Place the white chocolate chips or finely chopped white chocolate bars in a heatproof bowl.
2. In a saucepan, heat the heavy cream and unsalted butter over medium heat until it begins to simmer. Be careful not to let it boil.
3. Pour the hot cream mixture over the white chocolate. Allow it to sit for a minute to soften the chocolate.
4. Stir the mixture until the white chocolate is completely melted and smooth.
5. Add the vanilla extract and mix until well combined.
6. Cover the bowl with plastic wrap and refrigerate the mixture for at least 2 hours or until it firms up.

Shape the Ghostly Truffles:

1. Once the truffle mixture has chilled and is firm enough to handle, use a spoon or a small scoop to portion out small amounts of the mixture.
2. Roll each portion into a round ball between your palms to create ghostly truffle shapes. Place them on a baking sheet lined with parchment paper.
3. Gently flatten the bottom of each truffle to make them stand upright.
4. Insert edible candy eyes into each truffle to create the ghostly eyes. You can also use a toothpick dipped in black gel food coloring to draw mouths on the ghosts if desired.

Dust with Powdered Sugar:

1. Place a small amount of powdered sugar in a fine-mesh strainer or sieve.
2. Hold the strainer over the truffles and lightly tap it to dust the truffles with powdered sugar, giving them a ghostly appearance.

Chill and Serve:

1. Once you've dusted the truffles with powdered sugar, refrigerate them for another 30 minutes to set.
2. Your Ghostly White Chocolate Truffles are now ready to serve. Arrange them on a spooky-themed platter or serve them in small paper cupcake liners for a festive touch.

These Ghostly White Chocolate Truffles are not only delicious but also a fun and whimsical addition to your Halloween festivities. They're sure to delight both kids and adults alike, making them the perfect treat for Halloween parties or as a homemade gift for friends and family. Enjoy the spookiness!

# Thanksgiving and Christmas Classics

*As the air turns crisp and the calendar flips to the latter months of the year, a sense of warmth and nostalgia fills our hearts. It's a time when family and friends gather, when homes are adorned with festive decorations, and when the comforting aroma of beloved dishes wafts through the air. In this chapter of our cookbook, "Thanksgiving and Christmas Classics," we invite you to step into the world of timeless traditions and celebrate the heartwarming flavors of the holiday season*

# Main Dishes

# Spatchcocked Turkey

Spatchcocking a turkey and smoking or grilling it is a fantastic way to achieve a flavorful and evenly cooked bird. Here's a recipe for Spatchcock Turkey with an optional oven-roasting method and a delicious marinade injection:

Ingredients:

For the Marinade:

- Butter (1 cup, melted)
- Garlic cloves (4-6, minced)
- Fresh rosemary (2 tablespoons, chopped)
- Fresh thyme (2 tablespoons, chopped)
- Paprika (1 tablespoon)
- Salt (1 tablespoon)
- Black pepper (1 teaspoon)
- Lemon juice (2 tablespoons)
- Optional: Red pepper flakes for a touch of heat (adjust to your preference)
- Injector Syringe

For the Turkey:

- Whole turkey (12-14 pounds, thawed if frozen)
- Marinade (prepared as per the above ingredients)
- Cooking oil (for the grill grates or smoker rack)
- Wood chips or chunks for smoking (apple, cherry, or hickory work well)

Instructions:

Preparing the Marinade:

1. In a saucepan over medium heat, melt the butter.
2. Add minced garlic to the melted butter and sauté for about 1-2 minutes until fragrant.
3. Stir in the chopped fresh rosemary, thyme, paprika, salt, black pepper, lemon juice, and optional red pepper flakes. Combine well and let the marinade cool to room temperature.

Preparing the Turkey:

1. Ensure the turkey is completely thawed if previously frozen. Remove the giblets and neck from the turkey cavity.
2. Place the turkey on a clean and sturdy surface, breast-side down.
3. Use poultry shears or a sharp knife to cut along both sides of the turkey's backbone. Remove the backbone completely.
4. Flip the turkey over and press down firmly on the breastbone to flatten it. You should hear a cracking sound. This is called spatchcocking or butterflying the turkey.

5. Carefully lift the skin of the turkey over the breasts and thighs. Be gentle to avoid tearing the skin.
6. Inject the marinade evenly into the turkey meat under the skin, concentrating on the breasts and thighs. Use an injector or a basting syringe for this step.
7. Place the turkey in a large resealable plastic bag or a roasting pan. Pour any remaining marinade over the turkey. Seal the bag or cover the pan, and refrigerate for at least 4 hours or overnight, allowing the flavors to meld.

Smoking or Grilling the Turkey:

1. Preheat your smoker or grill to a temperature of 225-250°F (107-121°C). Use indirect heat if possible.
2. Add wood chips or chunks (soaked in water for about 30 minutes) to create smoke. Apple, cherry, or hickory wood works well with poultry.
3. Brush the grill grates or smoker rack with cooking oil to prevent sticking.
4. Place the marinated and spatchcocked turkey on the grill or smoker, breast-side up.
5. Close the lid and smoke or grill the turkey until it reaches an internal temperature of 165°F (74°C) in the thickest part of the thigh, typically about 3-4 hours, but cooking times may vary based on your grill or smoker and the size of the turkey.
6. During the cooking process, baste the turkey with any remaining marinade or melted butter every hour to keep it moist and flavorful.
7. Once the turkey reaches the desired temperature, remove it from the grill or smoker and let it rest for about 20-30 minutes before carving.

Optional Oven-Roasting Method:

1. Preheat your oven to 325°F (163°C).
2. Place the marinated and spatchcocked turkey on a roasting rack inside a roasting pan, breast-side up.
3. Roast in the preheated oven until the turkey reaches an internal temperature of 165°F (74°C) in the thickest part of the thigh, typically about 2.5-3 hours.
4. Baste the turkey with pan juices every 30 minutes to keep it moist and flavorful.
5. Once done, remove the turkey from the oven and let it rest for about 20-30 minutes before carving.
6. Carve and serve your delicious spatchcock turkey with your favorite sides.

Enjoy your flavorful and tender spatchcock turkey, whether it's smoked, grilled, or roasted in the oven. It's sure to be a hit at your next gathering or holiday feast!

# Deep Fried Turkey

Deep-frying a turkey results in a crispy, golden-brown skin and tender, juicy meat. Here's a recipe for deep-frying a turkey:

Ingredients:

- Whole turkey (10-15 pounds)
- Cooking oil (peanut oil is recommended, enough to submerge the turkey)
- Turkey injection marinade (optional, for flavor)
- Dry rub or seasoning mix (optional, for additional flavor)
- Equipment: Turkey fryer kit (including a propane burner, large pot, and thermometer), fire extinguisher, and turkey stand

Instructions:

1. Safety First:

- Safety is paramount when deep-frying a turkey. Set up your turkey fryer outdoors on a flat, non-flammable surface, away from any structures, and keep a fire extinguisher nearby.

2. 2. Prepare the Turkey:

- • Make sure the turkey is completely thawed and dry both inside and out. Any moisture can cause the hot oil to splatter.

3. Inject the Marinade (Optional):

- Using a turkey injector, inject your choice of marinade into various parts of the turkey to add flavor. Be cautious not to over-inject, as it can cause the skin to rupture.

4. Season the Turkey (Optional):

- Rub the turkey with your favorite dry rub or seasoning mix for added flavor. Ensure the turkey is evenly coated.

5. Heat the Oil:

- Place the large pot on the propane burner and add enough cooking oil to submerge the turkey completely. Heat the oil to 350°F (175°C). Use a thermometer to monitor the oil temperature.

6. Prepare the Turkey Stand:

- Attach the turkey stand to the turkey, making sure it's secure. The stand will help you lower and raise the turkey into the hot oil.

7. Lower the Turkey into the Oil:

- With the burner off, carefully lower the turkey into the hot oil using the turkey stand. Be slow and cautious to avoid splatters. Wear heavy-duty oven mitts and safety goggles for protection.

8. Fry the Turkey:

- Turn the burner back on and maintain the oil temperature at 350°F (175°C). Fry the turkey for about 3-4 minutes per pound. Use a turkey frying calculator to determine the exact frying time based on the turkey's weight.

9. Check the Internal Temperature:

- Use a meat thermometer to check the internal temperature of the turkey. The turkey is done when it reaches 165°F (74°C) in the thickest part of the thigh and the juices run clear.

10. Carefully Remove the Turkey:

- Turn off the burner and carefully lift the turkey out of the hot oil using the turkey stand. Allow the excess oil to drain back into the pot.

11. Let the Turkey Rest:

- Place the fried turkey on a clean surface lined with paper towels to absorb any remaining oil. Allow it to rest for at least 20-30 minutes before carving.

12. Carve and Serve:

- Carve the deep-fried turkey and serve it with your favorite side dishes.

Deep-frying a turkey can be a delicious and impressive way to prepare this holiday classic. Remember to follow safety precautions and be cautious when handling hot oil to ensure a safe and enjoyable cooking experience. Enjoy your crispy and juicy deep-fried turkey!

# Traditional Roasted Turkey

A traditional roasted turkey is a classic centerpiece for holiday feasts. Here's a simple recipe for roasting a turkey to perfection:

Ingredients:

- Whole turkey (12-15 pounds)
- Unsalted butter (1/2 cup, softened)
- Salt (1 tablespoon)
- Black pepper (1 teaspoon)
- Fresh herbs (rosemary, thyme, and sage, a few sprigs of each)
- Onion (1, quartered)
- Carrots (2-3, cut into chunks)
- Celery (2-3 stalks, cut into chunks)
- Garlic cloves (4-6, peeled)
- Chicken or turkey broth (2 cups)
- Cooking twine

Instructions:

1. Prep the Turkey:

- Preheat your oven to 325°F (163°C).
- Remove the turkey from its packaging and rinse it inside and out under cold running water. Pat it dry with paper towels.

2. Season the Turkey:

- In a small bowl, mix the softened butter, salt, and black pepper to create a seasoned butter mixture.
- Gently separate the skin from the turkey breast by sliding your fingers between the skin and meat. Be careful not to tear the skin.
- Rub the seasoned butter mixture under the turkey's skin, covering the breast meat.
- Season the cavity of the turkey with salt and pepper.

3. Add Aromatics:

- Place a few sprigs of fresh herbs (rosemary, thyme, sage), quartered onion, garlic cloves, carrots, and celery inside the turkey cavity. These aromatics will infuse flavor during roasting.

4. 4. Truss the Turkey (Optional):

- • Trussing helps the turkey cook evenly and maintain its shape. Use cooking twine to tie the legs together and secure the wings close to the body.

5. Roasting the Turkey:

- Place the turkey on a roasting rack inside a roasting pan, breast-side up.
- Pour the chicken or turkey broth into the bottom of the roasting pan. This will keep the turkey moist and flavorful.

- Cover the turkey loosely with aluminum foil to prevent the skin from getting too brown too quickly.
- Roast the turkey in the preheated oven. Calculate the cooking time based on the turkey's weight, allowing roughly 13-15 minutes per pound. A 12-15 pound turkey will take about 3-4 hours.

6. Baste the Turkey:

- Every 30 minutes, remove the foil and use a baster to drizzle the pan juices over the turkey. This helps keep the meat moist and adds flavor.

7. Check the Temperature:

- After about 3 hours of roasting, start checking the turkey's internal temperature using a meat thermometer. The turkey is done when the thickest part of the thigh reaches 165°F (74°C) and the juices run clear.

8. Rest the Turkey:

- Once the turkey reaches the desired temperature, remove it from the oven and tent it loosely with aluminum foil. Allow it to rest for at least 20-30 minutes. Resting allows the juices to redistribute, resulting in a juicier turkey.

9. Carve and Serve:

- Carve the roasted turkey and arrange it on a platter. Serve with your favorite side dishes and gravy made from the pan drippings.

Enjoy your traditional roasted turkey as the centerpiece of a delicious holiday meal!

# Smoked Prime Rib

Smoked prime rib, also known as a standing rib roast, is a flavorful and impressive dish for special occasions. Here's a recipe for smoking prime rib to perfection:

Ingredients:

- Prime rib roast (bone-in or boneless, 4-6 pounds)
- Olive oil (2-3 tablespoons)
- Kosher salt (2-3 tablespoons)
- Black pepper (1-2 tablespoons)
- Garlic powder (1-2 teaspoons)
- Onion powder (1-2 teaspoons)
- Fresh rosemary sprigs (3-4)
- Cherry or oak wood chunks or chips (for smoking)

Instructions:

1. Prepare the Prime Rib:

- Remove the prime rib from the refrigerator and let it sit at room temperature for about 1-2 hours before smoking. This allows for even cooking.
- Trim any excess fat from the surface of the meat, leaving a thin layer for flavor.

2. Season the Prime Rib:

- Preheat your smoker to 225°F (107°C) using your choice of wood chunks or chips (cherry or oak are great options). The smoking wood should be soaked in water for about 30 minutes before use.
- In a small bowl, mix the kosher salt, black pepper, garlic powder, and onion powder to create a rub.
- Rub the olive oil over the entire surface of the prime rib roast.
- Apply the spice rub generously to the prime rib, covering all sides. Be sure to press the rub into the meat to adhere.

3. Smoke the Prime Rib:

- Place the seasoned prime rib roast on the smoker's cooking grate, fat side up. Add the fresh rosemary sprigs on top of the meat.
- Smoke the prime rib at 225°F (107°C) for about 30-40 minutes per pound, or until it reaches your desired level of doneness. Use a meat thermometer to monitor the internal temperature. Aim for 120-125°F (49-52°C) for rare, 130-135°F (54-57°C) for medium-rare, and adjust accordingly.

4. Rest the Prime Rib:

- Once the prime rib reaches your desired temperature, remove it from the smoker and tent it loosely with aluminum foil. Allow it to rest for at least 20-30 minutes. This resting period allows the juices to redistribute, resulting in a juicy and tender roast.

5. Carve and Serve:

- After resting, carve the smoked prime rib into thick slices. Serve it with your favorite side dishes and au jus or horseradish sauce.

Smoked prime rib is a decadent and flavorful dish that's perfect for holiday feasts and special occasions. Enjoy the rich smoky flavor and tender meat with your family and friends!

# Roasted Prime Rib

Roasting prime rib in the oven is a classic and delicious way to prepare this special cut of meat. Here's a recipe for oven--roasted prime rib:

Ingredients:

- Prime rib roast (bone-in or boneless, 4-6 pounds)
- Olive oil (2-3 tablespoons)
- Kosher salt (2-3 tablespoons)
- Black pepper (1-2 tablespoons)
- Garlic powder (1-2 teaspoons)
- Onion powder (1-2 teaspoons)
- Fresh rosemary sprigs (3-4)
- Meat thermometer

Instructions:

1. Prepare the Prime Rib:
- Remove the prime rib roast from the refrigerator and let it sit at room temperature for about 1-2 hours before roasting. This ensures even cooking.

2. Preheat the Oven:
- Preheat your oven to 450°F (232°C). A high initial temperature will help create a flavorful crust on the prime rib.

3. Season the Prime Rib:
- In a small bowl, mix the kosher salt, black pepper, garlic powder, and onion powder to create a seasoning rub.
- Rub the olive oil over the entire surface of the prime rib roast.
- Generously coat the roast with the seasoning rub, making sure to cover all sides. Press the rub into the meat to adhere.

4. Roast at High Heat:
- Place the seasoned prime rib roast on a roasting rack inside a roasting pan, bone side down.
- Insert a meat thermometer into the thickest part of the meat without touching the bone.
- Roast the prime rib at 450°F (232°C) for about 15-20 minutes to sear the exterior and create a crust.

5. Reduce the Heat:
- After the initial searing, reduce the oven temperature to 325°F (163°C). This lower temperature will allow for slower, even cooking.

6. Continue Roasting:
- Continue roasting the prime rib for about 13-15 minutes per pound. Use the meat thermometer to monitor the internal temperature. Aim for 120-125°F (49-52°C) for rare, 130-135°F (54-57°C) for medium--rare, and adjust accordingly.

7. Rest the Prime Rib:
- Once the prime rib reaches your desired level of doneness, remove it from the oven and tent it loosely with aluminum foil. Allow it to rest for at least 20-30 minutes. Resting allows the juices to redistribute, resulting in a juicy and tender roast.

8. Carve and Serve:
- After resting, carve the oven-roasted prime rib into thick slices. Serve it with your favorite side dishes and au jus or horseradish sauce.

Oven-roasted prime rib is a classic and elegant choice for special occasions. Enjoy the flavorful crust and tender, juicy meat with your loved ones!

# Baked Ham

Baked ham is a delightful dish that's perfect for special occasions and holidays. Here's a classic recipe for baked ham:

Ingredients:

- Bone-in ham (8-10 pounds)
- Whole cloves (for scoring, optional)
- Brown sugar (1 cup)
- Dijon mustard (1/4 cup)
- Maple syrup (1/4 cup)
- Pineapple juice (1/4 cup)
- Apple cider vinegar (2 tablespoons)
- Ground cloves (1/2 teaspoon, optional)

Instructions:

1. Preheat the Oven:
- Preheat your oven to 325°F (163°C).

2. Prepare the Ham:
- Place the ham in a large roasting pan, fat side up. If desired, score the surface of the ham in a diamond pattern and insert whole cloves into the intersections.

3. Create the Glaze:
- In a mixing bowl, combine the brown sugar, Dijon mustard, maple syrup, pineapple juice, apple cider vinegar, and ground cloves (if using). Mix until well combined.

4. Apply the Glaze:
- Brush the glaze generously over the surface of the ham, making sure to coat it evenly.

5. Cover and Bake:
- Cover the ham with aluminum foil to prevent excessive browning during the initial part of cooking.
- Bake the ham in the preheated oven for approximately 15-20 minutes per pound. Use a meat thermometer to monitor the internal temperature. The ham is done when it reaches an internal temperature of 140°F (60°C).

6. Baste:
- Every 30 minutes or so, baste the ham with the pan juices to keep it moist and flavorful.

7. Uncover and Caramelize:
- In the last 30 minutes of cooking, remove the foil to allow the ham to caramelize and develop a beautiful glaze. You can baste it once more during this time.

8. Rest and Carve:
- Once the ham reaches 140°F (60°C) and has a nice caramelized exterior, remove it from the oven.
- Allow the ham to rest for about 15-20 minutes before carving. This resting period allows the juices to redistribute, resulting in a juicy and tender ham.

9. Carve and Serve:
- Carve the baked ham into slices and serve it with your favorite sides and any remaining glaze as a drizzle.

Baked ham is a classic and savory dish that's sure to impress your guests at any gathering or holiday meal. Enjoy!

# Sides

# Traditional Stuffing

Ingredients:

- 12 cups cubed stale bread (white or wheat)
- 1 cup unsalted butter
- 2 cups diced onion
- 2 cups diced celery
- 1/4 cup chopped fresh parsley
- 2 teaspoons dried sage
- 2 teaspoons dried thyme
- 1 teaspoon dried rosemary
- 1 teaspoon dried marjoram
- 1/2 teaspoon salt (adjust to taste)
- 1/2 teaspoon black pepper (adjust to taste)
- 2-3 cups low-sodium chicken or vegetable broth
- 2 large eggs, beaten (optional, for binding)
- Cooking spray or additional butter for greasing

Instructions:

1. Prepare the Bread:

- Preheat your oven to 250°F (120°C) to dry out the bread cubes. Spread the cubed stale bread on baking sheets in a single layer. Bake for about 45 minutes, turning the cubes occasionally until they are dry but not browned. Alternatively, you can leave the bread cubes out to stale for a day or two.

2. Sauté Vegetables:

- In a large skillet or frying pan, melt the butter over medium heat. Add the diced onions and celery. Sauté for about 5-7 minutes, or until the vegetables are softened.

3. Season:

- Stir in the chopped fresh parsley, dried sage, dried thyme, dried rosemary, dried marjoram, salt, and black pepper. Cook for an additional 2-3 minutes until fragrant. Remove from heat.

4. Combine Bread and Vegetable Mixture:

- In a large mixing bowl, combine the dried bread cubes with the sautéed vegetable and herb mixture. Toss everything together until well mixed.

5. Add Broth:

- Gradually pour in the chicken or vegetable broth, starting with 2 cups. The amount of broth needed may vary depending on how dry your bread is. You want the stuffing to be moist but not soggy. Mix well, ensuring the bread is evenly coated. Add more broth if needed.

6. Bind with Eggs (Optional):

- If you prefer a firmer stuffing, you can beat the eggs and mix them into the stuffing at this point.

7. Bake:

- Transfer the stuffing mixture to a greased 9x13-inch baking dish or a casserole dish. Cover with aluminum foil.
- Bake in a preheated oven at 350°F (175°C) for 30 minutes. Then, remove the foil and bake for an additional 15-20 minutes, or until the top is golden brown and crispy.

8. Serve:

- Remove from the oven and let it cool for a few minutes before serving. Garnish with additional fresh parsley if desired.

9. Enjoy:

- Serve this classic Thanksgiving stuffing as a delicious side dish alongside your turkey and other holiday favorites.

This traditional stuffing is flavorful, aromatic, and the perfect complement to your Thanksgiving feast.

# Stuffing with Italian Sausage

Sausage and cashew stuffing is a flavorful and hearty side dish that's perfect for Thanksgiving or any festive meal. Here's a traditional recipe:

Ingredients:

- 1 pound mild pork sausage
- 1 cup unsalted cashews
- 8 cups day-old white bread cubes (about 1-inch pieces)
- 1 large onion, chopped
- 2 celery stalks, chopped
- 4 cloves garlic, minced
- 1/2 cup unsalted butter
- 2 teaspoons dried sage
- 1 teaspoon dried thyme
- 1/2 teaspoon dried rosemary
- 1/2 teaspoon dried parsley
- Salt and black pepper to taste
- 2-3 cups chicken or turkey broth (adjust for desired moisture)
- Fresh parsley for garnish (optional)

Instructions:

1. Cook the Sausage:

- In a large skillet over medium heat, cook the pork sausage until browned and crumbled. Remove the sausage from the skillet and set it aside.

2. Toast the Cashews:

- In the same skillet, add the unsalted cashews and toast them over medium heat until they are lightly golden. Remove the cashews and set them aside.

3. Sauté Vegetables:

- In the same skillet, melt the unsalted butter. Add the chopped onion, celery, and minced garlic. Sauté until the vegetables are softened, about 5-7 minutes.

4. Add Herbs and Spices:

- Stir in the dried sage, dried thyme, dried rosemary, dried parsley, salt, and black pepper. Cook for an additional 1-2 minutes to release the flavors.

5. Combine Ingredients:

- In a large mixing bowl, combine the cooked sausage, toasted cashews, sautéed vegetable mixture, and bread cubes. Toss everything together until well mixed.

6. Moisten with Broth:

- Gradually pour the chicken or turkey broth over the mixture. Start with 2 cups and add more if needed to reach your desired level of moisture. The mixture should be moist but not overly soggy.

7. Bake:

- Transfer the stuffing mixture to a greased baking dish. Cover the dish with aluminum foil.
- Bake in a preheated oven at 350°F (175°C) for 25-30 minutes.

8. Uncover and Brown:

- Remove the foil and continue baking for an additional 15-20 minutes or until the top is golden brown and crispy.

9. Garnish and Serve:

- If desired, garnish the sausage and cashew stuffing with fresh parsley before serving.

This savory and nutty stuffing is a delightful addition to your holiday feast. Enjoy it alongside roasted turkey or your favorite main dishes!

# Traditional Mashed Potatoes

Traditional mashed potatoes are a classic side dish that pairs well with many meals. Here's a simple recipe for creamy and delicious mashed potatoes:

Ingredients:

- 4 large russet potatoes
- 1/2 cup unsalted butter
- 1/2 cup milk (or more for desired consistency)
- Salt, to taste
- Black pepper, to taste
- Optional garnish: chopped fresh parsley or chives

Instructions:

1. Prepare the Potatoes:

- Peel the russet potatoes and cut them into evenly sized chunks. This ensures that they cook evenly.

2. Boil the Potatoes:

- Place the potato chunks in a large pot and cover them with cold water. Add a generous pinch of salt to the water.
- Bring the water to a boil over high heat, then reduce the heat to medium and let the potatoes simmer for about 15-20 minutes or until they are tender when pierced with a fork.

3. Drain the Potatoes:

- Once the potatoes are tender, drain them in a colander.

4. Mash the Potatoes:

- Return the drained potatoes to the pot. Use a potato masher or a potato ricer to mash the potatoes until they are smooth and free of lumps.

5. Add Butter:

- Cut the unsalted butter into small pieces and add it to the mashed potatoes. Stir until the butter is completely melted and incorporated.

6. Add Milk:

- Pour in the milk and continue to stir. Add more milk if needed to achieve your desired creamy consistency.

7. Season:

- Season the mashed potatoes with salt and black pepper to taste. Adjust the seasoning to your preference.

8. Serve:

- Transfer the creamy mashed potatoes to a serving bowl. If desired, garnish with chopped fresh parsley or chives for a pop of color and flavor.

9. Enjoy:

- Serve the traditional mashed potatoes hot alongside your favorite main dishes, such as roast chicken, turkey, or beef.

These creamy and buttery mashed potatoes are a comforting classic that complements a wide range of meals. Enjoy the simple goodness of homemade mashed potatoes!

# Baked Macaroni and Cheese

Baked macaroni and cheese is a classic comfort dish loved by many. Here's a delicious recipe to prepare it:

Ingredients:

- 2 cups elbow macaroni
- 4 cups shredded sharp cheddar cheese
- 1/2 cup grated Parmesan cheese
- 3 cups milk
- 1/4 cup butter
- 2 1/2 cups shredded mozzarella cheese
- 2 1/2 cups breadcrumbs
- 2 teaspoons salt
- 1/2 teaspoon black pepper
- 1/2 teaspoon paprika
- 1/2 teaspoon garlic powder
- 1/4 teaspoon nutmeg (optional)
- 2 tablespoons all-purpose flour
- Cooking spray (for greasing the baking dish)

Instructions:

1. Cook the Macaroni:

- Preheat your oven to 350°F (175°C). Grease a 9x13-inch baking dish with cooking spray.

- Bring a large pot of salted water to a boil. Add the elbow macaroni and cook until just al dente (slightly undercooked). Drain and set aside.

2. Make the Cheese Sauce:

- In a large saucepan, melt the butter over medium heat. Stir in the flour to create a roux, and cook for about 1-2 minutes until it turns a light golden color.

- Slowly whisk in the milk to the roux, making sure to whisk out any lumps. Continue to cook and stir until the sauce thickens, about 3-5 minutes.

- Reduce the heat to low, then add the shredded sharp cheddar cheese, grated Parmesan cheese, salt, black pepper, paprika, garlic powder, and nutmeg (if using). Stir until the cheeses are melted, and the sauce is smooth and creamy.

3. 3. Combine with Macaroni:

- • Add the cooked elbow macaroni to the cheese sauce and stir to coat the pasta evenly with the cheesy mixture.

4. Layer in Baking Dish:

- Transfer half of the macaroni and cheese mixture into the greased baking dish. Sprinkle with half of the shredded mozzarella cheese. Repeat with the remaining macaroni and cheese, and top with the rest of the mozzarella cheese.

5. Prepare Breadcrumb Topping:

- In a small bowl, combine the breadcrumbs with a little melted butter to moisten them. Sprinkle the breadcrumb mixture evenly over the top of the macaroni and cheese.

6. Bake:

- Place the baking dish in the preheated oven and bake for about 30-35 minutes or until the top is golden brown and the cheese is bubbling.

7. Serve:

- Remove the baked macaroni and cheese from the oven and let it cool for a few minutes before serving. Scoop out servings and enjoy this deliciously creamy and cheesy comfort food.

Baked macaroni and cheese is a crowd-pleaser and a perfect dish for a Holiday side. Enjoy its rich, cheesy goodness!

# Slow Cooker Green Bean Casserole

Using a slow cooker to make a traditional green bean casserole is not only convenient but also frees up oven space, making it perfect for holiday gatherings. Here's a recipe:

Ingredients:

- 2 cans (14.5 ounces each) of French-cut green beans, drained
- 1 can (10.5 ounces) of condensed cream of mushroom soup
- 1/2 cup milk
- 1 cup crispy fried onions (reserve some for topping)
- 1/2 cup shredded cheddar cheese (optional)
- Salt and black pepper, to taste

Instructions:

1. Prepare the Slow Cooker:

- Grease the inside of your slow cooker with cooking spray or a small amount of butter to prevent sticking.

2. Combine Ingredients:

- In a mixing bowl, combine the drained French-cut green beans, condensed cream of mushroom soup, milk, shredded cheddar cheese (if using), and half of the crispy fried onions. Stir until all the ingredients are well combined.

3. Season:

- Season the mixture with salt and black pepper to taste. Be mindful of the salt, as the condensed soup and fried onions are already salted.

4. Transfer to the Slow Cooker:

- Pour the green bean mixture into the prepared slow cooker.

5. Cook:

- Cover the slow cooker and set it to LOW. Cook the green bean casserole for 3-4 hours. It's important to use the LOW setting to prevent overcooking and ensure a creamy texture.

6. Top with Onions:

- About 30 minutes before serving, sprinkle the remaining crispy fried onions over the top of the casserole.

7. Serve and Keep Warm:

- Once the casserole is heated through and the onions on top are crispy and golden, it's ready to serve. The slow cooker will keep it warm, making it convenient for serving during your meal.

8. Enjoy:

- Spoon out servings of the green bean casserole and enjoy this classic side dish with your holiday feast.

By using a slow cooker for your traditional green bean casserole, you not only save oven space but also ensure that the dish stays warm and ready to serve throughout your meal. It's a convenient and delicious addition to any holiday gathering.

# *Roasted Green Beans*

Roasted green beans with almond slivers make for a delightful and nutritious side dish. Here's a simple recipe to prepare them:

Ingredients:

- 1 pound fresh green beans, trimmed
- 2 tablespoons olive oil
- 1/4 cup almond slivers
- 2 cloves garlic, minced
- Salt and black pepper, to taste
- Zest of 1 lemon (optional)
- Lemon wedges for serving (optional)

Instructions:

1. Preheat the Oven:
- Preheat your oven to 425°F (220°C). This high temperature will help roast the green beans quickly, giving them a nice crisp texture.

2. Prepare the Green Beans:
- Wash and thoroughly dry the green beans. Trim the ends if necessary.

3. Toss with Olive Oil:
- In a large bowl, toss the green beans with the olive oil until they are evenly coated.

4. Season:
- Sprinkle the minced garlic over the green beans and toss to distribute it evenly. Season the green beans with salt and black pepper to taste.

5. Arrange on a Baking Sheet:
- Spread the seasoned green beans in a single layer on a baking sheet. This allows them to roast evenly.

6. Roast in the Oven:
- Place the baking sheet in the preheated oven and roast the green beans for 12-15 minutes or until they are tender and slightly browned, but still crisp.

7. Toast the Almond Slivers:
- While the green beans are roasting, heat a dry skillet over medium heat. Add the almond slivers and toast them, stirring frequently, until they turn golden brown. This should take about 3-5 minutes. Be careful not to burn them.

8. Combine Green Beans and Almonds:
- Once the green beans are done roasting, remove them from the oven and transfer them to a serving platter. Sprinkle the toasted almond slivers over the top of the green beans.

9. Optional Lemon Zest:
- For a burst of fresh flavor, you can sprinkle lemon zest over the green beans and almonds. It adds a delightful citrusy aroma and taste.

10. Serve:
- Serve the roasted green beans with almond slivers immediately as a side dish. You can also garnish with lemon wedges for an extra zing.

These roasted green beans with almond slivers are a tasty and elegant addition to any meal. They pair wonderfully with roasted meats, poultry, or as a standalone side dish for a vegetarian or vegan feast. Enjoy!

# Roasted Root Vegetables

Roasted root vegetables are a delicious and hearty side dish. You can use a variety of root vegetables, such as carrots, potatoes, parsnips, and beets, to create a colorful and flavorful dish. Here's a basic recipe:

Ingredients:

- 4 cups of mixed root vegetables (carrots, potatoes, parsnips, beets, etc.),
- peeled and cut into bite-sized pieces
- 2 tablespoons olive oil
- 2 cloves garlic, minced
- 1 teaspoon fresh rosemary (or other herbs of your choice), chopped
- Salt and pepper, to taste

Instructions:

1. Preheat the Oven:

- Preheat your oven to 425°F (220°C).

2. Prepare the Vegetables:

- Wash, peel, and cut the root vegetables into uniform bite-sized pieces. This ensures even cooking.

3. Season the Vegetables:

- In a large mixing bowl, combine the root vegetables, olive oil, minced garlic, chopped rosemary (or other herbs), salt, and pepper. Toss everything together until the vegetables are evenly coated with the oil and seasonings.

4. Arrange on a Baking Sheet:

- Spread the seasoned vegetables out in a single layer on a baking sheet. You can line the sheet with parchment paper for easier cleanup if desired.

5. Roast in the Oven:

- Place the baking sheet in the preheated oven and roast the root vegetables for about 30-40 minutes or until they are tender and golden brown. Stir the vegetables halfway through the cooking time to ensure even roasting.

6. Serve:

- Once the vegetables are roasted to your liking, remove them from the oven. Transfer them to a serving dish and garnish with fresh herbs if desired.

7. Enjoy:

Serve the roasted root vegetables as a delightful side dish to complement your main course.

Variations:

- Feel free to customize your roasted root vegetables by adding other seasonings or ingredients like balsamic vinegar, honey, thyme, or grated Parmesan cheese.
- You can also mix and match different types of root vegetables to create a colorful and diverse dish.

Roasted root vegetables are not only delicious but also a versatile side dish that pairs well with various meals. Enjoy their natural sweetness and earthy flavors in this simple and satisfying recipe.

# Creamed Spinach

Creamed spinach is a classic side dish known for its creamy, flavorful sauce. Here's a recipe to prepare it:

Ingredients:

- 1 pound fresh spinach, washed and trimmed
- 2 tablespoons butter
- 2 cloves garlic, minced
- 2 tablespoons all-purpose flour
- 1 cup milk (whole or 2%)
- 1/4 cup heavy cream
- 1/4 cup grated Parmesan cheese
- Salt and black pepper, to taste
- A pinch of ground nutmeg (optional)

Instructions:

1. Prepare the Spinach:

- Wash the fresh spinach thoroughly to remove any dirt or grit. Trim any tough stems. You can also use pre-washed baby spinach for convenience.

2. Blanch the Spinach:

- Bring a large pot of water to a boil. Add the spinach and blanch it for about 1-2 minutes until it wilts. Immediately transfer the wilted spinach to a bowl of ice water to stop the cooking process. Drain and squeeze out excess water from the spinach using a clean kitchen towel. Chop the blanched spinach roughly.

3. Make the Cream Sauce:

- In a large skillet or saucepan, melt the butter over medium heat. Add the minced garlic and sauté for about 1 minute until fragrant but not browned.
- Sprinkle the flour over the melted butter and garlic, and whisk continuously for 1-2 minutes to create a roux (a thickening agent).
- Gradually pour in the milk while whisking to prevent lumps. Continue to cook and whisk until the sauce thickens, which should take about 3-5 minutes.
- Reduce the heat to low, then stir in the heavy cream, grated Parmesan cheese, salt, black pepper, and a pinch of ground nutmeg (if using). Continue to stir until the cheese is melted and the sauce is smooth and creamy.

4. Add the Spinach:

- Add the chopped, blanched spinach to the cream sauce. Stir well to combine and coat the spinach with the creamy mixture.

5. Simmer:

- Allow the creamed spinach to simmer on low heat for an additional 5-7 minutes, stirring occasionally, to heat the spinach thoroughly and meld the flavors.

6. Serve:

- Once the creamed spinach is heated through and has reached your desired consistency, remove it from the heat. Taste and adjust the seasoning if needed.
- Transfer the creamed spinach to a serving dish and serve hot as a delectable side dish.

Creamed spinach is a classic accompaniment to many meals and adds a delightful touch of creamy goodness to your dinner table. Enjoy!

# Sweet Potato Casserole

Sweet Potato Casserole is a beloved side dish, especially during the holidays. Here's a delightful recipe to make this comforting dish:

Ingredients:

For the Sweet Potato Filling:

- 4 cups mashed sweet potatoes (about 3-4 medium sweet potatoes, cooked
- and peeled)
- 1/2 cup brown sugar, packed
- 1/4 cup unsalted butter, melted
- 2 large eggs
- 1/2 cup milk
- 1 teaspoon vanilla extract
- 1/2 teaspoon ground cinnamon
- 1/4 teaspoon ground nutmeg
- 1/4 teaspoon salt

For the Topping:

- 1 cup mini marshmallows OR 1 cup chopped pecans (choose one, or use half of each for a combination)

Instructions:

1. Preheat the Oven:

- Preheat your oven to 350°F (175°C). Grease a 9x13-inch baking dish.

2. Prepare the Sweet Potatoes:

- Peel the sweet potatoes, chop them into chunks, and boil or steam them until they are tender. Drain and mash them in a large bowl until smooth.

3. Make the Sweet Potato Filling:

- To the mashed sweet potatoes, add the brown sugar, melted butter, eggs, milk, vanilla extract, ground cinnamon, ground nutmeg, and salt. Stir until all the ingredients are well combined and the mixture is smooth.

4. Transfer to Baking Dish:

- Transfer the sweet potato mixture to the greased 9x13-inch baking dish, spreading it out evenly.

5. Add Topping:

- Choose either mini marshmallows or chopped pecans for your topping (or use a combination). If using marshmallows, spread them evenly over the sweet potato mixture. If using pecans, sprinkle them over the top.

6. Bake:

- Place the baking dish in the preheated oven and bake for about 25-30 minutes, or until the casserole is heated through, and the marshmallows are golden brown and gooey (if using marshmallows) or the pecans are toasted.

7. Serve:

- Remove the sweet potato casserole from the oven and let it cool for a few minutes before serving. The marshmallows will be melty, and the pecans will add a delightful crunch.

8. Enjoy:

- Serve this delicious Sweet Potato Casserole as a side dish for your holiday feast or any special meal. It's sure to be a crowd-pleaser!

This Sweet Potato Casserole is the perfect combination of creamy, sweet, and slightly crunchy, making it a delightful addition to any dinner table.

# Baked Yams

Baked yams, also known as sweet potatoes, are a simple and nutritious side dish. Here's a classic recipe to prepare them:

Ingredients:

- 4 medium-sized yams or sweet potatoes
- 2 tablespoons olive oil
- Salt, to taste
- Ground black pepper, to taste
- Optional toppings: butter, brown sugar, cinnamon, marshmallows (for a sweeter version)

Instructions:

1. Preheat the Oven:

- Preheat your oven to 375°F (190°C).

2. Wash and Prepare the Yams:

- Scrub the yams under running water to remove any dirt. Pat them dry with a clean kitchen towel.

3. Prick the Yams:

- Use a fork to prick each yam several times. This helps steam escape during baking and prevents the yams from bursting.

4. Coat with Olive Oil:

- Place the pricked yams on a baking sheet or in a baking dish. Drizzle olive oil over the yams and use your hands to rub the oil evenly over their surfaces.

5. Season with Salt and Pepper:

- Sprinkle salt and ground black pepper over the oiled yams. You can adjust the amount of salt and pepper to your taste.

6. Bake:

- Place the yams in the preheated oven and bake for approximately 45-60 minutes, depending on the size of the yams. They are done when a fork or knife easily pierces the flesh.

7. Rest and Serve:

- Remove the baked yams from the oven and allow them to rest for a few minutes before serving. This helps them firm up slightly.

8. Serve:

- Serve the classic baked yams with optional toppings like butter, brown sugar, cinnamon, or even marshmallows for a sweeter twist.

9. Enjoy:

- Enjoy your classic baked yams as a delicious and nutritious side dish.

Baked yams are a versatile side dish that pairs well with various main courses. They are naturally sweet and full of flavor, making them a favorite for many occasions. Customize the toppings to suit your taste, and savor the goodness of this classic dish.

# Traditional Turkey Gravy

Traditional turkey gravy made with the turkey neck is rich and flavorful. Here's a classic recipe to prepare it:

Ingredients:

- 1 turkey neck (from the turkey you're roasting)
- 1 onion, chopped
- 1 carrot, chopped
- 1 celery stalk, chopped
- 2 cloves garlic, minced
- 4 cups turkey or chicken broth
- 1/4 cup all-purpose flour
- 1/4 cup unsalted butter
- Salt and black pepper, to taste

Instructions:

1. Prepare the Turkey Neck:

- Rinse the turkey neck under cold water and pat it dry with paper towels.

2. Sauté the Vegetables:

- In a large saucepan or skillet, melt the butter over medium heat. Add the chopped onion, carrot, celery, and minced garlic. Sauté for about 5-7 minutes until the vegetables become soft and fragrant.

3. Brown the Turkey Neck:

- Push the sautéed vegetables to one side of the pan and add the turkey neck to the other side. Brown the turkey neck on all sides for about 5 minutes. This step adds depth of flavor to the gravy.

4. Create the Roux:

- Sprinkle the flour over the vegetables and turkey neck. Stir well to combine, creating a roux. Continue to cook and stir for another 2-3 minutes until the roux turns a light golden color.

5. Add Broth:

- Gradually pour in the turkey or chicken broth while continuously whisking to avoid lumps. Bring the mixture to a gentle simmer.

6. 6. Simmer:

- Reduce the heat to low and let the gravy simmer, uncovered, for about 30-40 minutes. Stir occasionally, and as the gravy simmers, the turkey neck will infuse it with flavor.

7. Strain:

- After simmering, remove the turkey neck and strain the gravy through a fine-mesh sieve or cheesecloth into a clean saucepan. Press down on the vegetables to extract as much flavor as possible.

8. Season:

- Season the gravy with salt and black pepper to taste. Adjust the seasoning as needed.

9. Serve:

- Keep the turkey neck for another use or discard it. Transfer the strained gravy to a gravy boat or serving dish.

10. Enjoy:

- Serve your traditional turkey gravy alongside your roasted turkey and other holiday dishes.

This homemade turkey gravy, infused with the flavors of the turkey neck and aromatic vegetables, is a delicious addition to your holiday meal. Pour it generously over your turkey, mashed potatoes, and stuffing for a truly traditional feast.

Note: if you are spatchcocking your Turkey, throw the turkey spine in too.

# *Traditional Cranberry Sauce*

Traditional cranberry sauce is a delightful accompaniment to roast turkey or chicken. Here's a classic recipe to make it:

Ingredients:

- 12 ounces (about 3 cups) fresh cranberries
- 1 cup granulated sugar
- 1 cup water
- Zest of one orange (optional)
- 2 tablespoons orange juice (optional)
- 1 cinnamon stick (optional)

Instructions:

1. Rinse the Cranberries:

- Place the fresh cranberries in a colander and rinse them thoroughly under cold running water. Remove any stems or bruised cranberries.

2. Combine Ingredients:

- In a medium saucepan, combine the rinsed cranberries, granulated sugar, and water. If desired, add the orange zest, orange juice, and a cinnamon stick for extra flavor.

3. Bring to a Simmer:

- Place the saucepan over medium heat and bring the mixture to a gentle simmer. Stir occasionally to dissolve the sugar.

4. Cook the Cranberries:

- Once the mixture starts simmering, reduce the heat to low. Let the cranberries cook for about 10-15 minutes, or until they burst and the sauce thickens. Stir occasionally.

5. Adjust Consistency:

- If the sauce seems too thick, you can add a little more water to achieve your desired consistency. Keep in mind that it will continue to thicken as it cools.

6. Remove from Heat:

- Remove the saucepan from the heat and discard the cinnamon stick if used. Let the cranberry sauce cool for a few minutes.

7. Serve or Chill:

- You can serve the cranberry sauce warm or at room temperature. If you prefer it chilled, transfer it to a serving dish, cover, and refrigerate until cold.

8. Enjoy:

- Cranberry sauce is a classic Thanksgiving and holiday side dish. Serve it alongside your roast turkey, chicken, or other main dishes.

Note: You can adjust the sweetness of the cranberry sauce by adding more or less sugar to suit your taste. Additionally, you can customize it with other flavorings like grated ginger or a splash of lemon juice for variation.

This traditional cranberry sauce balances the tartness of cranberries with the sweetness of sugar, creating a flavorful and vibrant condiment for your holiday table.

# Traditional Holiday Desserts

# Pumpkin Pie

Pumpkin pie is a classic dessert, especially popular during the fall and Thanksgiving season. Here's a traditional recipe for homemade pumpkin pie:

Ingredients:

For the Pie Crust:

- 1 1/4 cups all-purpose flour
- 1/2 teaspoon salt
- 1/2 cup (1 stick) unsalted butter, cold and cut into small cubes
- 3-4 tablespoons ice water

For the Pumpkin Filling:

- 1 15-ounce can of pumpkin puree (not pumpkin pie filling)
- 3/4 cup granulated sugar
- 1 teaspoon ground cinnamon
- 1/2 teaspoon ground ginger
- 1/4 teaspoon ground cloves
- 1/2 teaspoon salt
- 2 large eggs
- 1 12-ounce can of evaporated milk

Instructions:

1. Prepare the Pie Crust:

- In a mixing bowl, combine the all-purpose flour and salt. Add the cold, cubed butter. Using a pastry cutter or your fingers, work the butter into the flour until the mixture resembles coarse crumbs.

- Gradually add ice water, 1 tablespoon at a time, and mix until the dough just comes together. Be careful not to overwork the dough. Form it into a disk, wrap it in plastic wrap, and refrigerate for at least 30 minutes.

2. Preheat the Oven:

- Preheat your oven to 425°F (220°C).

3. Roll Out the Pie Crust:

- On a lightly floured surface, roll out the chilled pie crust into a circle large enough to fit a 9-inch pie dish. Carefully transfer the crust to the pie dish, pressing it gently into the bottom and up the sides. Trim any excess crust hanging over the edge.

4. Prepare the Pumpkin Filling:

- In a large mixing bowl, combine the pumpkin puree, granulated sugar, ground cinnamon, ground ginger, ground cloves, and salt. Mix until well com-bined.

- In a separate bowl, beat the eggs, and then add them to the pumpkin mixture. Stir until fully incorporated.

- Gradually add the evaporated milk and mix until the filling is smooth.

5. Assemble and Bake:

- Pour the pumpkin filling into the prepared pie crust.

- Bake the pie in the preheated oven at 425°F (220°C) for 15 minutes. Then, reduce the oven temperature to 350°F (175°C) and continue baking for an additional 40-50 minutes, or until the filling is set and a toothpick inserted into the center comes out clean.

6. Cool and Serve:

- Allow the pumpkin pie to cool completely on a wire rack. You can refrigerate it for a few hours or overnight before serving.

7. Optional Toppings:

- Serve your pumpkin pie with a dollop of whipped cream or a scoop of vanilla ice cream for extra deliciousness.

Enjoy your homemade pumpkin pie as a classic dessert for fall celebrations and Thanksgiving gatherings!

244

# Pumpkin Cheesecake

Pumpkin cheesecake is a delightful dessert that combines the creamy richness of cheesecake with the warm, spicy flavors of pumpkin. Here's a recipe to make a delicious pumpkin cheesecake from scratch:

Ingredients:

For the Crust:

- 1 1/2 cups graham cracker crumbs
- 1/4 cup granulated sugar
- 1/2 cup unsalted butter, melted

For the Cheesecake Filling:

- 3 (8-ounce) packages cream cheese, softened
- 1 cup granulated sugar
- 1 teaspoon vanilla extract
- 3 large eggs
- 1 cup canned pumpkin puree (not pumpkin pie filling)
- 1 teaspoon ground cinnamon
- 1/2 teaspoon ground nutmeg
- 1/2 teaspoon ground cloves
- 1/2 teaspoon ground ginger

For the Topping:

- 1 cup sour cream
- 1/4 cup powdered sugar
- 1 teaspoon vanilla extract

Instructions:

1. Preheat the Oven:
- Preheat your oven to 325°F (160°C).

2. Prepare the Crust:
- In a mixing bowl, combine the graham cracker crumbs, granulated sugar, and melted butter. Mix until the crumbs are evenly coated with butter.
- Press the mixture firmly into the bottom of a 9-inch springform pan to create the crust. You can use the bottom of a glass to help compact the crumbs.

3. Prepare the Cheesecake Filling:
- In a large mixing bowl, beat the softened cream cheese until it's smooth and creamy.
- Add the granulated sugar and vanilla extract to the cream cheese and continue to beat until well combined.

- Add the eggs one at a time, mixing well after each addition.
- In a separate bowl, combine the pumpkin puree, ground cinnamon, ground nutmeg, ground cloves, and ground ginger. Mix until the spices are evenly distributed.
- Gradually add the pumpkin mixture to the cream cheese mixture and blend until smooth.

4. Bake the Cheesecake:
- Pour the cheesecake filling over the prepared crust in the springform pan.
- Bake the cheesecake in the preheated oven for about 45-50 minutes, or until the edges are set, but the center is slightly jiggly.

5. Prepare the Topping:
- In a small bowl, combine the sour cream, powdered sugar, and vanilla extract. Mix until smooth.

6. Apply the Topping:
- Remove the cheesecake from the oven and let it cool for about 10 minutes.
- Gently spread the sour cream topping evenly over the surface of the cheesecake.

7. Bake Again:
- Return the cheesecake to the oven and bake for an additional 10 minutes to set the topping.

8. Cool and Refrigerate:
- Allow the cheesecake to cool to room temperature, and then refrigerate it for at least 4 hours or overnight to chill and set.

9. Serve:
- Before serving, you can garnish the pumpkin cheesecake with whipped cream, caramel sauce, or chopped nuts if desired.

Enjoy your homemade pumpkin cheesecake, a perfect dessert for fall and Thanksgiving celebrations!

# Classic Apple Pie

Classic apple pie is a beloved dessert that features tender, spiced apples baked in a flaky pie crust. Here's a traditional recipe for homemade apple pie:

Ingredients:

For the Pie Crust:

- 2 1/2 cups all-purpose flour
- 1 teaspoon salt
- 1 cup (2 sticks) unsalted butter, cold and cubed
- 6-8 tablespoons ice water

For the Apple Filling:

- 6-7 cups peeled, cored, and thinly sliced apples (such as Granny Smith, Honeycrisp, or Fuji)
- 3/4 cup granulated sugar
- 1 tablespoon lemon juice
- 1 teaspoon ground cinnamon
- 1/4 teaspoon ground nutmeg
- 2 tablespoons all-purpose flour
- 1 tablespoon unsalted butter, cut into small pieces

Instructions:

1. Prepare the Pie Crust:

- In a large mixing bowl, combine the all-purpose flour and salt. Add the cold, cubed butter.
- Use a pastry cutter or your fingers to work the butter into the flour until the mixture resembles coarse crumbs.
- Gradually add ice water, 1 tablespoon at a time, and mix until the dough just comes together. Be careful not to overwork the dough. Divide it into two equal portions, shape each into a disk, wrap in plastic wrap, and refrigerate for at least 30 minutes.

2. Preheat the Oven:

- Preheat your oven to 425°F (220°C).

3. Prepare the Apple Filling:

- In a large mixing bowl, combine the sliced apples, granulated sugar, lemon juice, ground cinnamon, ground nutmeg, and all-purpose flour. Toss everything together until the apples are evenly coated.

4. Roll Out the Pie Crust:

- On a lightly floured surface, roll out one of the chilled pie crust disks into a circle large enough to fit a 9-inch pie dish. Carefully transfer the crust to the pie dish.

5. Add the Apple Filling:

- Pour the prepared apple filling into the pie crust, spreading it out evenly. Dot the top of the filling with small pieces of butter.

6. Roll Out the Top Crust:

- Roll out the second chilled pie crust disk into a circle. You can leave it whole to cover the pie or cut it into strips for a lattice design.

7. Seal and Vent:

- Place the top crust over the apples and trim any excess dough. Seal the edges of the crust by crimping them together with a fork or your fingers. If using a whole top crust, don't forget to cut a few slits or create a decorative pattern in the center to allow steam to escape.

8. Bake:

- Place the pie in the preheated oven and bake at 425°F (220°C) for 45-55 minutes, or until the crust is golden brown, and the apple filling is bubbling.

9. Cool and Serve:

- Allow the apple pie to cool on a wire rack for at least 2-3 hours before serving. This helps the filling set.

10. Enjoy:

- Serve your classic homemade apple pie with a scoop of vanilla ice cream or a dollop of whipped cream, if desired.

This classic apple pie is a timeless dessert that captures the comforting flavors of apples and spices in a flaky, buttery crust. Perfect for any occasion!

# Pecan Praline Pie

Pecan praline pie is a delicious and decadent dessert that combines the rich flavors of pecans and caramelized sugar. Here's a recipe to make a mouthwatering pecan praline pie:

Ingredients:

For the Pie Crust:

- 1 9-inch unbaked pie crust (homemade or store--bought)

For the Pecan Filling:

- 1 1/2 cups pecan halves
- 3 large eggs
- 1 cup granulated sugar
- 1 cup light corn syrup
- 1/4 cup unsalted butter, melted
- 1 teaspoon vanilla extract
- 1/4 teaspoon salt

For the Praline Topping:

- 1/2 cup light brown sugar, packed
- 1/4 cup unsalted butter
- 1/4 cup heavy cream
- 1/2 cup pecan halves, toasted (for garnish)

Instructions:

1. Preheat the Oven:
- Preheat your oven to 350°F (175°C).

2. Prepare the Pie Crust:
- If using a homemade or store-bought pie crust, place it in a 9-inch pie dish and crimp the edges. Set it aside.

3. Toast the Pecans:
- Spread the pecan halves on a baking sheet and toast them in the preheated oven for about 8-10 minutes until fragrant. Remove them from the oven and let them cool. Reserve 1/2 cup for garnish.

4. Prepare the Pecan Filling:
- In a mixing bowl, whisk together the eggs, granulated sugar, light corn syrup, melted butter, vanilla extract, and salt until well combined.
- Stir in the toasted pecan halves (excluding the reserved 1/2 cup) into the filling mixture.

5. Pour into Pie Crust:
- Pour the pecan filling mixture into the prepared pie crust.

6. Bake:

- Place the pie in the preheated oven and bake for 45-55 minutes or until the filling is set, and the top is golden brown. If the edges of the crust begin to brown too quickly, you can cover them with a pie shield or aluminum foil.

7. Prepare the Praline Topping:
- In a saucepan over medium heat, combine the light brown sugar, unsalted butter, and heavy cream. Stir continuously until the mixture comes to a boil. Let it boil for 1-2 minutes, stirring constantly.

8. Cool and Pour Over Pie:
- Remove the praline topping from the heat and let it cool for a few minutes. It will thicken as it cools.
- After the pie has baked and is still warm, pour the praline topping evenly over the top of the pie.

9. Garnish:
- Decorate the top of the pie with the reserved toasted pecan halves.

10. Cool and Serve:
- Allow the pecan praline pie to cool to room temperature before serving. This will allow the filling to set.

11. Enjoy:
- Slice and serve your delicious pecan praline pie. It's perfect on its own or with a scoop of vanilla ice cream for an extra treat.

This pecan praline pie is sure to be a hit, with its sweet, nutty filling and praline topping that adds a delightful caramel flavor. Enjoy!

247

# Sweet potato pie

Sweet potato pie is a classic Southern dessert known for its rich, creamy filling and warm spices. Here's a recipe to make a delicious homemade sweet potato pie:

Ingredients:

For the Pie Crust:

- 1 9-inch unbaked pie crust (homemade or store-bought)

For the Sweet Potato Filling:

- 2 cups mashed sweet potatoes (about 2 large sweet potatoes, cooked and
- peeled)
- 1/2 cup granulated sugar
- 1/2 cup brown sugar, packed
- 2 large eggs
- 1/2 cup evaporated milk
- 1/2 cup whole milk
- 1/4 cup unsalted butter, melted
- 1 teaspoon vanilla extract
- 1/2 teaspoon ground cinnamon
- 1/4 teaspoon ground nutmeg
- 1/4 teaspoon salt

Instructions:

1. Preheat the Oven:
- Preheat your oven to 350°F (175°C).

2. Prepare the Sweet Potatoes:
- Wash, peel, and chop the sweet potatoes into chunks. Place them in a pot of boiling water and cook until they are tender when pierced with a fork, about 15-20 minutes. Drain and mash the sweet potatoes until smooth.

3. Prepare the Pie Crust:
- If using a homemade or store-bought pie crust, place it in a 9-inch pie dish and crimp the edges. Set it aside.

4. Make the Sweet Potato Filling:
- In a large mixing bowl, combine the mashed sweet potatoes, granulated sugar, brown sugar, eggs, evaporated milk, whole milk, melted butter, vanilla extract, ground cinnamon, ground nutmeg, and salt. Mix until all the ingredients are well combined and the filling is smooth.

5. Pour into Pie Crust:
- Pour the sweet potato filling into the prepared pie crust.

6. Bake:
- Place the pie in the preheated oven and bake for 45-50 minutes, or until the filling is set and a toothpick inserted into the center comes out clean.

7. Cool:
- Allow the sweet potato pie to cool on a wire rack for at least 1 hour before serving. This helps the pie set and enhances the flavor.

8. Serve:
- Slice and serve your homemade sweet potato pie. You can enjoy it as is or with a dollop of whipped cream or a scoop of vanilla ice cream.

9. Enjoy:
- Enjoy the warm, comforting flavors of this classic Southern dessert.

Sweet potato pie is perfect for holidays and special occasions, and it's sure to be a crowd-pleaser with its sweet and spiced filling.

# Mincemeat Pie

Mincemeat pie is a classic holiday dessert that's rich, flavorful, and filled with a mixture of dried fruits, spices, and sometimes a bit of brandy or rum. Here's a traditional recipe for making a delicious mincemeat pie:

Ingredients:

For the Pastry Crust:

- 2 1/2 cups all-purpose flour
- 1 cup (2 sticks) cold unsalted butter, cubed
- 1 teaspoon salt
- 1 teaspoon granulated sugar
- 6-8 tablespoons ice water

For the Mincemeat Filling:

- 2 cups prepared mincemeat (store-bought or homemade)
- 1/4 cup brandy or rum (optional)
- 1/4 cup chopped nuts (such as almonds or walnuts, optional)
- Zest and juice of 1 lemon
- 1 egg, beaten (for egg wash)
- Granulated sugar, for sprinkling

Instructions:

1. Prepare the Pastry Crust:

- In a large mixing bowl, combine the flour, salt, and sugar.
- Add the cold, cubed butter to the flour mixture. Using a pastry cutter or your fingertips, work the butter into the flour until it resembles coarse crumbs.
- Gradually add ice water, one tablespoon at a time, and mix until the dough comes together. Be careful not to overwork the dough.
- Divide the dough into two equal portions, shape each into a disc, wrap them in plastic wrap, and refrigerate for at least 30 minutes.

2. Prepare the Mincemeat Filling:

- In a mixing bowl, combine the prepared mincemeat, brandy or rum (if using), chopped nuts (if using), lemon zest, and lemon juice. Mix well. Allow the mixture to sit for about 30 minutes to let the flavors meld.

3. Preheat the Oven:

- Preheat your oven to 375°F (190°C).

4. Roll Out the Pastry:

- On a lightly floured surface, roll out one of the pastry discs into a circle large enough to line a 9-inch pie dish. Carefully transfer the rolled pastry to the pie dish, and trim any excess dough hanging over the edges.

5. Add the Mincemeat Filling:

- Spoon the prepared mincemeat filling into the pastry-lined pie dish, spreading it evenly.

6. Create the Top Crust:

- Roll out the second pastry disc into a circle large enough to cover the pie. You can create a solid top crust or use the pastry to create a lattice design. If using a solid top crust, be sure to cut a few slits in the pastry to allow steam to escape.

7. Seal and Decorate:

- Trim and crimp the edges of the pastry to seal the pie. If you've created a lattice design, weave the strips of pastry over the filling. Brush the top crust with the beaten egg and sprinkle with granulated sugar for a golden finish.

8. Bake:

- Place the pie on a baking sheet to catch any drips. Bake in the preheated oven for 45-55 minutes or until the crust is golden brown and the filling is bubbling.

9. Cool and Serve:

- Allow the mincemeat pie to cool on a wire rack for at least 2 hours before serving. Serve slices with a dollop of whipped cream or a scoop of vanilla ice cream if desired.

Enjoy your homemade mincemeat pie as a delightful holiday treat!

# *Pumpkin Roll*

The Pumpkin Roll is not only a delicious dessert but also a symbol of cozy gatherings and holiday celebrations. Whether you're preparing it for a Thanksgiving feast, a family get-together, or simply to savor the flavors of fall, this recipe will guide you through the steps to create a perfect, rolled sponge cake filled with a creamy pumpkin filling.

Ingredients:

For the Pumpkin Roll:

- 3/4 cup all-purpose flour
- 1/2 teaspoon baking powder
- 1/2 teaspoon baking soda
- 1/2 teaspoon ground cinnamon
- 1/2 teaspoon ground nutmeg
- 1/4 teaspoon salt
- 3 large eggs
- 1 cup granulated sugar
- 2/3 cup canned pumpkin puree
- 1 teaspoon vanilla extract
- Powdered sugar (for dusting)
- Kitchen towel or parchment paper

For the Cream Cheese Filling:

- 8 oz cream cheese, softened
- 1 cup powdered sugar
- 6 tablespoons unsalted butter, softened
- 1 teaspoon vanilla extract

Instructions:

1. Prepare the Pumpkin Roll:
- Preheat your oven to 375°F (190°C). Grease and flour a 15x10-inch jelly roll pan or line it with parchment paper.

2. Mix Dry Ingredients:
- In a small bowl, whisk together the flour, baking powder, baking soda, cinnamon, nutmeg, and salt. Set aside.

3. Beat Eggs and Sugar:
- In a large mixing bowl, beat the eggs and granulated sugar until thick and pale, about 2 minutes.

4. Add Pumpkin and Vanilla:
- Mix in the canned pumpkin and vanilla extract until well combined.

5. Add Dry Ingredients:
- Gradually add the dry ingredients to the pumpkin mixture and fold until just combined.

6. Spread Batter:
- Spread the batter evenly into the prepared jelly roll pan.

7. Bake:
- Bake in the preheated oven for 12-15 minutes, or until the cake springs back when touched.

8. Prepare Towel or Parchment:
- While the cake is baking, lay a clean kitchen towel or a piece of parchment paper on the counter and dust it generously with powdered sugar.

9. Roll the Cake:
- Immediately after removing the cake from the oven, invert it onto the prepared towel or parchment paper. Carefully peel off the parchment paper, if used.
- Starting from one of the shorter ends, carefully roll up the warm cake and towel (or parchment paper) together. This will create the rolled shape. Let it cool completely while rolled.

10. Prepare the Cream Cheese Filling:
- In a mixing bowl, beat together the softened cream cheese, powdered sugar, softened butter, and vanilla extract until smooth and creamy.

11. Unroll and Fill:
- Gently unroll the cooled cake and remove the towel or parchment paper. Spread the cream cheese filling evenly over the cake.

12. Roll it Up Again:
- Carefully roll the cake back up, this time without the towel or parchment paper. Place it seam side down.

13. Chill:
- Wrap the pumpkin roll in plastic wrap and refrigerate for at least an hour, or until ready to serve.

14. Slice and Serve:
- Before serving, dust the pumpkin roll with powdered sugar. Slice and enjoy!

This Pumpkin Roll is a delightful fall dessert with a creamy filling and a hint of spice. It's perfect for holiday gatherings or as a sweet treat during the autumn season.

# Leftover Magic

Our refrigerators often become treasure troves of leftover delights in the wake of holiday feasts like Easter, Thanksgiving, and Christmas. These remnants of grand celebrations hold the potential for delicious second acts, where yesterday's meal can be transformed into today's culinary masterpiece. In this chapter, aptly named "Leftover Magic: Transforming Easter, Thanksgiving, and Christmas Leftovers," we will show you how to turn those surplus ingredients into mouthwatering creations that are as exciting as the original meal.

# Turkey Pot Pie Recipe

Transform your leftover turkey into a comforting and delicious Turkey Pot Pie. This recipe combines tender turkey, mixed vegetables, and a creamy sauce, all topped with a flaky pie crust. It's the perfect way to enjoy those Thanksgiving leftovers.

Ingredients:

For the Pie Filling:

- 2 cups diced leftover turkey
- 2 cups mixed vegetables (carrots, peas, corn, and green beans), cooked
- 1/2 cup diced onion
- 1/2 cup diced celery
- 1/2 cup diced carrots
- 1/4 cup unsalted butter
- 1/4 cup all-purpose flour
- 2 cups chicken or turkey broth
- 1 cup whole milk or half-and-half
- 1 teaspoon dried thyme
- Salt and pepper to taste

For the Pie Crust:

- 2 store-bought pie crusts (top and bottom), or homemade if preferred

Instructions:

1. Preheat your oven to 375°F (190°C).

2. Prepare the Pie Filling:

- In a large skillet, melt the butter over medium heat. Add the diced onion, celery, and carrots. Cook until the vegetables are tender, about 5-7 minutes.

- Stir in the flour and cook for 2-3 minutes, stirring constantly to create a roux.

- Gradually whisk in the chicken or turkey broth and milk, ensuring there are no lumps. Continue to cook and stir until the mixture thickens, about 5-7 minutes.

- Add the diced turkey, cooked mixed vegetables, dried thyme, salt, and pepper to the creamy sauce. Stir well to combine. Taste and adjust seasonings as needed.

- Remove the skillet from heat, and set the filling aside while you prepare the pie crust.

3. Assemble the Pot Pie:

- Place one pie crust in the bottom of a 9-inch (23 cm) pie dish, pressing it gently to fit the shape. Trim any excess hanging over the edge.

- Pour the turkey and vegetable filling into the pie crust.

- Place the second pie crust on top of the filling. Trim any excess dough, leaving a 1-inch overhang.

- Crimp the edges of the two pie crusts together to seal the pot pie.

- Make a few small slits in the top crust to allow steam to escape during baking.

- Optional: You can brush the top crust with an egg wash (one beaten egg with a tablespoon of water) for a shiny finish.

4. Bake:

- Place the pot pie in the preheated oven and bake for 35-45 minutes, or until the crust is golden brown and the filling is bubbling.

- Allow the pot pie to cool for a few minutes before serving.

- Serve your delicious Turkey Pot Pie warm, and enjoy a comforting meal made from your leftover turkey and vegetables.

This hearty and creamy pot pie is the perfect way to make the most of your leftover turkey, and it's sure to become a family favorite.

# Turkey and Mascarpone Stuffed Shells

Ingredients:

- 20 jumbo pasta shells
- 2 cups leftover cooked turkey, shredded
- 1 cup mascarpone cheese
- 1/2 cup grated Parmesan cheese
- 1/4 cup fresh parsley, chopped
- 1/4 cup fresh basil, chopped
- 2 cloves garlic, minced
- 1 egg, beaten
- Salt and pepper to taste
- 2 cups marinara sauce
- 1 cup shredded mozzarella cheese
- Fresh basil leaves for garnish (optional)

Instructions:

1. Cook the Pasta Shells:

- Bring a large pot of salted water to a boil. Cook the jumbo pasta shells according to the package instructions until al dente. Drain and set aside.

2. Prepare the Filling:

- In a large mixing bowl, combine the shredded leftover turkey, mascarpone cheese, grated Parmesan cheese, chopped parsley, chopped basil, minced garlic, beaten egg, salt, and pepper. Mix until all the ingredients are well combined.

3. Stuff the Shells:

- Using a spoon, carefully fill each cooked pasta shell with the turkey and mascarpone filling mixture. Place the filled shells in a greased 9x13-inch baking dish.

4. Top with Marinara Sauce:

- Pour the marinara sauce evenly over the stuffed shells.

5. Add Mozzarella Cheese:

- Sprinkle the shredded mozzarella cheese over the top of the shells.

6. Bake:

- Cover the baking dish with aluminum foil and bake in a preheated oven at 350°F (175°C) for 25-30 minutes, or until the filling is hot and bubbly, and the cheese is melted.

7. Garnish and Serve:

- Remove from the oven and garnish with fresh basil leaves if desired.

8. Enjoy:

- Serve the Turkey and Mascarpone Stuffed Shells hot, and enjoy this creamy and comforting dish made with your leftover turkey and rich mascarpone cheese.

This recipe is a great way to repurpose leftover turkey into a satisfying and flavorful meal.

# Creamy Turkey Casserole

Ingredients:

- 3 cups cooked turkey, diced or shredded
- 8 oz cream cheese, softened
- 1/2 cup sour cream
- 1/2 cup mayonnaise
- 1/2 cup grated Parmesan cheese
- 1/2 cup shredded mozzarella cheese
- 1/4 cup chopped green onions
- 1/4 cup chopped fresh parsley
- 1 teaspoon garlic powder
- 1 teaspoon onion powder
- Salt and pepper to taste
- 2 cups cooked pasta (such as penne or rotini)
- 1 cup breadcrumbs
- 2 tablespoons melted butter

Instructions:

1. Preheat the Oven:
- Preheat your oven to 350°F (175°C). Grease a 9x13-inch baking dish.

2. Prepare the Cream Cheese Mixture:
- In a large mixing bowl, combine the softened cream cheese, sour cream, mayonnaise, grated Parmesan cheese, shredded mozzarella cheese, chopped green onions, chopped fresh parsley, garlic powder, onion powder, salt, and pepper. Mix until the mixture is smooth and well combined.

3. Combine with Turkey and Pasta:
- Add the diced or shredded cooked turkey and cooked pasta to the cream cheese mixture. Gently fold everything together until the turkey and pasta are evenly coated.

4. Transfer to Baking Dish:
- Transfer the mixture to the greased 9x13-inch baking dish and spread it out evenly.

5. Prepare the Topping:
- In a small bowl, mix the breadcrumbs with melted butter until well combined. Sprinkle the breadcrumb mixture evenly over the casserole.

6. Bake:
- Place the casserole in the preheated oven and bake for 25-30 minutes, or until the casserole is hot and bubbly, and the breadcrumb topping is golden brown.

7. Serve:
- Remove from the oven and let it cool for a few minutes before serving.

8. Enjoy:
- Serve the Creamy Turkey Casserole hot, and enjoy the creamy, cheesy goodness with a crunchy breadcrumb topping.

This creamy turkey casserole with cream cheese is a wonderful way to use leftover turkey, and its rich and savory flavors make it a comforting meal for any occasion.

# Ham and Pea Soup Recipe

Ingredients:

- 1 pound (450g) diced ham
- 2 cups frozen peas
- 1 medium onion, finely chopped
- 2 carrots, peeled and diced
- 2 celery stalks, chopped
- 3 cloves garlic, minced
- 6 cups chicken or vegetable broth
- 2 bay leaves
- 1 teaspoon dried thyme
- Salt and pepper to taste
- 2 tablespoons olive oil
- 1/2 cup heavy cream (optional, for added richness)
- Fresh parsley, for garnish (optional)

Instructions:

1. Heat a large soup pot or Dutch oven over medium heat. Add the olive oil and let it heat up for a minute or two.

2. Add the chopped onion and celery to the pot. Sauté for about 3-4 minutes, or until the vegetables start to soften and the onion becomes translucent.

3. Stir in the diced ham and garlic. Cook for an additional 2-3 minutes, allowing the ham to brown slightly.

4. Add the diced carrots and frozen peas to the pot. Stir well to combine all the ingredients.

5. Pour in the chicken or vegetable broth, and add the bay leaves and dried thyme. Season with salt and pepper to taste. Bring the mixture to a boil.

6. Once the soup is boiling, reduce the heat to low, cover, and let it simmer for about 20-25 minutes, or until the vegetables are tender and the flavors have melded together.

7. If you'd like a creamier soup, you can add the optional heavy cream at this point. Stir it in and let the soup simmer for an additional 5 minutes. If you prefer a lighter soup, you can skip this step.

8. Remove the bay leaves from the soup and discard them.

9. Taste the soup and adjust the seasoning with more salt and pepper if necessary.

10. Ladle the hot ham and pea soup into bowls. Garnish with fresh parsley if desired.

11. Serve the soup hot with some crusty bread or rolls for a complete meal.

Enjoy your comforting and delicious homemade Ham and Pea Soup!

# Ham and Cheese Breakfast Casserole

Ingredients:

- 2 cups diced ham
- 2 cups shredded cheddar cheese (or your preferred cheese)
- 1 cup diced bell peppers (any color you prefer)
- 1 cup diced onions
- 1 cup diced mushrooms
- 6 large eggs
- 1 1/2 cups milk
- 1 teaspoon salt
- 1/2 teaspoon black pepper
- 1/2 teaspoon garlic powder
- 1/2 teaspoon dried thyme (optional)
- Cooking spray

Instructions:

1. Preheat your oven to 350°F (175°C). Grease a 9x13-inch (23x33 cm) baking dish with cooking spray.
2. In a large skillet over medium heat, add a bit of cooking oil or butter and sauté the diced ham until it's slightly browned, about 3-5 minutes. Remove the ham from the skillet and set it aside.
3. In the same skillet, add a little more oil if needed, then sauté the diced onions, bell peppers, and mushrooms until they are tender, about 5-7 minutes. Season with a pinch of salt and black pepper. Once done, remove the vegetables from the skillet and set them aside.
4. In a large mixing bowl, whisk together the eggs, milk, salt, pepper, garlic powder, and dried thyme (if using). Mix until well combined.
5. Spread half of the diced ham in an even layer in the greased baking dish. Next, add half of the sautéed vegetables on top of the ham. Sprinkle half of the shredded cheese over the vegetables.
6. Repeat the layering process with the remaining ham, vegetables, and cheese.
7. Pour the egg mixture evenly over the layers in the baking dish. Make sure the ingredients are evenly distributed.
8. Gently press down on the casserole with a spatula to ensure the egg mixture soaks into the layers.
9. Cover the baking dish with aluminum foil and bake in the preheated oven for 40-45 minutes.
10. After 40-45 minutes, remove the foil and bake for an additional 10-15 minutes or until the casserole is set and the top is golden brown.
11. Once done, remove the casserole from the oven and let it cool for a few minutes before serving.
12. Slice the ham and cheese breakfast casserole into squares or rectangles and serve hot. Enjoy your hearty morning meal!

This casserole is versatile and can be customized with your favorite vegetables or additional seasonings to suit your taste. It's perfect for breakfast or brunch gatherings and can be prepared in advance for a convenient morning meal.

# Ham and Broccoli Pasta Bake

Ingredients:

- 2 cups elbow macaroni or your favorite pasta
- 2 cups diced cooked ham
- 2 cups steamed broccoli florets
- 2 cups shredded cheddar cheese
- 1 cup shredded mozzarella cheese
- 1/2 cup grated Parmesan cheese
- 2 cups whole milk
- 3 tablespoons all-purpose flour
- 3 tablespoons unsalted butter
- 1/2 teaspoon salt
- 1/2 teaspoon black pepper
- 1/2 teaspoon garlic powder
- 1/2 teaspoon onion powder
- 1/4 teaspoon paprika
- 1/4 teaspoon dried thyme (optional)
- Cooking spray

Instructions:

1. Preheat your oven to 375°F (190°C) and grease a 9x13-inch baking dish with cooking spray.

2. Cook the Pasta:
   - Bring a large pot of salted water to a boil.
   - Cook the pasta according to the package instructions until al dente.
   - Drain the pasta and set it aside.

3. Prepare the Cheese Sauce:
   - In a medium saucepan over medium heat, melt the butter.
   - Stir in the flour to create a roux, and cook for 1-2 minutes, or until it turns lightly golden.
   - Slowly whisk in the milk, stirring continuously to avoid lumps.
   - Cook the sauce until it thickens, which should take about 5-7 minutes.
   - Remove the saucepan from the heat and stir in 1 1/2 cups of cheddar cheese, 1/2 cup of mozzarella cheese, and 1/2 cup of Parmesan cheese until the mixture is smooth.
   - Season the cheese sauce with salt, black pepper, garlic powder, onion powder, paprika, and dried thyme (if using). Stir to combine.

4. Assemble the Pasta Bake:
   - In a large mixing bowl, combine the cooked pasta, diced ham, and steamed broccoli.
   - Pour the prepared cheese sauce over the pasta mixture and gently stir until everything is well coated.

5. Bake the Pasta:
   - Transfer the mixture into the greased baking dish.
   - Sprinkle the remaining 1/2 cup of cheddar cheese on top.
   - Cover the baking dish with aluminum foil.

6. Bake in the preheated oven for 25-30 minutes, or until the pasta is heated through and the cheese is melted and bubbly.

7. For a golden brown crust, remove the foil during the last 5-10 minutes of baking and let it bake uncovered until the top is golden and slightly crispy.

8. Once done, remove the pasta bake from the oven and let it cool for a few minutes before serving.

9. Serve your delicious Ham and Broccoli Pasta Bake hot, garnished with extra grated Parmesan cheese and fresh parsley if desired. Enjoy!

This creamy and cheesy pasta bake makes for a comforting and hearty meal the whole family will love.

# Ham and Vegetable Quiche Recipe

This delicious ham and vegetable quiche is the perfect savory dish for brunch. With diced ham, eggs, cheese, and your choice of vegetables, it's a satisfying and flavorful option that will please your guests. Follow these simple steps to create a mouthwatering quiche:

Ingredients:

For the Quiche Crust:

- 1 1/4 cups all-purpose flour
- 1/2 teaspoon salt
- 1/2 cup unsalted butter, cold and cubed
- 3-4 tablespoons ice water

For the Quiche Filling:

- 1 cup diced ham
- 1 cup shredded cheese (cheddar, Swiss, or your favorite)
- 1 cup your choice of vegetables (spinach, bell peppers, mushrooms, onions,
- etc.), chopped and sautéed if needed
- 4 large eggs
- 1 cup milk
- Salt and pepper to taste
- 1/4 teaspoon nutmeg (optional)
- Fresh herbs (such as chives or parsley) for garnish

Instructions:

1. Prepare the Quiche Crust:

- In a food processor, combine the flour and salt.
- Add the cold, cubed butter and pulse until the mixture resembles coarse crumbs.
- Slowly add ice water, one tablespoon at a time, and pulse until the dough begins to come together.
- Gather the dough into a ball, flatten it into a disk, wrap it in plastic wrap, and refrigerate for at least 30 minutes.
- Preheat the oven to 375°F (190°C). Roll out the chilled dough on a floured surface to fit a 9-inch (23 cm) pie dish. Press the dough into the pie dish and trim any excess. Prick the bottom with a fork to prevent bubbles during baking. Line the crust with parchment paper and add pie weights or dried beans.

2. Blind Bake the Crust:

- Place the prepared crust in the preheated oven and bake for about 10-12 minutes or until the edges are lightly golden.
- Remove the parchment paper and pie weights, then return the crust to the oven for an additional 5 minutes to ensure the bottom cooks.

3. Prepare the Filling:

- In a bowl, whisk together the eggs and milk until well combined.
- Season the mixture with salt, pepper, and nutmeg (if using).
- Sprinkle diced ham, sautéed vegetables, and shredded cheese evenly over the prebaked crust.
- Pour the egg and milk mixture over the ham, vegetables, and cheese in the crust.

4. Bake:

- Place the quiche in the oven and bake for 30-35 minutes, or until the center is set, and the top is golden brown.

5. Let the quiche cool for a few minutes before slicing. Garnish with fresh herbs.

6. Serve warm and enjoy your homemade ham and vegetable quiche for a delicious brunch!

This ham and vegetable quiche is versatile, so feel free to customize it with your favorite ingredients. It's perfect for a leisurely brunch with family and friends.

# Prime Rib Hash with Fried or Poached Egg

Ingredients:

- 2 cups diced prime rib (cooked)
- 2 cups diced potatoes (precooked or parboiled)
- 1 cup diced onions
- 2 cloves garlic, minced
- 2 tablespoons butter or cooking oil
- 1 teaspoon dried thyme
- 1 teaspoon dried rosemary
- Salt and black pepper to taste
- Chopped fresh parsley for garnish (optional)
- Eggs (1 per serving)
- Cooking oil (for frying or poaching eggs)

Instructions:

1. Start by preparing the ingredients: Dice the leftover prime rib into small, bite-sized pieces. If you don't have precooked potatoes, dice them into small cubes and either parboil them until they're slightly tender or microwave them for a few minutes to soften.

2. In a large skillet, melt the butter or heat the cooking oil over mediumhigh heat.

3. Add the diced onions to the skillet and sauté them until they become translucent and start to caramelize, about 5 minutes.

4. Stir in the minced garlic and cook for an additional 1-2 minutes until fragrant.

5. Add the diced potatoes to the skillet, spreading them out in an even layer. Allow them to cook undisturbed for a few minutes until they develop a crispy crust on one side. Then, flip and brown the other side, stirring occasionally to ensure even cooking.

6. Once the potatoes are nicely browned, add the diced prime rib to the skillet. Cook for about 5-7 minutes, stirring occasionally, until the prime rib is heated through and slightly crispy on the edges.

7. Sprinkle the dried thyme and rosemary over the hash. Season with salt and black pepper to taste. Continue to cook for an additional 2-3 minutes, allowing the flavors to meld.

8. While the hash is cooking, prepare your fried or poached eggs in a separate pan or pot according to your preference.

9. Serve the prime rib hash hot, topped with a fried or poached egg. Garnish with chopped fresh parsley if desired.

10. Enjoy your delicious Prime Rib Hash with a perfectly cooked egg for a satisfying brunch or breakfast. The combination of tender prime rib, crispy potatoes, and flavorful seasonings is sure to impress your taste buds.

Feel free to customize your hash by adding other ingredients like bell peppers, cheese, or hot sauce to suit your taste.

# *Prime Rib Sandwich Recipe*

Ingredients:

For the Prime Rib:

- 1 boneless prime rib roast (3-4 pounds)
- 2 tablespoons olive oil
- 2 cloves garlic, minced
- 1 tablespoon fresh rosemary, finely chopped
- 1 tablespoon fresh thyme, finely chopped
- Salt and freshly ground black pepper, to taste

For the Horseradish Sauce:

- 1/2 cup mayonnaise
- 2 tablespoons prepared horseradish (adjust to taste)
- 1 teaspoon Dijon mustard
- 1 teaspoon white wine vinegar
- Salt and freshly ground black pepper, to taste

For Assembling the Sandwiches:

- Your favorite bread or rolls (e.g., ciabatta, baguette, or soft sandwich rolls)
- Thinly sliced prime rib (cooked and cooled)
- Horseradish sauce
- Sliced red onions (optional)
- Fresh lettuce leaves (optional)
- Sliced tomatoes (optional)

Instructions:

Preparing the Prime Rib:

1. Preheat your oven to 450°F (232°C).
2. In a small bowl, mix together the olive oil, minced garlic, chopped rosemary, and chopped thyme to create a herb-infused oil.
3. Place the boneless prime rib roast on a roasting rack set inside a roasting pan. Pat the meat dry with paper towels.
4. Rub the herb-infused oil mixture all over the prime rib, ensuring it's evenly coated. Season generously with salt and freshly ground black pepper.
5. Roast the prime rib in the preheated oven for about 15 minutes to sear the outside and develop a crust.
6. Reduce the oven temperature to 325°F (163°C) and continue roasting for approximately 15-20 minutes per pound for medium-rare doneness, or adjust the time to your desired level of doneness. Use a meat thermometer to check the internal temperature; it should reach about 130°F (54°C) for medium-rare.
7. Remove the prime rib from the oven and let it rest for at least 15-20 minutes before slicing. This allows the juices to redistribute and keeps the meat tender.

Preparing the Horseradish Sauce:

1. In a small bowl, combine the mayonnaise, prepared horseradish, Dijon mustard, white wine vinegar, salt, and pepper. Adjust the amount of horseradish to your preferred level of spiciness. Mix well and set aside. Assembling the Sandwiches:
2. Slice the prime rib thinly against the grain.
3. Slice your favorite bread or rolls in half horizontally.
4. Spread a generous amount of horseradish sauce on the bottom half of each bread or roll.
5. Layer the sliced prime rib on top of the sauce.
6. If desired, add optional toppings like sliced red onions, lettuce leaves, and sliced tomatoes.
7. Place the top half of the bread or roll over the sandwich fillings.
8. If you like, you can wrap the sandwiches in foil and warm them in a preheated oven at 350°F (177°C) for a few minutes to melt the flavors together.
9. Serve your prime rib sandwiches immediately, and enjoy the delicious combination of tender prime rib and zesty horseradish sauce!

These gourmet Prime Rib Sandwiches are perfect for a special lunch or dinner.

# *Prime Rib Fried Rice*

Ingredients:

- 2 cups diced prime rib (cooked and leftover)
- 3 cups cooked and cooled white rice (preferably day-old)
- 1 cup mixed vegetables (peas, carrots, bell peppers, and corn), diced
- 3 tablespoons vegetable oil
- 3 cloves garlic, minced
- 1 small onion, finely chopped
- 3 tablespoons soy sauce
- 2 eggs, beaten
- 1/2 teaspoon salt, or to taste
- 1/4 teaspoon black pepper, or to taste
- 2 green onions, thinly sliced (for garnish)

Instructions:

1. Prepare the Ingredients:
- Dice the leftover prime rib into small, bite-sized pieces.
- Ensure that the cooked rice is cold and not too sticky. You can use day-old rice for the best results.
- Dice the mixed vegetables into small, uniform pieces.
- Mince the garlic and finely chop the onion.
- Beat the eggs in a small bowl.

2. Heat the Wok or Large Skillet:
- Heat a large wok or skillet over medium-high heat.

3. Sauté the Aromatics:
- Add the vegetable oil to the heated wok or skillet.
- Add the minced garlic and chopped onion.
- Stir-fry for 2-3 minutes until the onion becomes translucent and fragrant.

4. Scramble the Eggs:
- Push the sautéed aromatics to one side of the wok or skillet.
- Pour the beaten eggs into the empty side.
- Allow them to cook for a minute or so until they start to set, then scramble them with a spatula until fully cooked.

5. Add the Diced Prime Rib:
- Add the diced prime rib to the wok or skillet.
- Stir-fry for 2-3 minutes until the prime rib pieces are heated through and begin to develop a slight sear.

6. Incorporate the Rice and Vegetables:
- Add the cold, cooked rice to the wok or skillet, breaking up any clumps.
- Stir-fry the rice and prime rib mixture together for 4-5 minutes until the rice is well coated with the flavors and starts to become slightly crispy.

7. Add the Vegetables and Soy Sauce:
- Stir in the diced mixed vegetables and continue stir-frying for another 2-3 minutes until the vegetables are tender.
- Drizzle the soy sauce evenly over the fried rice mixture.
- Season with salt and black pepper to taste.
- Stir-fry for an additional 2 minutes to ensure all ingredients are well combined and heated through.

8. Garnish and Serve:
- Remove the prime rib fried rice from the heat.
- Garnish with sliced green onions.
- Transfer the fried rice to a serving platter or individual plates.

9. Serve hot as a delicious and satisfying main dish or side dish.

Enjoy your homemade Prime Rib Fried Rice, which combines the rich flavors of prime rib with the classic comfort of fried rice!

Thank you for embarking on this culinary journey with "Season's Eatings." I hope you've enjoyed exploring the delicious recipes and flavors that each season has to offer. If you've found these recipes inspiring and your taste buds delighted, I invite you to continue your culinary adventure on my author page at https://www.amazon.com/stores/Brandee-Jankoski/ author/B0CP9GQG64.

There, you'll discover more of my cookbooks, each filled with delectable dishes and culinary inspiration. Your support and feedback mean the world to me, so please consider leaving a review on Amazon. Your reviews help other food enthusiasts find their way to these recipes and share in the joy of cooking.

*May your kitchen be filled with warmth, your meals be shared with loved ones, and your Season's Eatings be nothing short of delightful!*

www.ingramcontent.com/pod-product-compliance
Lightning Source LLC
Chambersburg PA
CBHW080838120626
46553CB00009B/2477